AF544932

A Model Workshop
Margaret Lowengrund and The Contemporaries

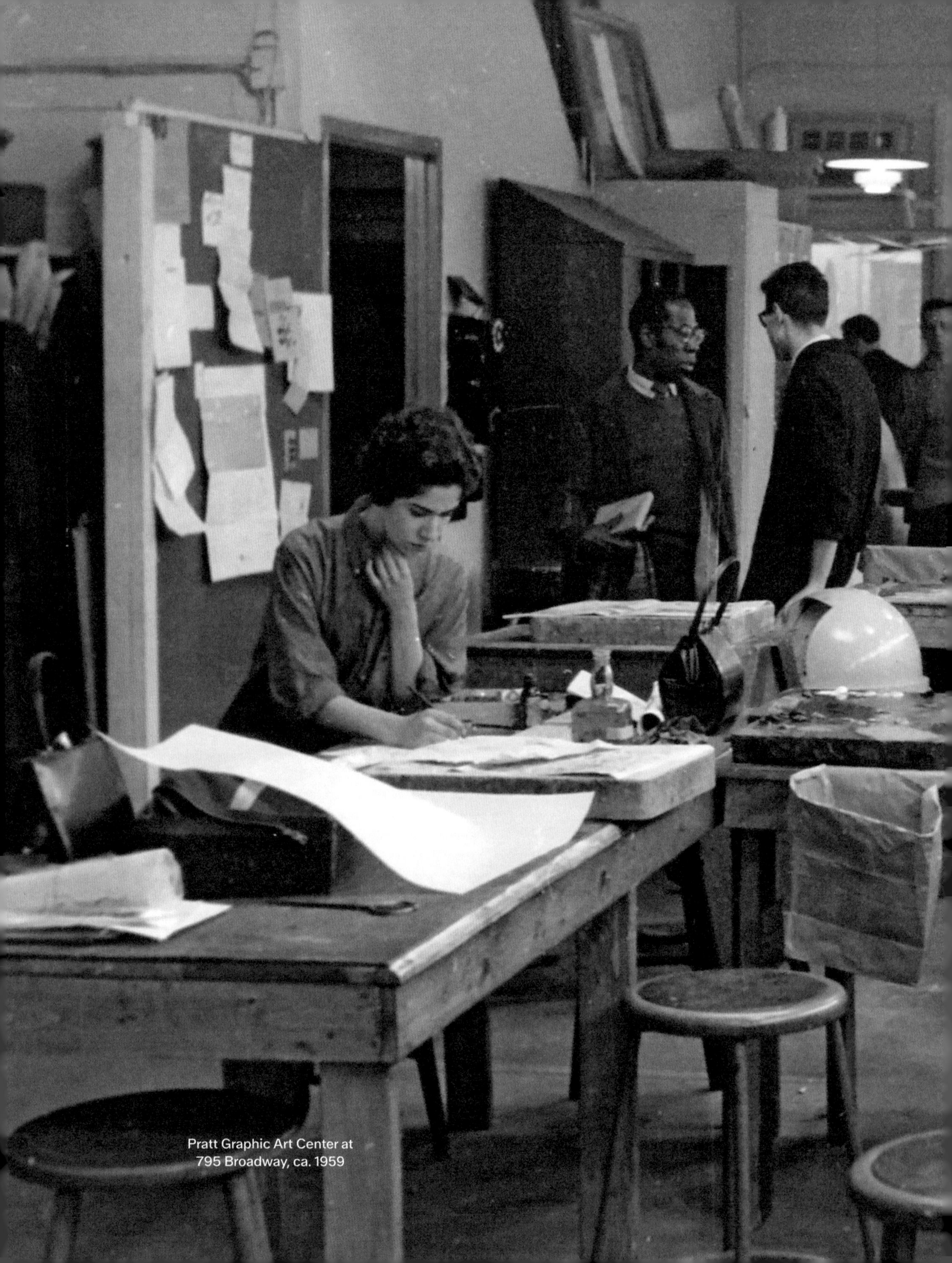

Pratt Graphic Art Center at
795 Broadway, ca. 1959

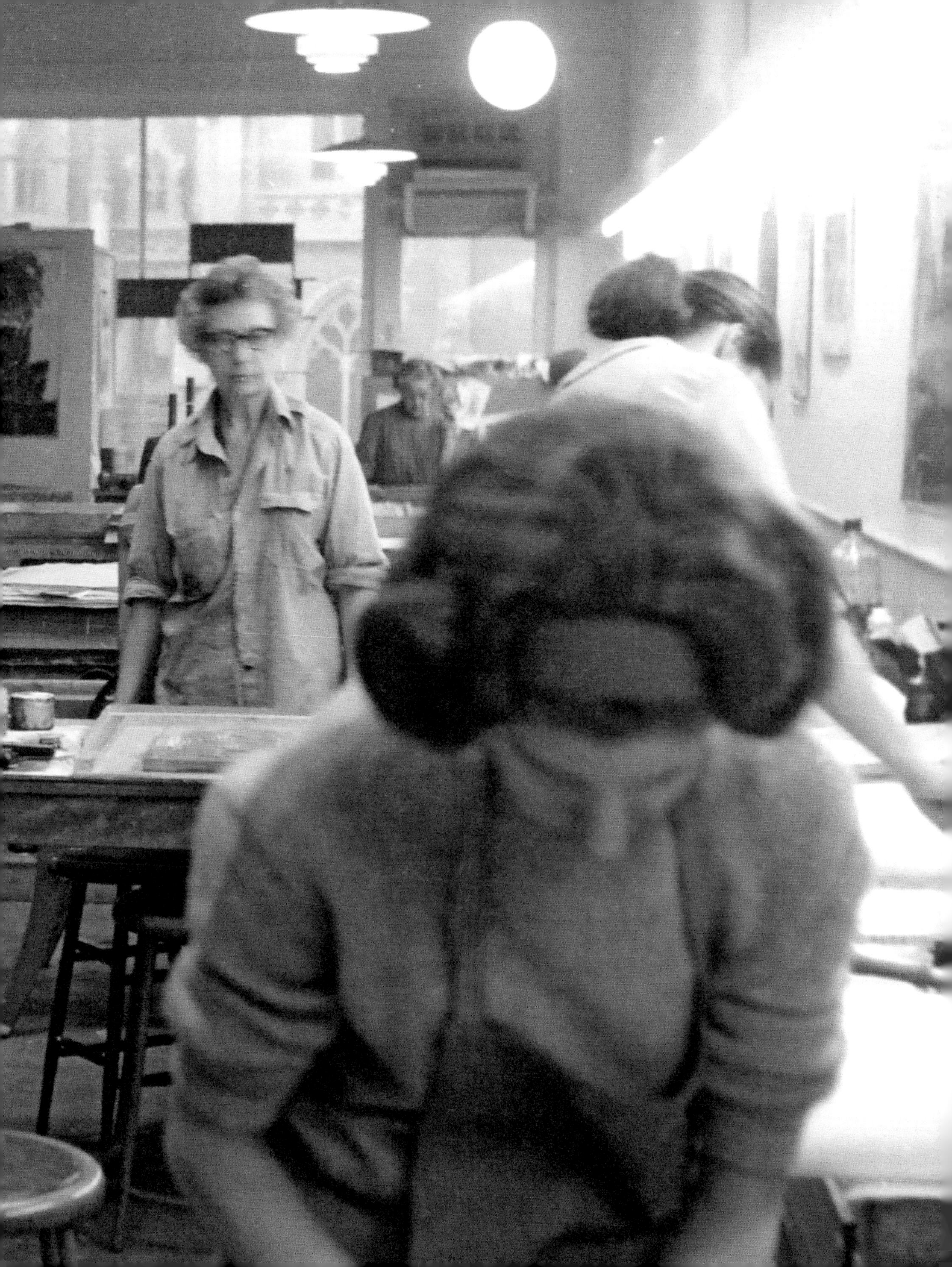

A MODEL WORKSHOP

Margaret Lowengrund and The Contemporaries

LAUREN ROSENBLUM AND CHRISTINA WEYL

With contributions by Sarah Archer, Ellen J. Benjamin,
Noriko Kuwahara, Jillian Russo, and Rachel Vogel

Print Center New York   Hirmer Publishers

FOREWORD AND ACKNOWLEDGMENTS

Judy Hecker and Jenn Bratovich

A Model Workshop: Margaret Lowengrund and The Contemporaries is the first exhibition and publication to chart the contributions of Margaret Lowengrund and the hybrid print workshop-gallery she founded in New York in 1951, The Contemporaries. An often overlooked figure, Lowengrund was an artist and printmaker herself—and so much more. She was a fierce advocate for printmaking; a critic, leader, and organizer; and a pioneering entrepreneur who developed a prescient model for community artistic activity that had a lasting impact in the field. For The Contemporaries, Lowengrund's vision was twofold: it was at once a workshop for collaborative print production and hands-on learning, *and* a gallery asserting the primacy of printmaking by exhibiting prints alongside painting, sculpture, and other media. Following The Contemporaries' 1956 merger with the Pratt Institute and Lowengrund's untimely death the following year, its legacy would live on as the long-running Pratt Graphic Art Center (PGAC).

With *A Model Workshop*, co-curators Lauren Rosenblum and Christina Weyl have excavated this story, mapping the far-reaching networks of artists who moved through The Contemporaries and PGAC and charting key exhibitions and activities that helped define these spaces. The exhibition and publication that Rosenblum and Weyl have organized are testaments to not only their impressive research and archival sleuthing, but also their clarity of vision and tenacious commitment to a story that was absent from the history of the postwar print renaissance in the United States. We thank them for bringing *A Model Workshop* to the Jordan Schnitzer Gallery at Print Center New York.

The success of this project is indebted to the lending institutions, galleries, individuals, and artists' estates who made it possible. Access to some materials was only possible through the generosity of many individuals who opened up their homes and personal collections to the curators and our team—we thank them for their time, warmth, and collaborative spirit. Chief among them is Ellen J. Benjamin, Margaret Lowengrund's grandniece, who has for many years worked to document Lowengrund's work and preserve her legacy by collecting primary materials such as personal documents, artworks, and interviews. Her contributions as a lender to our exhibition, a research resource, and an essayist have been invaluable.

We also thank our many colleagues in curatorial departments, archives, and libraries who have opened up their collections and facilitated Rosenblum and Weyl's research over the last three years. For research assistance, we thank especially Emily Jones (The Woodstock Artists Association and Museum); Cristina Fontánez Rodríguez and Caitlin Riordan (Pratt Institute); Elizabeth Seaton (The Marianna Kistler Beach Museum of Art); Margaret Glover and Alvaro Lazo (The New York Public Library); and Marisa Bourgoin and colleagues (The Archives of American Art).

In realizing this publication, we are indebted to our brilliant guest essayists for engaging so rigorously with their topics. We also thank Flatpage for their speedy copyediting; William Howze for his expertise in image acquisition and licensing; and Argenis Apolinario and Evan Jenkins for new photography. We owe thanks to a fantastic team at Hirmer Verlag: Elisabeth Rocheau-Shalem, Senior Editor, believed in this project from the start and gave us the opportunity to create this lasting document of our curators'—and Lowengrund's—work. Her colleague in Munich, Rainer Arnold, expertly managed the book's production. On the book's design, we are fortunate to have worked with Adam Squires of CHIPS, who has been a thoughtful and creative collaborator in developing this publication and its visual sensibility.

The dedicated staff at Print Center New York realized this ambitious project over three years of development. Marina Avia Estrada, Research Assistant, performed instrumental research support for the curators, especially in the early stages of their work. Exhibitions and Programs Coordinator Robin Siddall, Curatorial Fellow Danielle Cooke, and Registrar and Facilities Manager Aaron Fisher have each worked tirelessly to support the curators' vision for both this publication and the *A Model Workshop* exhibition. We also thank our former team members Diana Perea and Tuesday Smillie, both of whom contributed to this project during their time with us.

We are grateful for Getty's instrumental vision and leadership support through its Paper Project, which transformed the scope of this project and allowed Weyl and Rosenblum to dream big. We extend thanks to The Wyeth Foundation for American Art and The Kaleta A. Doolin Foundation for their support of this publication; and the Helen Frankenthaler Foundation for their support of the project overall. Finally, we thank Print Center New York's Board of Trustees for their continued support of our exhibitions and programming that, like *A Model Workshop*, uncover new stories and push our field forward.

Judy Hecker
Executive Director

Jenn Bratovich
Director of Exhibitions and Programs

Editor's Note: Following Japanese convention, Japanese artists are referred to in this publication with their surname first, followed by their given name.

Margaret Lowengrund, detail of *Manhattan*, ca. 1928.
Drypoint, plate 8 ½ × 10 ¼ in.

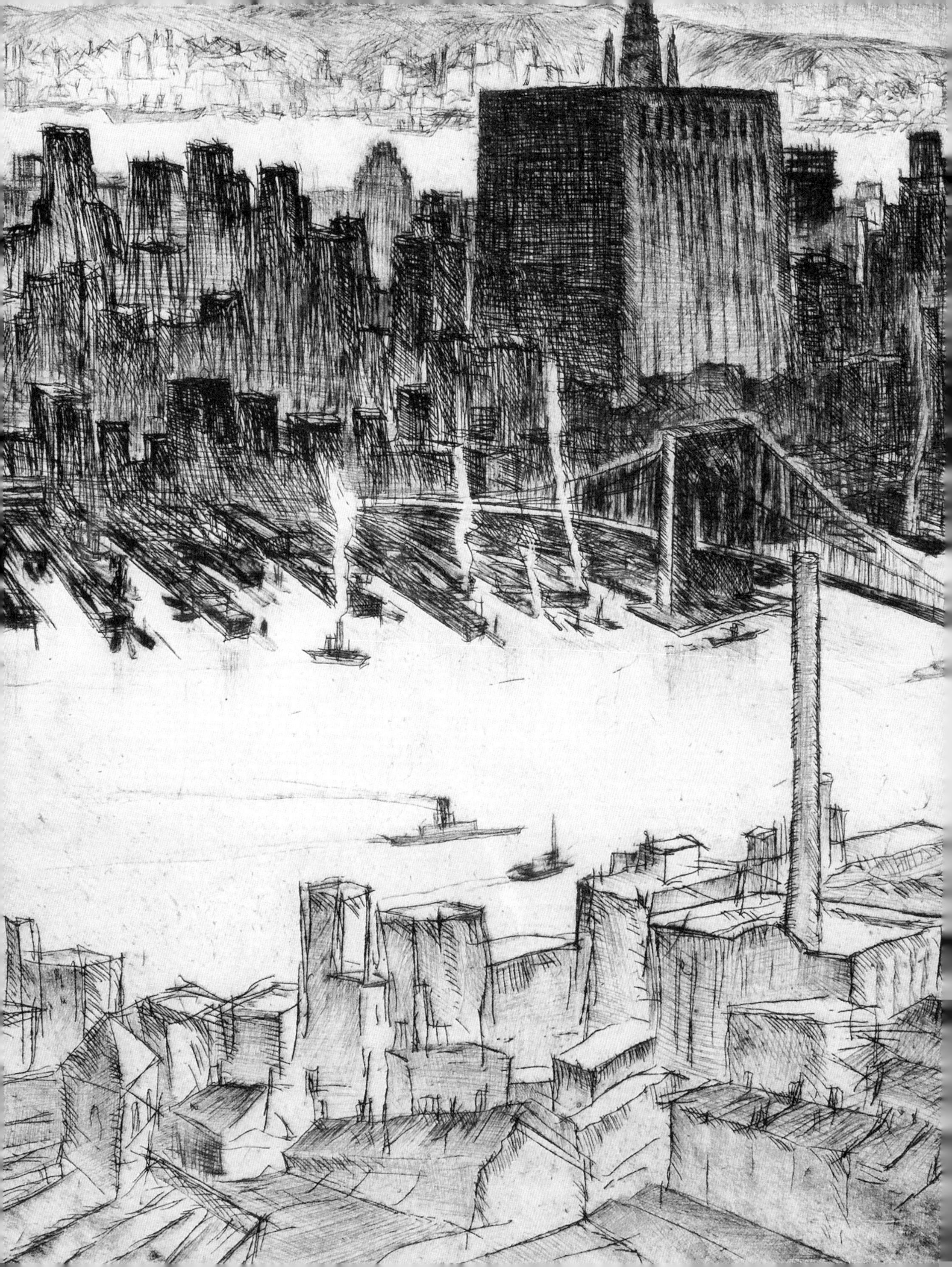

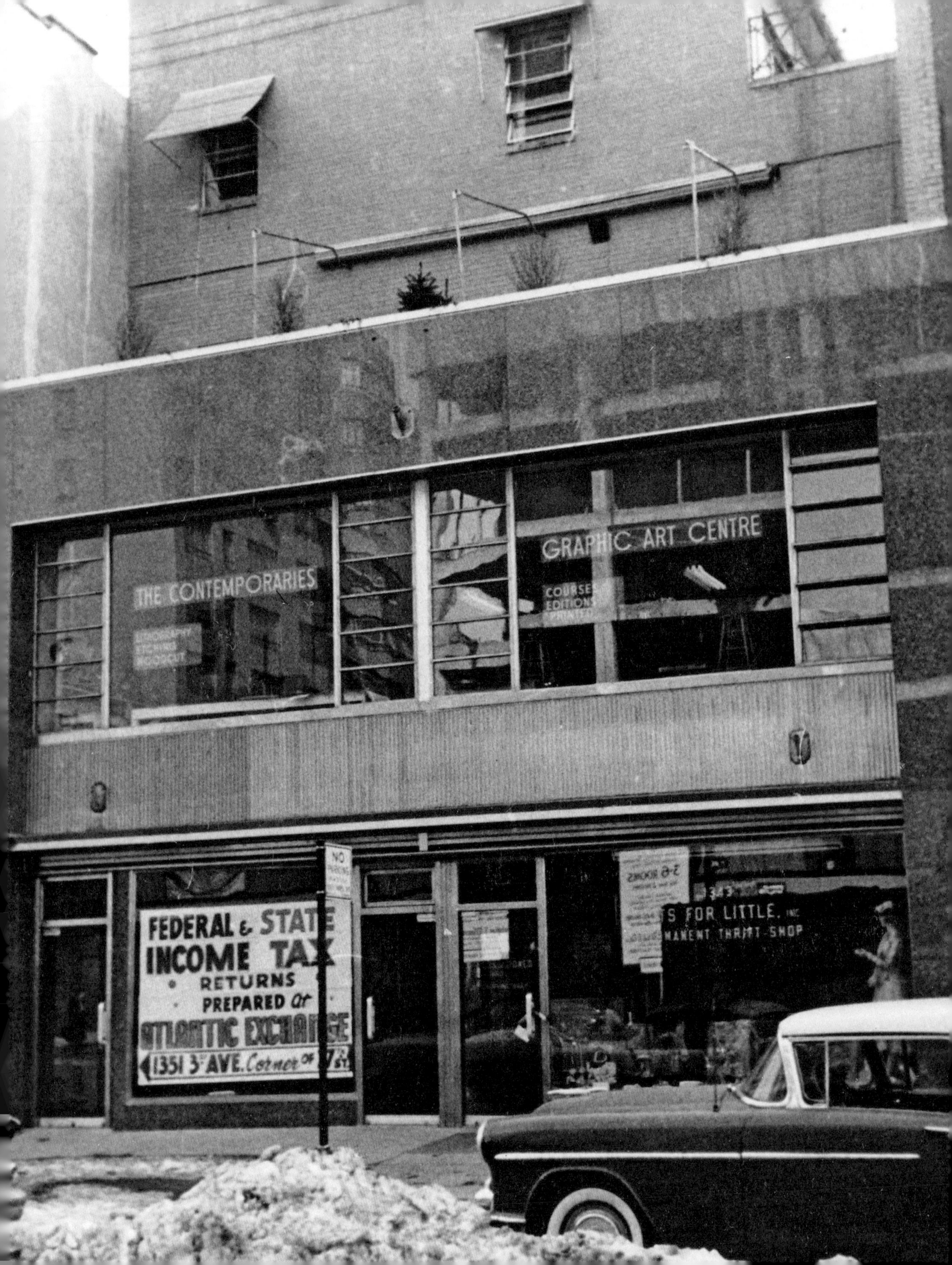
GRAPHIC ART CENTRE
THE CONTEMPORARIES
COURSES
EDITIONS
PRINTED
NO PARKING
FEDERAL & STATE
INCOME TAX
RETURNS
PREPARED At
ATLANTIC EXCHANGE
1351 3rd AVE. Corner OF

INTRODUCTION

Lauren Rosenblum and Christina Weyl

In late November 1951, a small bifold announcement card arrived at the New York Public Library's Art Division with handwritten instructions from the sender to "please post" (Fig. 1). The mailing, which originated from an entirely unknown entity called The Contemporaries, included little practical information—neither artist roster nor hours of operation. Instead, the inside of the small, folded flyer outlined this unconventional enterprise, which fused production, education, exhibition, and sales of prints under one roof—representing the first such entity in the United States. Under headers "The Gallery" and "The Studio," director Margaret Lowengrund (1902–1957) laid out ambitious goals for her hybrid space located on Madison Avenue at Seventy-Fifth Street, far removed from the bustling hub of the midtown gallery scene. The studio was an innovative workshop that advertised a range of educational and professional services across the spectrum of printmaking processes—lithography, intaglio, and "all related printing techniques." In addition to instruction at all levels, from beginners

The Gallery:

An exhibition place for present-day graphic art, painting and sculpture.

Work in graphics is a creative impetus to artists in other fields when the means is made available.

Exhibiting all fine arts media side by side extends the scope of contemporary art.

The Studio:

A workshop for artists, professional or student.

We offer instruction in lithography, etching and all related printing techniques at moderate rates.

Special attention given to beginners. Editions printed for professionals in color or black and white.

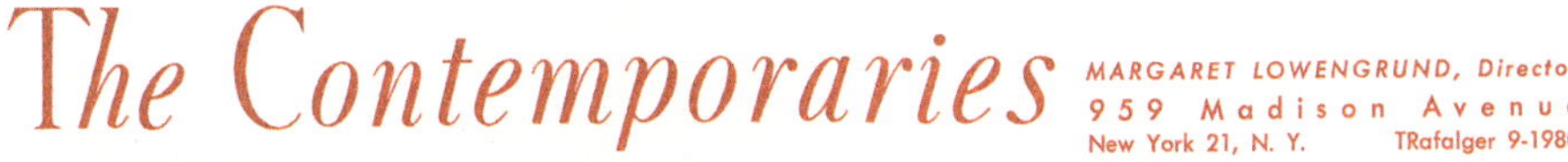

Fig. 1 Card announcing the opening of The Contemporaries, 1951

to professionals, artists could pay to have editions printed in either color or black and white. For the gallery, Lowengrund asserted a bold vision. By "exhibiting all fine arts media side by side," The Contemporaries would reveal the graphic arts as a "creative impetus," inspiring artists working in all media, including painting and sculpture. Lowengrund's concept aimed to disrupt traditional artistic hierarchies and to reverse the conventional direction of creative practice that held that prints derived from artists' work in other media. With this small announcement card, Lowengrund provocatively claimed that prints were essential—not secondary—to the contemporary artist.

Exterior of The Contemporaries Graphic Art Centre at 1343–45 Third Avenue, ca. 1955–56

A Model Workshop: Margaret Lowengrund and The Contemporaries explores the generative legacies of this visionary artist-advocate and her hybrid workshop-gallery. Over its first fifteen years (1951–66), The Contemporaries and its successor institution—Pratt Graphic Art Center (PGAC)—supported and inspired countless artists who arrived in New York City from all over the world seeking to train in the graphic arts, to join a creative community, and to exhibit their work in contexts emphasizing the primacy of printmaking. Although Lowengrund's direct involvement with The Contemporaries ended in 1957 with her premature death, her founding vision and aspirations continued to carry significant impact. In her lifetime, she touched countless artists, curators, and dealers active in the bourgeoning field of postwar printmaking, and the course of PGAC's first ten years of activities and programming reflect the continuation of her influence. Lowengrund pioneered a model of the printer-publisher that was ahead if its time and hugely consequential to the history of the graphic arts in the United States during the twentieth century.

While rebuilding the complex institutional history of The Contemporaries and PGAC, *A Model Workshop* brings into focus a picture of the bustling printmaking scene of the 1950s that largely contradicts historical accounts describing the decade as devoid of innovative printmaking activity. The standard narrative implies that the founding of several collaborative printmaking workshops stretching from the late 1950s through the 1960s—including Tamarind Lithography Workshop, Universal Limited Art Editions (ULAE), Gemini G.E.L. (Graphic Editions Ltd.), and Crown Point Press—sparked a resurgence of interest in printmaking variously called the "Print Boom" or "Graphic Revival."[1] *A Model Workshop*'s deep exploration of archival materials—about Lowengrund specifically, but also about the artists and institutions with whom she interreacted—shows that the Print Boom began at least a decade earlier and that The Contemporaries was central to sparking this surge.[2] *A Model Workshop* describes the interest in contemporary printmaking that took shape across the 1950s as a slow and sometimes circuitous crescendo, rather than a burst of spontaneous activity. Indeed, this project contends that Lowengrund's unwavering advocacy—she was, according to one colleague, "completely dedicated to making fine and original prints"—and her hybrid workshop-gallery were both vital precedents and catalysts for the collaborative workshops and printer-publishers that proliferated and profited during the 1960s.[3]

For a host of reasons, Lowengrund and The Contemporaries have been only a blip charted on historical accounts of twentieth-century printmaking. One of the largest stumbling blocks integrating this history fully is that Lowengrund restructured The Contemporaries several times across six years, relocating the gallery and workshop and reimagining the connection between the two entities. While it is possible to reconstruct Lowengrund's professional career—given her extensive exhibition history, plus her active participation in many art organizations—existing scholarship about The Contemporaries and PGAC has not yet captured the complexity of these shifts and moves. Along with this catalogue's essays, the chronology assembled for this publication maps this institutional history for the first time.

The dearth of archival material and the lack of one consolidated resource about Lowengrund, The Contemporaries, and PGAC has kept this rich institutional history under wraps. In 2004, Lowengrund's daughter donated a slim collection of papers pertaining to The Contemporaries to the New York Public Library.[4] Pratt Institute, which merged with The Contemporaries workshop in 1956, holds a sliver of material in its archives from PGAC's earliest years. Thankfully, the Rockefeller Foundation maintained copious notes related to its two grants to PGAC, and these records at the Rockefeller Archive Center form the backbone of this study. A large group of PGAC's early documentation also remained with Fritz Eichenberg, who took over directorship

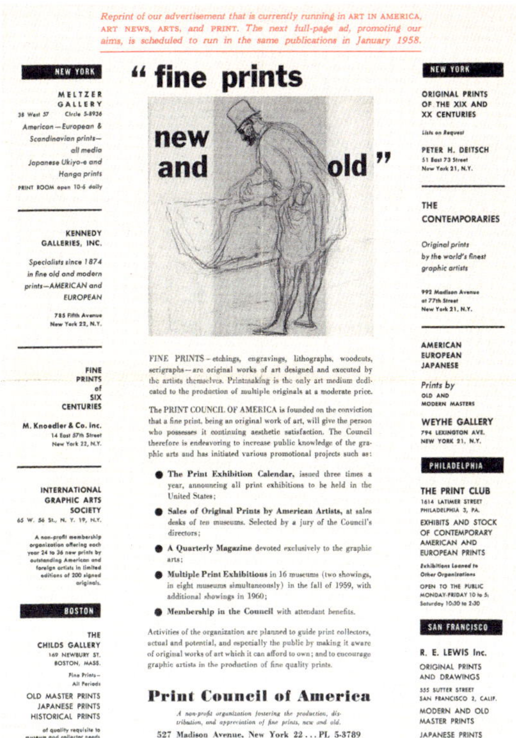

Fig. 2 Advertisement for the Print Council of America, reproduced in *Art News* 56, no. 6 (October 1957)

of PGAC after Lowengrund's death and later donated his papers to Yale University. The Lowengrund family has generously facilitated access to its private archives, which assisted in developing a vibrant portrait of this artist-advocate. Beyond these resources, research for *A Model Workshop* has relied on scattered reference to The Contemporaries or PGAC in individual artists' papers.

These archival documents paint a new, previously untold picture of Lowengrund's advocacy and leadership within the larger ecosystem of the Print Boom of the 1950s. Over the last fifty years, a handful of scholars have acknowledged Lowengrund's central role in reinvigorating postwar lithography.[5] This scholarship, however, misses Lowengrund's more catholic approach to supporting graphic artists across all media and her broader goals of stimulating the public's interest in printmaking in the United States. She was, for example, actively involved in the earliest years of the Print Council of America (PCA), an organization founded to provide education and to foster print collecting among new audiences.[6] Lowengrund enthusiastically supported the PCA's first full-page advertisement, which ran in several national art magazines in 1957–58, introducing the organization and promoting reputable galleries offering original prints (Fig. 2).

Lowengrund has, at times, been positioned alongside June Wayne and Tatyana Grosman as one of three enterprising women who spurred the explosion of collaborative printmaking workshops during the 1960s.[7] In these accounts, Lowengrund is the much lamented third figure, whose premature death factors into her relative obscurity behind Wayne and Grosman. Interestingly, the women's activities are described as if they were acting independent of one another in their own geographic vacuums—Grosman running ULAE on Long Island, Wayne opening Tamarind in Los Angeles, and Lowengrund operating in New York City. New archival discoveries for *A Model Workshop* reveal, for the first time, that Lowengrund served

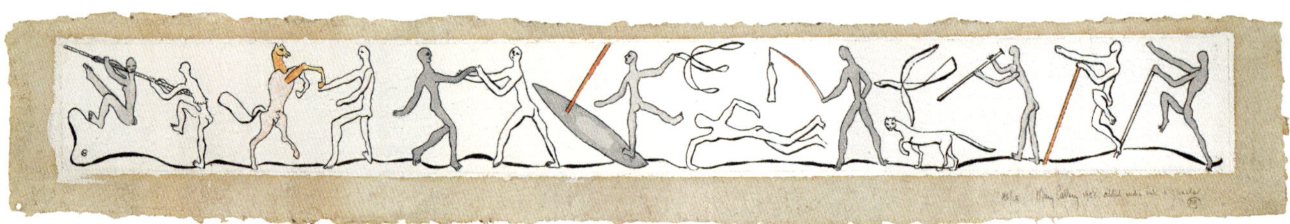

Fig. 3 Mary Callery, *Sons of Morning*, 1955–56. Screenprint, edition of 48, sheet: 8 × 54 in. Published by Universal Limited Art Editions, Bayshore, NY

as a foremother to both Wayne and Grosman, whom she knew and inspired with her advocacy. With the hybrid model she established at The Contemporaries, Lowengrund blazed the trail for Grosman and Wayne to make their own contributions only a few years later.

Like Lowengrund, Tatyana Grosman was aware of the growing graphic revival, but she and her husband Maurice initially entered the field from a slightly different angle. Around the same time that Lowengrund opened The Contemporaries to showcase "original" prints by leading contemporary artists, the Grosmans began to screenprint reproductions of artworks by others.[8] The channels and spaces for selling the Grosmans' facsimiles, however, were distinct from Lowengrund's upscale Upper East Side gallery. Seeing the trending popularity of original prints, Grosman shifted course by early 1955 and began reproducing original drawings, which artist friends supplied specifically for this purpose.[9] Although these screenprints were not produced in the type of collaborative workshop that Lowengrund was pioneering, the Grosmans' new publications were now within the realm of prints offered at The Contemporaries. In fact, Mary Callery's *Sons of Morning* (1955–56), the Grosmans' first original screenprint, was exhibited in *Today: An Exhibition of Sculpture and Graphic Art* (September 1955), the show inaugurating The Contemporaries' reopening at 992 Madison Avenue (Figs. 3 and 4).[10] The Grosmans' publishing entity—Limited Art Editions, which would later evolve into ULAE—was launched a few weeks later on November 16, 1955.[11] The Grosmans' storied printshop would not have been possible without the example Lowengrund set with The Contemporaries.

Lowengrund significantly influenced artist June Wayne, founder of Tamarind Lithography Workshop, by showing her the enormous benefit of training professional printers to collaborate with artists. Though she never availed herself of Lowengrund's professional printers, Wayne was closely associated with The Contemporaries, showing in several group shows and a duo exhibition (1953). When Lowengrund died in 1957, Wayne mourned her both as a friend and a professional artist interested in making lithographs, fearing the loss of Lowengrund's estimable model of artist-printer collaboration.[12] Wayne's somber mood at Lowengrund's death no doubt affected her decision to approach the Ford Foundation in 1958 for a major grant to establish Tamarind, which opened in 1960 and reshaped the landscape of lithography in the United States.

The catalogue essays for *A Model Workshop* proceed in roughly chronological order. Lauren Rosenblum's essay focuses on Lowengrund's activist formulation of The Contemporaries as "A Model Workshop"—the headline used to describe Lowengrund's hybrid workshop-gallery in a 1954 issue of *Art News*—by documenting how she adapted and reshaped the varied models of printmaking studios encountered across her professional career. Christina Weyl's essay recounts the

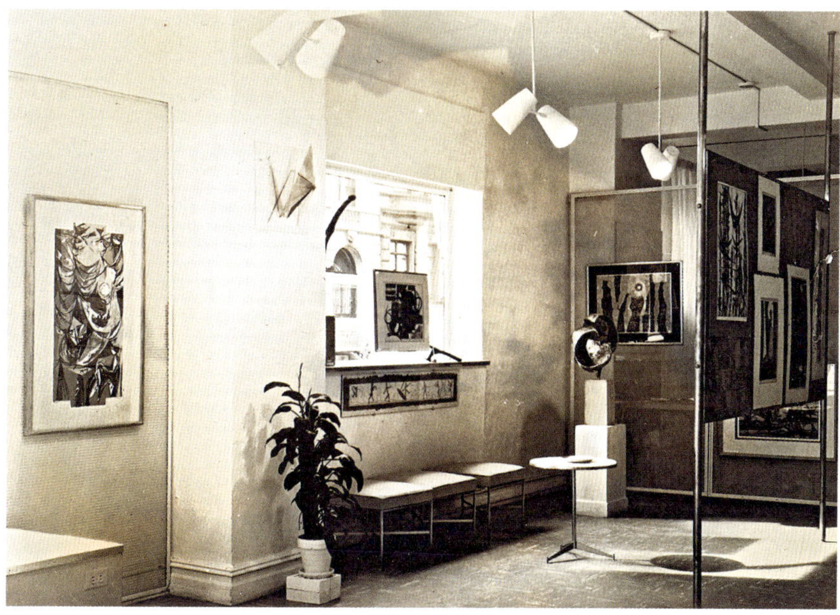

Fig. 4 Installation view of *Today: An Exhibition of Sculpture and Graphic Art*, at The Contemporaries, 992 Madison Avenue, 1955, with Mary Callery's *Sons of Morning* hanging below the window. Gelatin silver print. Photo by Robert Delson

institutional history of The Contemporaries and PGAC, looking back on Lowengrund's writings and other contemporary trends to understand how she not only catalyzed but also supported the development of contemporary printmaking.

Five shorter essays lay out major themes in Lowengrund's professional career and in midcentury printmaking by highlighting varied dialogues, activities, and innovations taking place within The Contemporaries and PGAC. Ellen J. Benjamin provides insights into Lowengrund's little-studied but extensive work as an illustrator and critic, noting how the artist was persistent across her career in making her voice and opinions known through her art and writing. Jillian Russo situates Lowengrund among the female gallerists who increasingly dominated the postwar art scene. Sarah Archer contextualizes Lowengrund's outreach to interior designers and decorators within the postwar housing boom and the push to bring contemporary printmaking to middle-class homes. Noriko Kuwahara charts the many instances of exchange between Japanese printmakers and The Contemporaries and PGAC, highlighting the mutual benefits to Lowengrund and the artists she supported. Finally, Rachel Vogel considers PGAC's generative legacy among the cohort of Latin American artists who founded the New York Graphic Workshop and pushed the definition of contemporary printmaking into a conceptional direction.

These essays and case studies collectively showcase Lowengrund's extensive influence on the graphic arts and the broad reach of her advocacy. She possessed the rare ability to identify structural problems that were impeding the creative growth of printmaking in the United States and to formulate specific and actionable plans to enact change. As June Wayne wrote in her condolence letter to Lowengrund's daughter, "She was rare and wonderful, full of courage, and vision, and she made the difference between a dark and a bright horizon for many artists in many places."[13] *A Model Workshop* represents a first step in opening the scholarly dialogue to Lowengrund's enormous impact on hundreds of artists during her lifetime and to her posthumous legacy on the trajectory of postwar print studios.

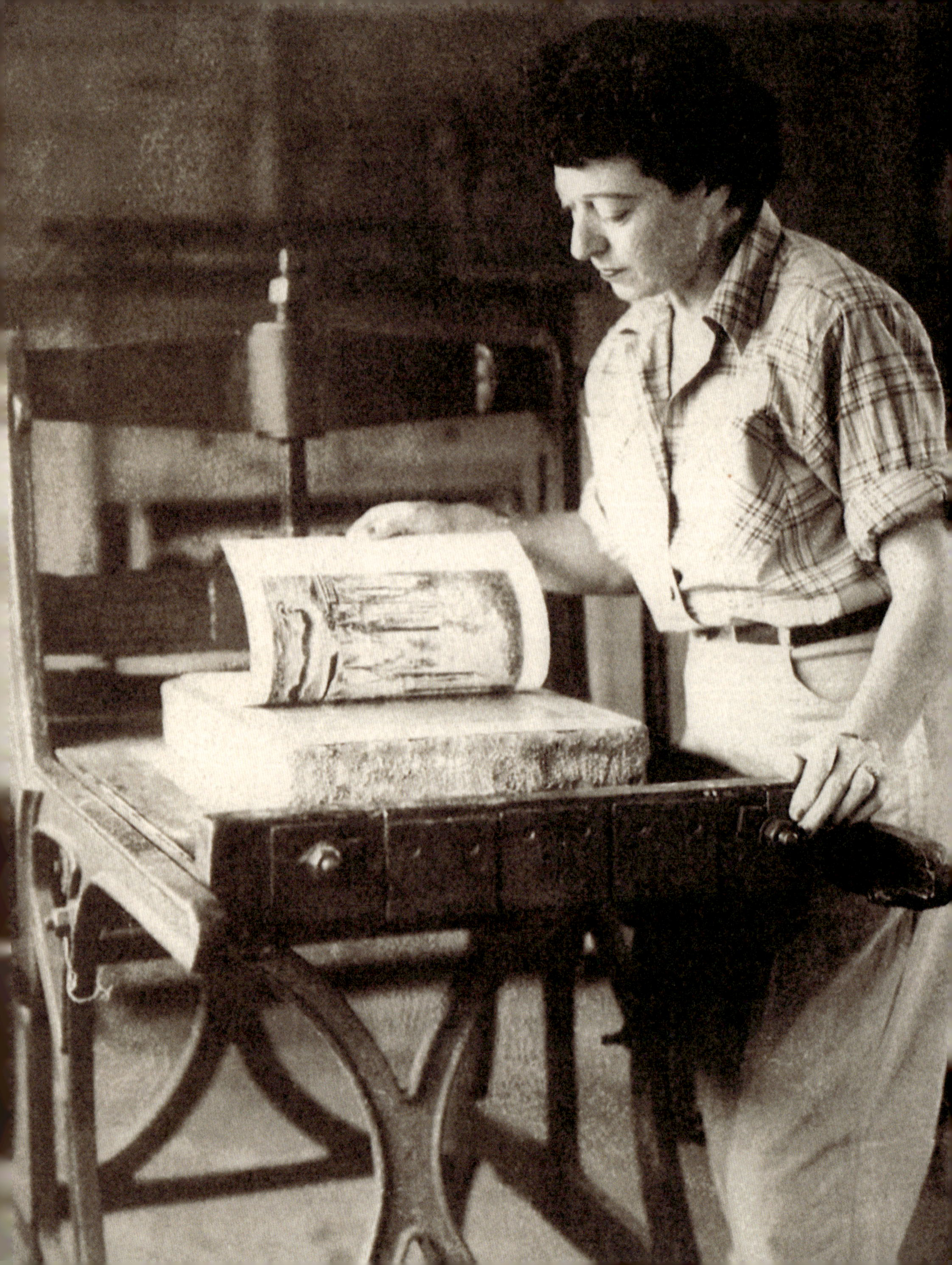

CONCEIVING A MODEL WORKSHOP: MARGARET LOWENGRUND BEFORE THE CONTEMPORARIES

Lauren Rosenblum

A 1954 article titled "A Model Workshop" updates the *Art Digest* reader on the status of The Contemporaries, the three-year-old gallery and workshop, by describing it as "one of the more ambitious galleries specializing in print media."[1] It reports that artists have been drawn to it, seeking out the studio space, "sensing and understanding the essence of the project and its need as a service and outlet for their creative work."[2]

From its inception, The Contemporaries was an unprecedented enterprise in the United States with its fusion of production, exhibition, and sales of modern graphics. Its mission and operation were expertly built upon founder Margaret Lowengrund's nearly thirty-five years of experience. During this time, work as a painter, printmaker, and illustrator brought her into traditional academic printshops, European ateliers, shared artists' studios, and modern art galleries, where she gained practical knowledge and formed a creative vision for her novel endeavor. In witnessing these workshop models, Lowengrund learned practicalities, like how to set up the physical space of a studio wholly dedicated to production. She observed how its rooms were efficiently organized to hold materials ranging from toxic chemicals to delicate papers, as well as a large press—or two, if lucky—used for a specific graphic process. Concurrently, she saw the print studio as an emergent site of socialization, with artists and printers clustered in tight quarters—sharing creative ideas, solving technical problems, and addressing sociopolitical concerns. Lastly, Lowengrund accrued pertinent insights into the financial viability of a print studio while circulating within the New York art world and a nationally networked community of print advocates dedicated to promoting a largely disregarded medium. She leveraged the totality of these experiences toward the founding of The Contemporaries, a commercial gallery with a focus on both production and sales, and unlike any that had come before it.

The course of Lowengrund's artistic career tracks many of the broad changes and dominant aesthetic trends as they emerged from the creative circles in which she moved. While an art school student and young professional during the 1920s, her creative output—lithographs, etchings, as well as sketches for newspaper illustration—mirrored the transformation of the contemporary artist into the mobile observer of modern life and city architecture, which became subjects of direct social commentary.[3] Building upon these experiences in the educational print

Margaret Lowengrund printing *River Traffic* in Woodstock, New York, ca. 1946 studios of her youth, Lowengrund became a participant and leader within several important artistic communities during the tumultuous decades of the 1930s and 1940s—from the idyllic artists' colony in Woodstock, New York, to the politically charged urban milieu of the Works Progress Administration's Federal Art Project. Paralleling shifts in her personal political beliefs, her artwork increasingly moved away from etching and toward an almost exclusive focus on lithography, which had a newfound association with leftist politics. During a brief stint as an art critic during the 1940s, she produced writing that attended to the postwar shift toward abstraction and the "art boom" catalyzed by the nation's economic prosperity. These same conditions motivated the founding of The Contemporaries. Through it all, Lowengrund saw the significance of graphics—and lithography specifically—in defining contemporary art for her own work and for that of her peers.

Lowengrund grew up in a middle-class Philadelphia family of German-Jewish origin with access to culture and a commitment to the visual arts from a young age.[4] Her earliest years were spent learning draftsmanship at the Graphic Sketch Club, a community art center. Her inherent skill as a drafter was recognized when she was awarded a prize in a national competition.[5] Lowengrund began a traditional art education in 1921. She spent two years studying illustration at the Philadelphia School of Design for Women and subsequently transferred to the Pennsylvania Academy of the Fine Arts (PAFA) in 1923—one of the country's oldest and most prestigious art schools—where women, though few in number, were attending, teaching, and exhibiting.[6] In class, students explored individual style, received one-on-one feedback, and participated in monthly critiques. A life drawing class exclusively for women fostered observational skills intended to teach students "to grasp and record quickly the spirit and character of the subject presented," which grounded the illustrative manner that formed Lowengrund's creative focus.[7]

But perhaps the most defining experience for Lowengrund was her continued tutelage at both schools under George Harding, whose illustration classes impacted her early style and her first career decisions.[8] According to a PAFA school circular, he offered "practical instruction" in drawing and composition that enabled the artist "to enter the professional field of magazine and book illustrating."[9] This instruction indeed proved to be practical, for soon, while still his student, Lowengrund started publishing illustrations in Philadelphia's *Evening Public Ledger* in a regular column called "Just Little Sketches 'Round Our Town."[10]

In fall 1924, Lowengrund moved to New York City and enrolled at the Art Students League (ASL), where she remained until spring 1926. If PAFA maintained its nineteenth-century pedagogical mission while accommodating the modernist tendencies of select faculty members, the ASL promoted itself as an alternative: it was democratically run with a modern pedagogy that fostered closer working relationships between students and their instructors.[11] Only two years before Lowengrund enrolled, the ASL had invited esteemed printmaker Joseph Pennell to revive its etching class and to establish one in lithography. With this imperative, Pennell aspired to seed, in the words of his biographer, "a great school of graphic art" that would surpass those educational workshops found in Europe, where he had built his career.[12] At first his poorly equipped classroom attracted mostly students interested in pursuing intaglio for its commercial appeal.[13] By the time Lowengrund arrived, Pennell had acquired several presses and new tools, and he soon hired a dedicated lithographer, Charles Locke.[14] While a student at the ASL, Lowengrund attended morning classes with Pennell and evening classes with Locke.

In this newly outfitted workshop, Pennell established a modern pedagogy in the graphic arts through an apprenticeship model whereby students worked alongside one another and the instructor. Lowengrund captured this studio dynamic

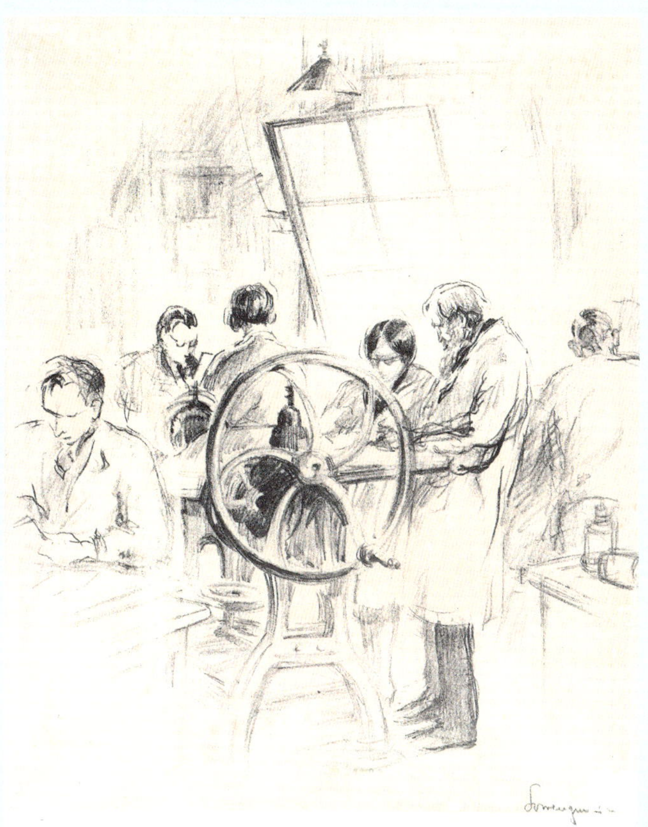

Fig. 1 Margaret Lowengrund, *Joseph Pennell at His Etching Press*, 1924/1925. Lithograph, sheet: 16 ¾ × 13 ½ in.

in a lithograph that conveys concentrated dedication to print production (Fig. 1). The scene centers around Pennell, the master printer, whom she defines with tusche—a liquid grease used to mark a lithograph stone—to outline his long smock and face. He and a nearby student stare downward, deep in conversation about a print in progress. The studio's large overhead windows illuminate the room, revealing the weighty printing presses at the center with a pride of place and students at tables cluttered with cans of solvent and sheets of paper. All are at work, each concentrating on a step in the process: marking a plate, cranking the printing press, smoking a plate, or regarding freshly etched markings.

Pennell charged his students with learning every step of the production process for both etching and lithography, representing a charge forward in how artists in the United States learned printmaking. He insisted on practical knowledge: he brought students to an industrial lithographic plant and provided commercial inks and etch recipes for students' experimentation at the ASL. Lowengrund's fellow classmate reflected on this well-rounded education:

> *We have learned a great deal about everything, from grinding stones and damping paper to the pulling of prints. We can now make drawings which without the intervention of any middle man can be printed directly from our stones in magazines, etc.*[15]

Notwithstanding this major pedagogical innovation, Pennell's operating model for the printmaking studio maintained standing divisions of labor. While his students learned every step in the printmaking process, he directed them to call upon professional printers to oversee the issuing of editions, as he had over the course of his own career.[16] While a student, Lowengrund encountered an institutionalized tension between the creative approach of the printmaker-artist and the skilled craft of the commercial printer engaged in mass production. Within printmaking, she experienced a traditional hierarchy that differentiated between the "refined" process of etching as an art form and the commercialism previously associated with lithography.[17] Lowengrund confronted this distinction in her artwork by experimenting with both intaglio and lithography at the ASL, while continuing to work as an illustrator.

Pennell also introduced a model of professional collegiality, facilitating his students' introduction to the art world and to print history. Elizabeth Robbins Pennell, her husband's biographer, describes the milieu both inside the ASL classroom, as sketched out in Lowengrund's lithograph, and outside in the city at large:

> *[Pennell] had the two classrooms—a second was given him for lithography—painted black on floor and high dado, white on the upper walls and ceiling, not solely for decorative effect but for concentration of the light. On the black dado he hung enlarged photographs of Rembrandts and Whistlers, determined to rescue his students from their outer darkness.... No fine exhibition of prints could open at the Metropolitan or the Grolier Club that he did not visit it with his class.... He lectured to his class, explaining his meaning with the aid of lantern slides.... He persuaded Mr. Mitchell Kennerley to hold his students' annual exhibition at the Anderson Galleries.*[18]

His enthusiasm for the practice of printmaking and the sociality inherent in the print world was not lost on Lowengrund: she participated in the aforementioned student exhibition, among her first professional presentations.[19]

As a student, Lowengrund explored both lithography and etching simultaneously, as was encouraged at the ASL, while making portraits of working people and the modern city. The lithograph *Untitled [Highbridge]* (ca. 1925), for example, depicts the oldest such structure in New York City as seen from the ground (Fig. 2). This viewpoint emphasizes the strong verticality of its stone barrel vaults, instead of the popular pedestrian promenade, and situates the area's landmark water tower to emphasize the composition's upward thrust, likely encouraged by an exploration of perspective observed in Pennell's prints. Lowengrund's intaglio prints of this period draw directly upon James McNeill Whistler's use of the etched line to both delineate form and mark out shadow. She also adopts his favored subject matter in images of shopfronts and doorways.[20]

Just as she had in Philadelphia, Lowengrund continued publishing an observational illustration series, retitled "Little Sketches About Town," in the *New York Evening Post*.[21] If at PAFA illustration was uneasily classified as a fine art, she recalled a different response from Pennell:

> *[He] criticized my newspaper stuff as roundly as my work in his class. He saved the clippings daily and went over them with me. When visitors to the graphics room came by, he always pointed out the fact that some students also worked for a living commercially, and did it as a part of professional training, not as a separate thing.*[22]

In support of Lowengrund's further development as a printmaker, Pennell wrote a letter of recommendation to his colleague, Archibald S. Hartrick, based at the Central School of Arts and Crafts in London, where she enrolled in the spring of

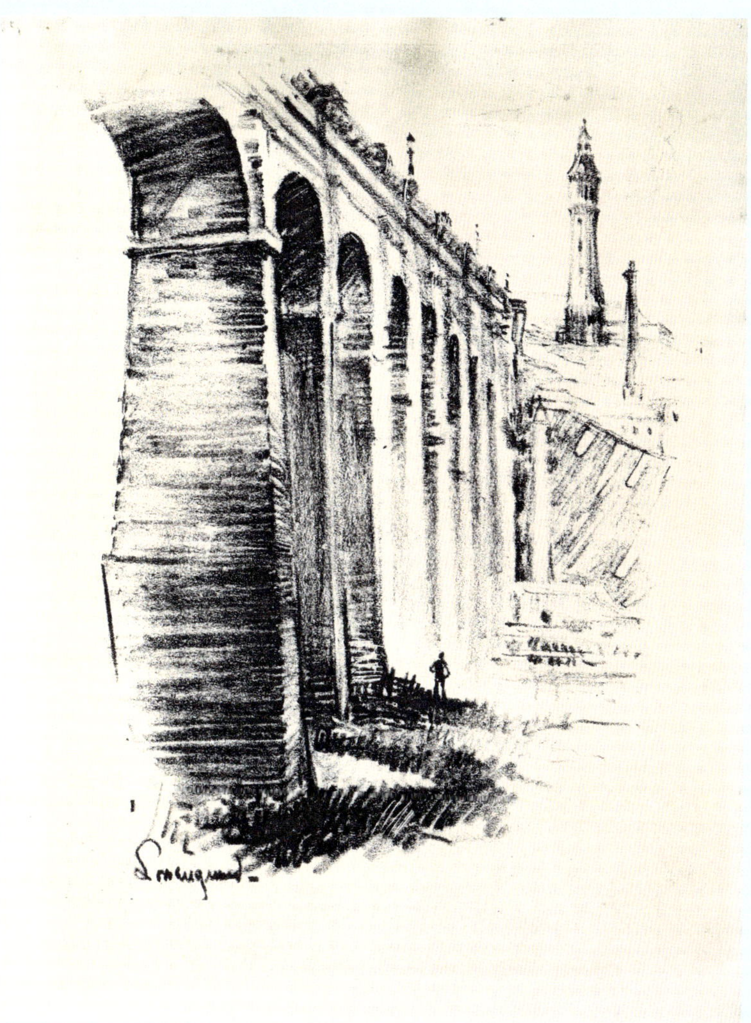

Fig. 2 Margaret Lowengrund, *Untitled [Highbridge]*, ca. 1925. Lithograph, sheet: 11 ½ × 9 in.

1926.[23] In 1909, Pennell and Hartrick had cofounded the Senefelder Club in London to promote lithography as an artistic medium among their peers, purchasing a shared press and hiring a printer to assist in experimentation.[24] The club also fostered a public for their prints by holding exhibitions and starting a lay members' collecting program—a model that Pennell, in part, exported to the United States. By the time of Lowengrund's arrival in London, the club had transformed into a social group coalesced around their shared interest in the process of lithography and exhibition opportunities.

Much like her experiences in New York and Philadelphia, Lowengrund continued to publish illustrations in European periodicals while also editioning unique prints concentrated on city life.[25] Extended trips to Paris, for example, resulted in impressions of the city's leisure activities and café culture during the interwar years. *L'apéritif* (1926), an etching depicting two sitters before a slightly filled glass containing a low pool of muddy liquid, emphasizes Lowengrund's mastery of the unique formal characteristics of the medium (page 33). Through the precision offered in intaglio, the woman's darkened, soft hat is rendered

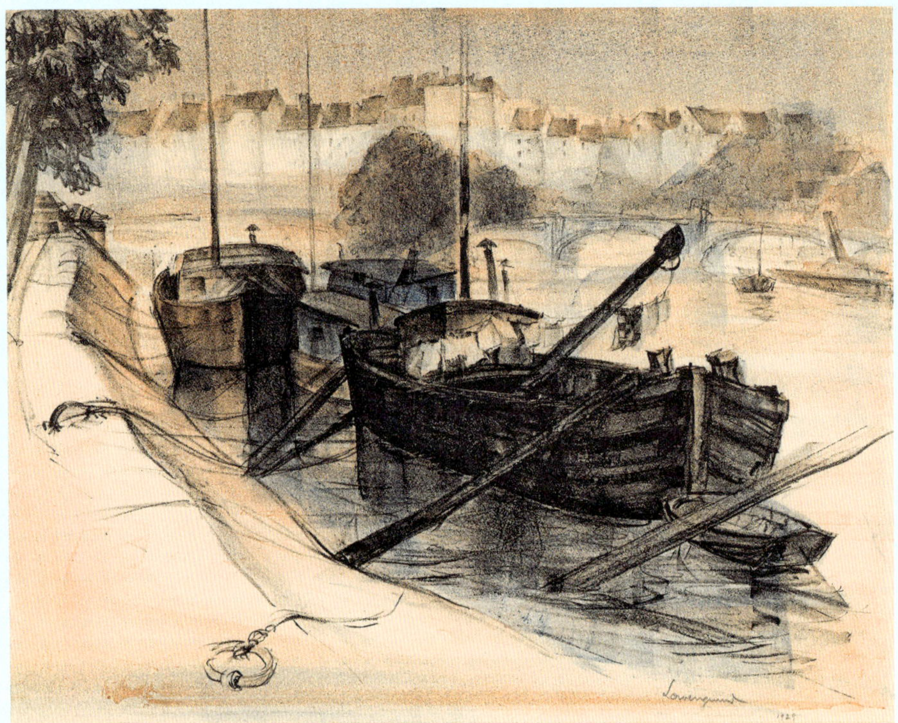

Fig. 3 Margaret Lowengrund, *Barges Along the Seine*, *Paris*, ca. 1927–29. Lithograph, image: 13 × 16 ½ in.

sparsely and with selective details; the man is defined by his delicate facial features and fuzzy hair. Inclusion of this print in the 1927 Salon d'Automne, one of Paris's independent juried art exhibitions that was receptive to nonacademic styles, signaled the recognition of Lowengrund's work as, in her own words, "daring" art associated with the cosmopolitanism of foreign artists in the School of Paris.[26]

Lowengrund also measured her successes abroad through honors such as the British Museum's purchase of her color lithograph, *Barges Along the Seine, Paris* (ca. 1927–29), facilitated by its curator Campbell Dodgson (Fig. 3).[27] Despite the support of her new associates and the institutional honor, she questioned the museum's selection, observing that it conformed too closely to an English preference for drawing that is "too conventional" and "too real."[28] She further admitted:

> *I don't like it myself.... Like other modernists I am not particularly concerned about having a beautiful scene or subject to paint. I want to recreate the commonplace through my own personality and make it interesting.*[29]

More than an observation of a British predilection, here the artist asserts the potential of modernity to be rendered in the graphic arts, just as it was in other media.

In 1928, Lowengrund returned to New York, and her newfound assuredness resonated from the artworks on display in her first solo exhibition at the Kleemann-Thorman Galleries. In addition to the paintings, drawings, and graphics Lowengrund had made abroad, the solo show introduced a new set of intaglio prints depicting the Manhattan skyline, which presented abstracted and geometrized facades of the city's ascendent skyscrapers, captured from increasingly dramatic perspectives.[30]

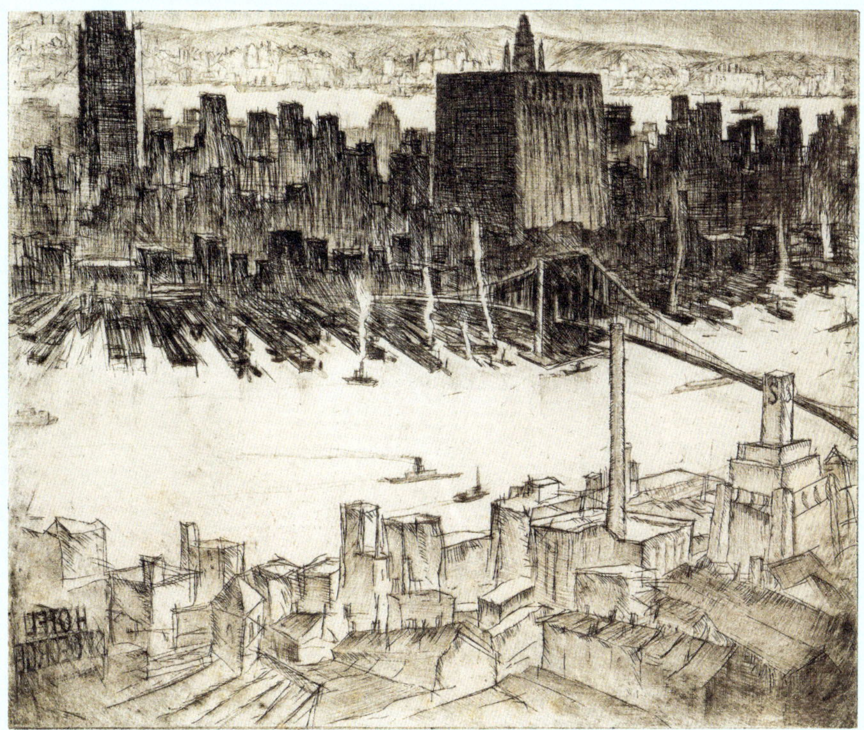

Fig. 4 Margaret Lowengrund, *Manhattan*, ca. 1928. Drypoint, plate: 8 ½ × 10 ¼ in.

Manhattan (ca. 1928), for example, approaches the city from above, showing the twenty-year-old suspension bridge spanning the vast East River as a connection between the neighboring boroughs (Fig. 4). She delineates the foreground buildings in light, blocklike shapes and the Manhattan skyline in inky shadow defined by vertical markmaking. In *Liberty* (ca. 1928), Lowengrund moves in and among the geometric angles of the city's skyscrapers to cast, again, a long view on the famous neoclassical sculpture—the Statue of Liberty—shrunk to the size of a figurine, afloat in New York Harbor (page 34). When viewed together, this group of prints shows Lowengrund's shift away from representation: her style became more pronounced as she attended to the changing cityscape under constant construction and boldly announced her new direction in modern printmaking.

Only a year after Lowengrund's debut exhibition, the stock market crashed and set off a widespread economic crisis. Her second marriage to Joseph Lilly, a respected journalist, brought personal and financial stability, and the two settled into a comfortable life in Great Neck, within commuting distance of the city.[31] During the early years of the Great Depression, Lowengrund continued to create new art that was featured steadily in exhibitions at the Kleemann Galleries and other important venues across the East Coast. She served as an illustrator for the *New York World-Telegram* and secured occasional magazine commissions that brought her and her husband to places such as Hollywood on behalf of Paramount News, the Caribbean via the Royal Netherlands Steamship Company, and Peru with the Grace Steamship Company.[32] However, the United States was a changed place. Like many artists of her time, Lowengrund's political convictions grew, and her preferred artistic subject matter turned to the afflictions of working people.

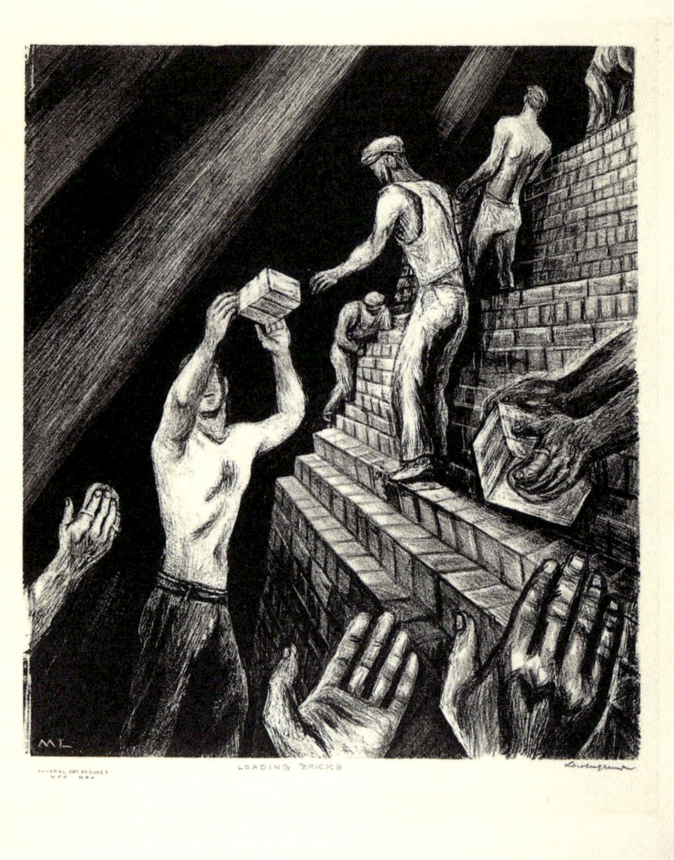

Fig. 5 Margaret Lowengrund, *Loading Bricks*, 1936. Lithograph, image: 10 7/16 × 9 3/8 in.; sheet: 15 7/8 × 11 1/2 in. Published by the Works Progress Administration, Federal Art Project, New York

Lowengrund worked productively and consistently across print processes throughout the mid-1930s. In a significant development, she was hired in 1936 by the Federal Art Project (FAP), a New Deal employment program of the Works Progress Administration (WPA). Lowengrund specifically worked in the Graphic Arts Division in 1936, the year its studio opened in Manhattan. There she completed five lithographs—identifiable by a signature stamp claiming the prints as government property—which were distributed to libraries, community centers, and public buildings across the country. Like the other artists working under the government's auspices, Lowengrund's subjects ranged from the everyday—including a scenic view of a landscape on Martha's Vineyard—to social commentary in the depiction of the working class in the United States. In a series of prints, Lowengrund presents frozen tableaux of laborers at a brick factory running the mechanized kiln and organizing its product. Such is the case in the background of *Loading Bricks* (1936), where men standing in a staggered formation along a brick wall pass dried clay blocks to one another (Fig. 5). Uniquely foregrounded, however, are two sets of enlarged disembodied hands floating on top of the routinized labor. One pair of hands remains upraised after releasing the brick to another pair that grasps the product tightly. Here, hands take on value beyond their service as a bodily appendage; they become the symbol of mechanized labor itself—brickworker and graphic artist alike—and a meeting point for their political solidarity.[33]

The federally funded printshop introduced Lowengrund to yet another model of workshop—this one attempting to maximize the employment of artists working in a small space in order to produce "art for the millions." (Fig. 6)[34] Abiding by the policies that governed access to the project's moderately sized printshop, Lowengrund and fellow artists—normally capped at sixty—visited only when the occasion demanded it.[35] After developing an image in her personal studio, Lowengrund presented the drawing for approval by committee. Once the image was accepted, she returned home to translate the image onto the heavy stone matrix, which had been delivered directly to her. Finally, she visited the government studio to work alongside the in-house, professional printer to run the edition on the press. While this collaborative relationship was already quite familiar to Lowengrund, it was new to many artists who made their first prints for the FAP. It set a widely adopted precedent that continued into the following decades.

Lowengrund, along with many of the others working in the Graphic Arts Division, saw lithography as a medium uniquely suited to images focused on the struggles of everyday life and labor during the Depression. These "social viewpoint printmakers," as they were called at the time, made "social art" that supported their leftist politics.[36] In this way, the workshop itself became a location of sociality where progressive ideology and activity were cultivated. It was in this context that lithography finally disentangled itself from long-standing commercial associations, transforming from a tool to circulate inexpensive, multiple originals into a "democratic" fine art—a cultural product of the political democracy.[37]

While the Graphic Arts Division's workshop was a hub for politicized printmaking, it was also a site of concentrated technical innovation.[38] There, Lowengrund likely honed her knowledge about recent developments in color lithography and within a short amount of time began teaching a course intended for both beginner

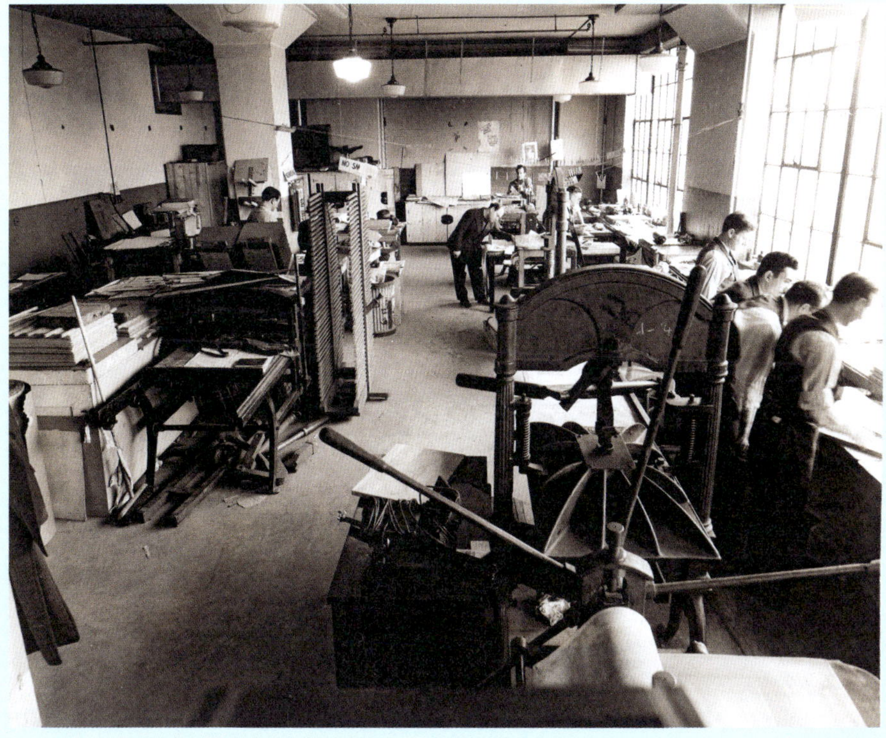

Fig. 6 Interior of the Graphic Arts Division of the Works Progress Administration Federal Art Project printmaking workshop, 110 King Street, New York, 1939. Photo by Max Yavno

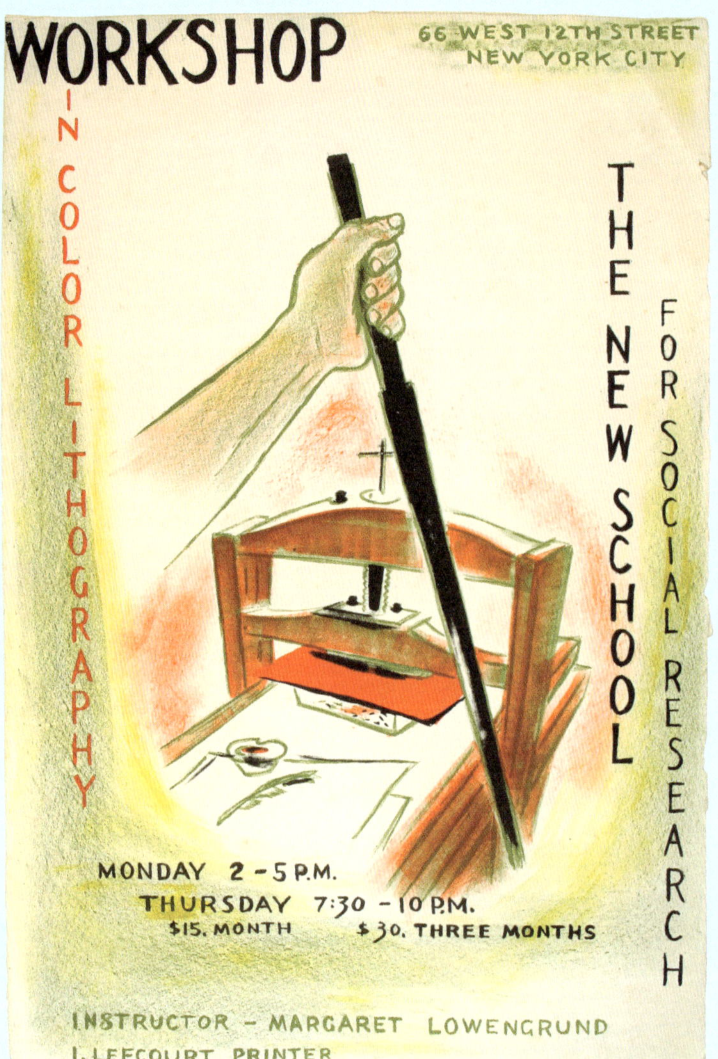

Fig. 7 Margaret Lowengrund, poster for workshop in color lithography at the New School for Social Research, 1938. Lithograph, 20 × 13 in.

and advanced students alike at the New School for Social Research.[39] The poster Lowengrund designed to advertise the class—itself a lithograph in dynamic yellows and reds—showcases the lithographic printing press. Reminiscent of *Loading Bricks*, a disembodied hand of the printer (identified on the poster as Irwin Lefcourt) grasps the press's lever in preparation to lift the scraper bar—another instance of the laboring hand moving in symbolic solidarity with all craftworkers (Fig. 7). The New School was founded on progressivism and had long been a home for political expression. In honor of this institutional imperative, the university hosted events by external organizations including the American Artists' Congress (AAC).[40] This large group worked to support the mandate of the Communist Party of the United States of America's (CPUSA) Popular Front initiative (1935–39) that aimed to rally radical and moderate leftists and to unify socioeconomic classes against fascism under the banner of "cultural democracy."

While Lowengrund's CPUSA membership card is not extant, scattered documentation registers her participation throughout the 1930s in arts organizations that clarify her political values.[41] Active within the AAC, Lowengrund was among the 401 signatories of its first declaration of purpose in February 1936 and served

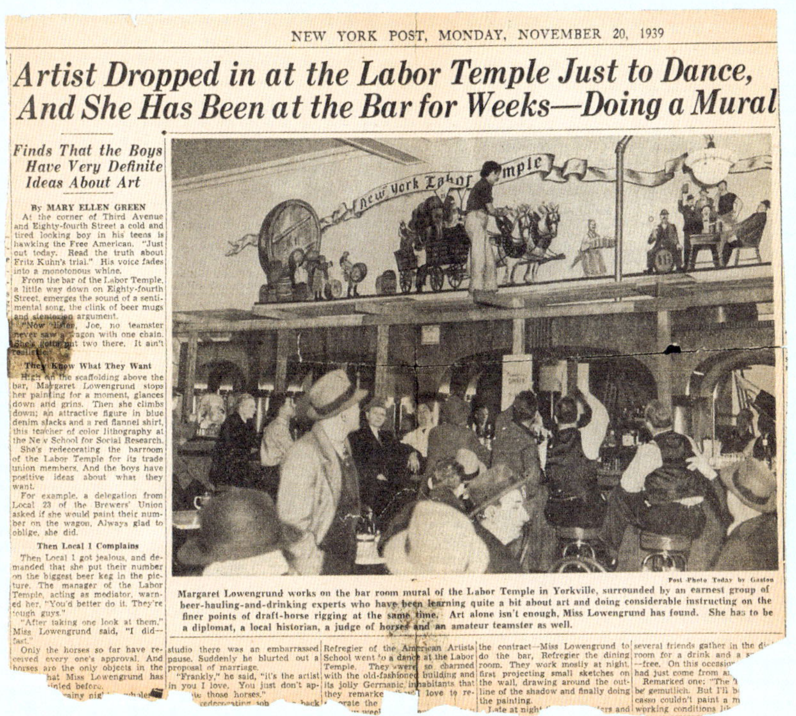

NEW YORK POST, MONDAY, NOVEMBER 20, 1939

Artist Dropped in at the Labor Temple Just to Dance, And She Has Been at the Bar for Weeks—Doing a Mural

Finds That the Boys Have Very Definite Ideas About Art

By MARY ELLEN GREEN

At the corner of Third Avenue and Eighty-fourth Street a cold and tired looking boy in his teens is hawking the Free American. "Just out today. Read the truth about Fritz Kuhn's trial." His voice fades into a monotonous whine.

From the bar of the Labor Temple, a little way down on Eighty-fourth Street, emerges the sound of a sentimental song, the clink of beer mugs and stentorian argument.

"Now listen, Joe, no teamster never saw a wagon with one chain. She's gotta put two there. It ain't realistic."

They Know What They Want

High on the scaffolding above the bar, Margaret Lowengrund stops her painting for a moment, glances down and grins. Then she climbs down; an attractive figure in blue denim slacks and a red flannel shirt, this teacher of color lithography at the New School for Social Research.

She's redecorating the barroom of the Labor Temple for its trade union members. And the boys have positive ideas about what they want.

For example, a delegation from Local 23 of the Brewers' Union asked if she would paint their number on the wagon. Always glad to oblige, she did.

Then Local 1 Complains

Then Local 1 got jealous, and demanded that she put their number on the biggest beer keg in the picture. The manager of the Labor Temple, acting as mediator, warned her, "You'd better do it. They're tough guys."

"After taking one look at them," Miss Lowengrund said, "I did—fast."

Only the horses so far have received every one's approval. And horses are the only objects in the [illegible]hat Miss Lowengrund has [illegible]inted before.

[illegible]

Post Photo Today by Gaston

Margaret Lowengrund works on the bar room mural of the Labor Temple in Yorkville, surrounded by an earnest group of beer-hauling-and-drinking experts who have been learning quite a bit about art and doing considerable instructing on the finer points of draft-horse rigging at the same time. Art alone isn't enough, Miss Lowengrund has found. She has to be a diplomat, a local historian, a judge of horses and an amateur teamster as well.

studio there was an embarrassed pause. Suddenly he blurted out a proposal of marriage.

"Frankly," he said, "it's the artist in you I love. You just don't ap[illegible] those horses."

[illegible]

Refregier of the American Artists School went to a dance at the Labor Temple. They were so charmed with the old-fashioned building and its jolly Germanic inhabitants that they remarke[illegible] love to re[illegible]orate the [illegible]

the contract—Miss Lowengrund to do the bar, Refregier the dining room. They work mostly at night, first projecting small sketches on the wall, drawing around the outline of the shadow and finally doing the painting.

Late at night [illegible]ers and several friends gather in the di[illegible] room for a drink and a [illegible] —free. On this occasio[illegible] had just come from a[illegible]

Remarked one: "The [illegible] be gemutlich. But I'll b[illegible] casso couldn't paint a m[illegible] working conditions li[illegible]

Fig. 8 Margaret Lowengrund painting the mural for the New York Labor Temple, 243–47 East Eighty-Fourth Street, reproduced in the *New York Post*, 1939

on the organizing committee of its second town hall in 1937.[42] She consistently presented paintings, etchings, and lithographs in its robust, thematic exhibitions held between 1936 and 1940, which brought together a broad coalition of artists working in various styles.[43] Lowengrund found further collectivism in exhibiting with An American Group, a more selective membership organization.[44] In addition, she contributed illustrations to *Art Project Reporter*, the newsletter of the Artists' Union, a trade group that took an activist stance in representing the collective labor interests of artists working for the FAP.[45] Lowengrund published images in leftist journals focusing on the aims of the Popular Front: two illustrations appeared in the magazine *Woman Today*, which advocated for anti-fascism, unionism, and broadly stated women's rights; and her lithograph, *Give Us a Program!*, appeared alongside an article in the radical *New Masses*, a journal known for publishing literature and visual arts.[46] A 1939 commission to execute a mural painting in the barroom of the New York Labor Temple, a community center for organized labor on Manhattan's Upper East Side, resulted in three vignettes showing the delivery of beer barrels to tables where they are drunk in good spirits by union worker patrons (Fig. 8).[47]

Only two years after the birth of her daughter Linda in 1934, Lowengrund and her husband relocated part-time to the rural artists' colony of Woodstock, approximately one hundred miles north of New York City. Over the course of the following twenty-three years—through the depths of the Great Depression, the turmoil of World War II, and the solace of a postwar nation—she cultivated an active civic and cultural life in Woodstock. Among her numerous projects there, Lowengrund's long-standing experience in news media led her to briefly host a radio program and to contribute a weekly column to several local newspapers

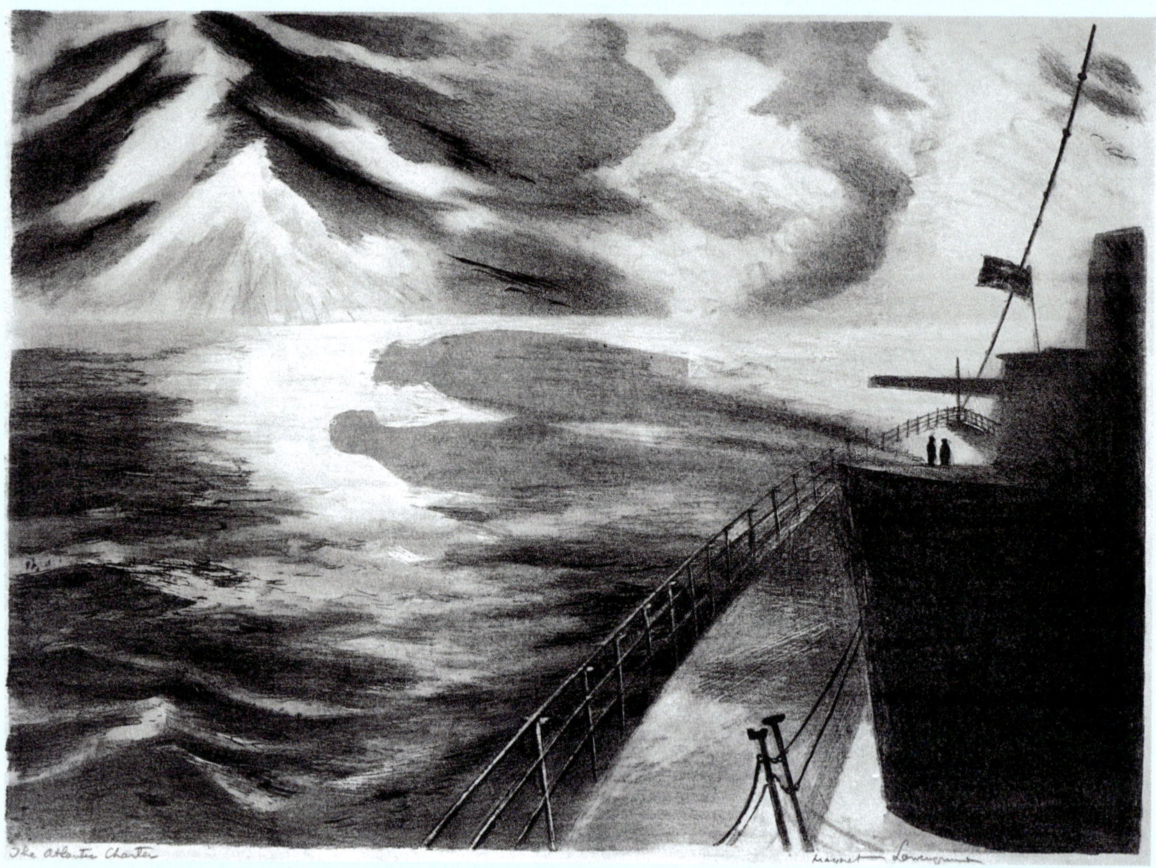

Fig. 9 Margaret Lowengrund, *The Atlantic Charter*, 1942. Lithograph, image: 12 ½ × 18 in.

that observed the activities of artists, critics, galleries, and museums in the Catskills and Manhattan.[48]

After the defining experiences of the FAP and its surrounding political movement, Lowengrund's membership in the Woodstock Artists Association (WAA) shaped the ensuing direction of her career.[49] The WAA served as a central hub of social and intellectual activity and was a major site of exhibitions for a large creative community of artists working in various media and competing styles.[50] In the 1940s, Lowengrund resumed painting in earnest; focusing on pastoral landscapes, still lifes, and portraits of her community members, her style shifted away from social commentary to more commonplace scenic images that recalled her previous illustration work and that were consistent with trends among Woodstock artists.[51] Alternately considered trite or modern by critics, these works were presented in her first solo exhibition at the local Rudolph Galleries in 1944, in regular shows at the ACA Gallery in Manhattan, and on the front of numerous greeting and holiday cards published by the American Artists Group.[52] Even when participating in the politically motivated wartime group exhibitions that circulated nationalist pictures—including *American Artists' Record of War and Defense* at the National Gallery of Art, Washington, DC in 1942 and *Artists for Victory* at the Metropolitan Museum of Art in 1943—Lowengrund often presented images of the home front or front line that communicated stillness instead of imagined acts of heroism. Her lithograph, *The Atlantic Charter* (1942), exhibited in *America in the War* (1943), an exhibition on view concurrently at twenty-six venues, sets an imposing warship off to the side of the image, with the shadows of its naval command cast out over the peaceful ocean (Fig. 9).[53]

While Lowengrund's work in graphics tapered during the 1940s, her ongoing commitment to the craft of lithography and its spaces of production is captured in a photograph taken in the basement of the WAA (page 18). She stands in work clothes next to a lithography press while peeling back a sheet of paper from the stone matrix resting on its bed.[54] Rather than the bustling studios of her past, she is alone pulling an edition of her *River Traffic* (1946), in which a long boat passes before the New York City skyline. These skyscrapers—geometric forms cast in light—resemble those from her etchings from the late 1920s. The lithograph is also reminiscent of her work as an illustrator in its stylized placemaking and narrative detail. Her final lithographs, completed in the years before her death, depicted alternately the natural—leaves and plants—or the architectural—images of midcentury apartment buildings.

Just before opening The Contemporaries in 1951, Lowengrund founded 7 Painter-Printmakers, a group of graphic artists who pursued both media with vigor.[55] Several of these printmakers' collectives had formed in the late 1940s and early 1950s, and Lowengrund's group explicitly sought to engage artists with color lithography—particularly artists with little or no previous experience in the medium.[56] Nearly all of the original members of 7 Painter-Printmakers, in fact, participated in an early exhibition organized by The Contemporaries, which opened at Chicago's Well of the Sea Gallery in February 1952.

By the dawn of her commercial venture in 1951, Lowengrund had spent her artistic career absorbing lessons from myriad printmaking workshops and artists' organizations that introduced her to varied models of collaboration and print production that would become significant to instituting The Contemporaries. Through academic training and professional experiences, she had become a proficient and accomplished practitioner of lithography and intaglio printmaking. Furthermore, she was keenly attuned to debates surrounding the function of various print media—from rarefied objects for elite consumption to images for mass distribution—and aware of the avenues for their dissemination into the commercial marketplace. Her experiences had also embedded her into networks—in Woodstock and among leftist organizers—that would become significant to her new venture. Lowengrund ably transformed these experiences into a new role as a business owner, a gallerist, and a workshop director. Ultimately with The Contemporaries, the culmination of her short-lived career, Lowengrund offered a new definition of what made printmaking and its artisanal process relevant to her contemporaries and to contemporary art in the United States.

Margaret Lowengrund

Balancing work in painting and graphic art, this selection of Margaret Lowengrund's prints conveys the range of her output. From her earliest student etchings through her final lithographs made at The Contemporaries, Lowengrund completed over 80 prints over the course of her lifetime.

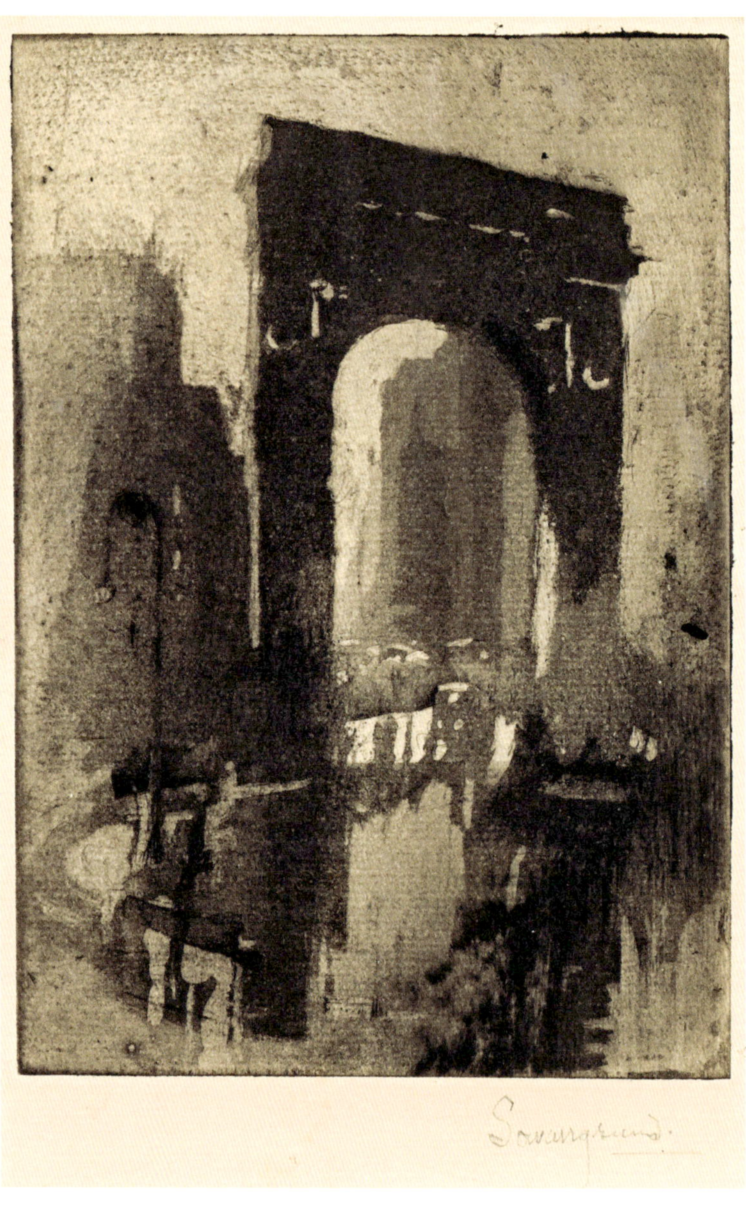

Margaret Lowengrund, *Washington Square*, ca. 1920s.
Aquatint, plate: 6 7/8 x 4 7/8 in.; sheet: 9 1/2 × 6 1/4 in.

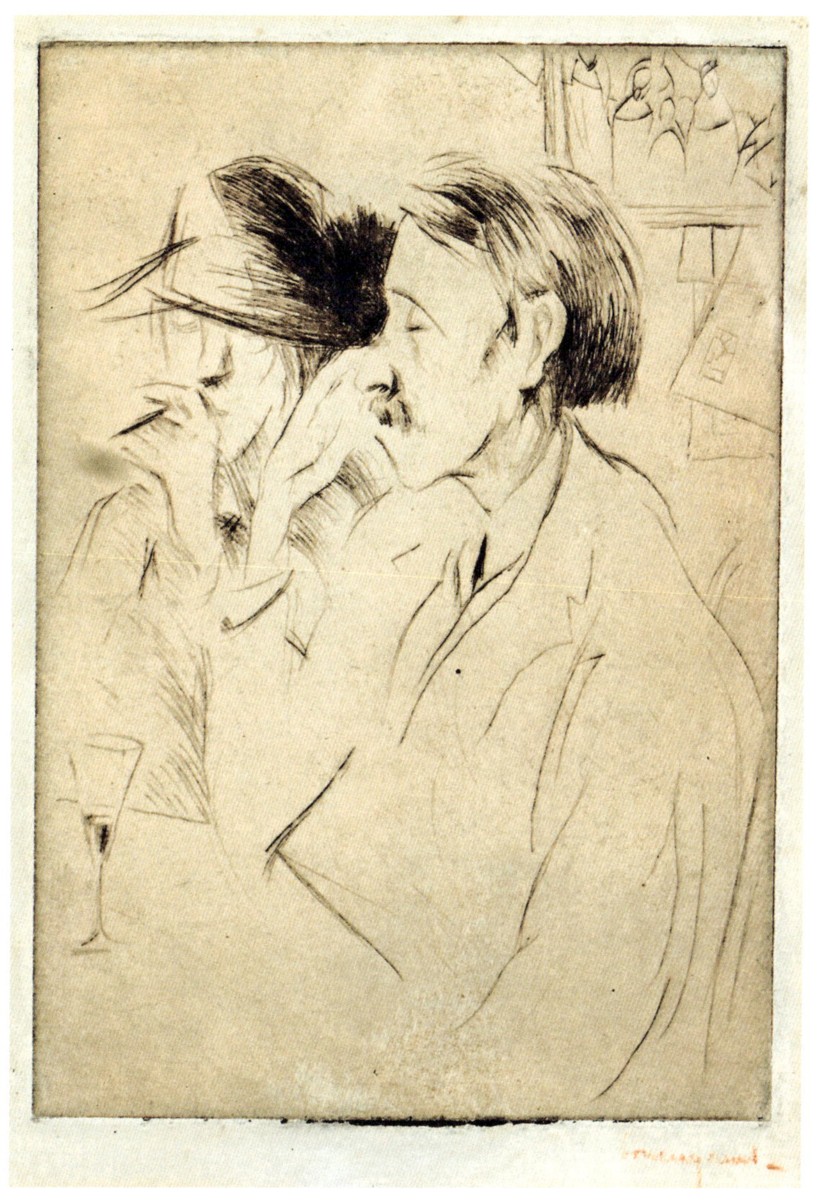

Margaret Lowengrund, *L'apéritif (The Appetizer)*, 1926.
Drypoint, plate: 6 15⁄16 × 4 15⁄16 in.

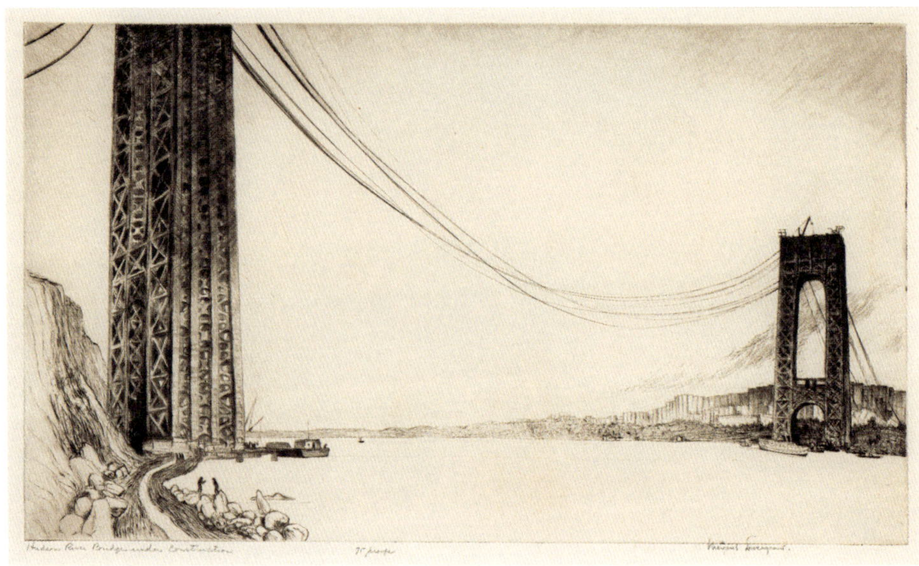

Margaret Lowengrund, *Hudson River Bridge Under Construction*, ca. 1928.
Etching, plate: 9 × 15 ¾ in.; sheet: 10 × 17 in.

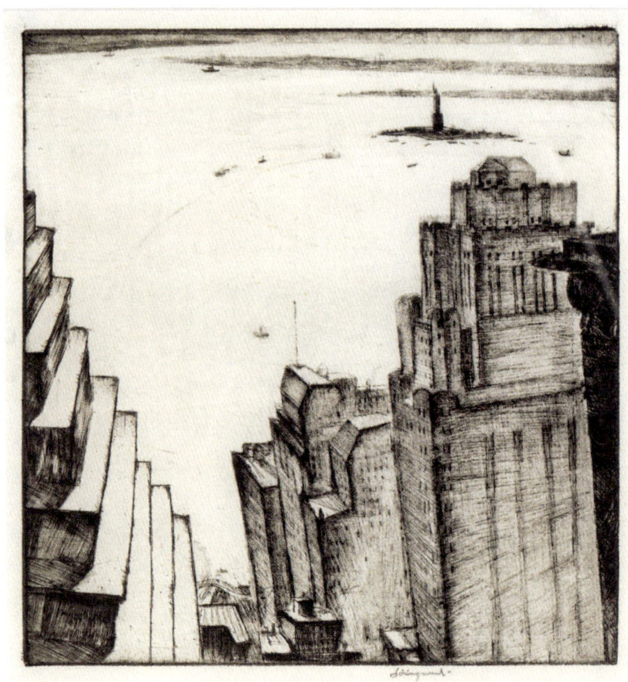

Margaret Lowengrund, *Liberty*, ca. 1928. Etching and drypoint, edition of 15, plate: 8 ¼ × 8 in.

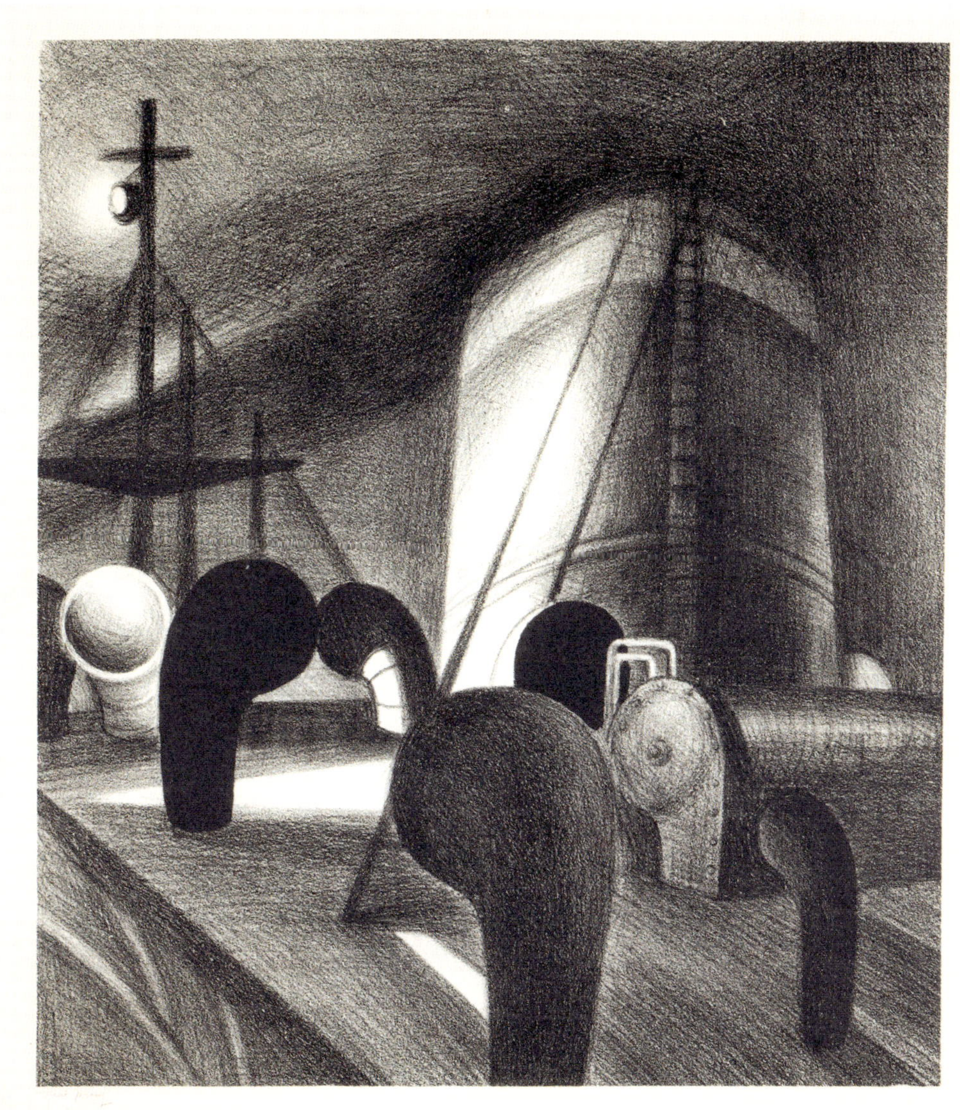

Margaret Lowengrund, *Top Deck*, 1932. Lithograph, edition of 20, sheet: 13 ¼ × 12 in.

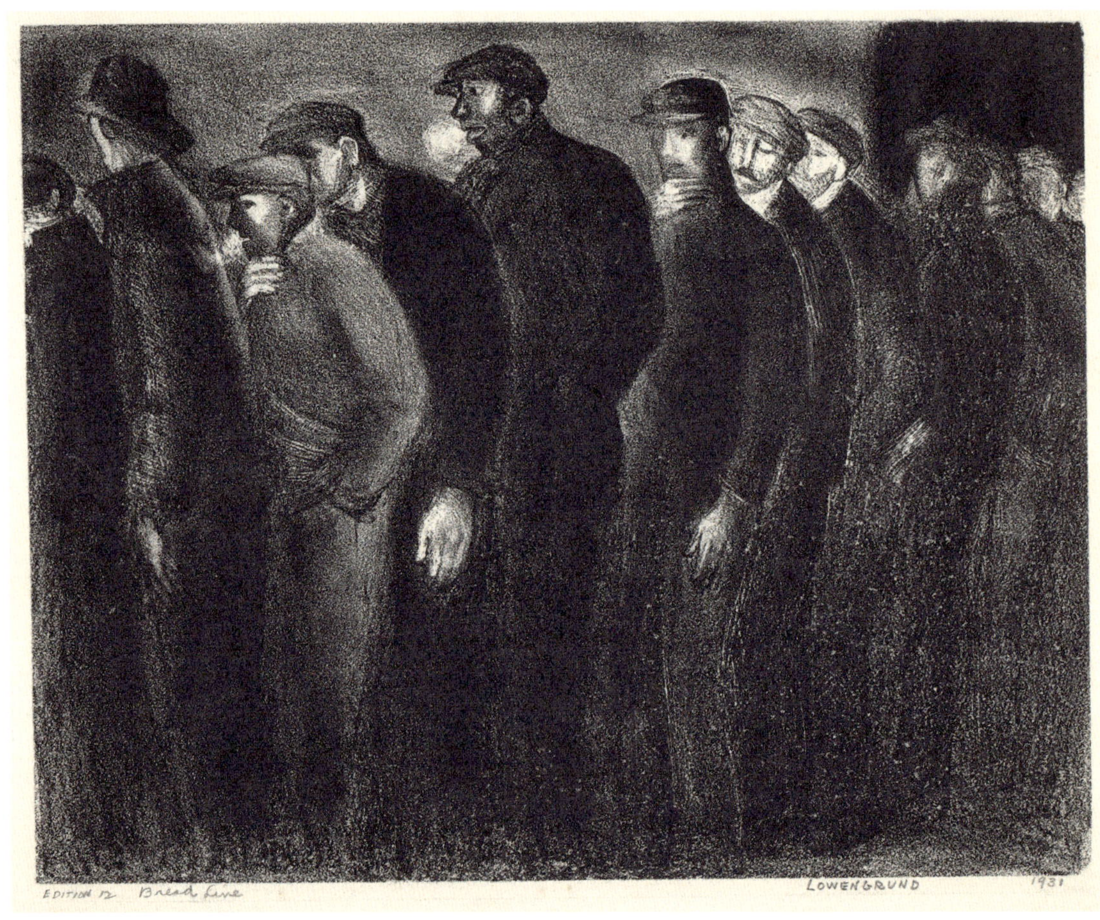

Margaret Lowengrund, *Breadline*, 1931. Lithograph, edition of 12, sheet: 8 × 10 in.

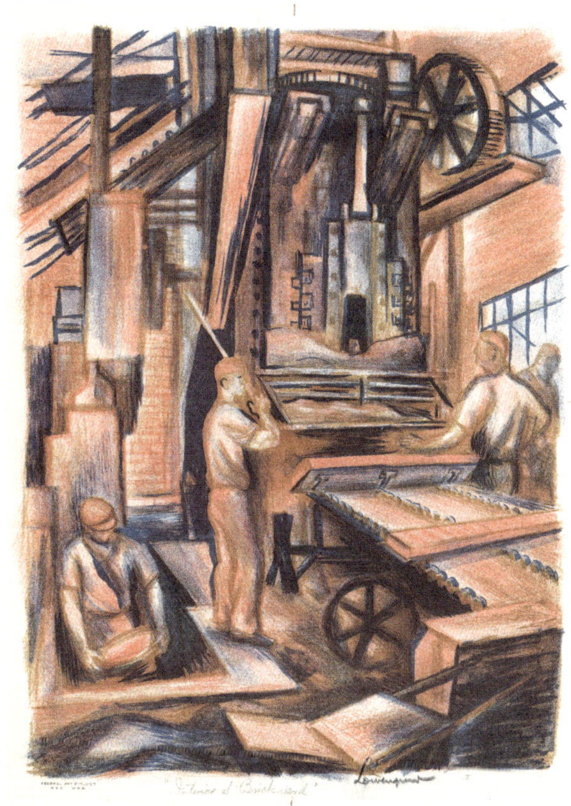

Margaret Lowengrund, *Interior of Brickyard*, 1936. Lithograph, image: 15 × 11 ⅜ in.; sheet: 19 × 12 ¾ in. Published by the Works Progress Administration, Federal Art Project, New York

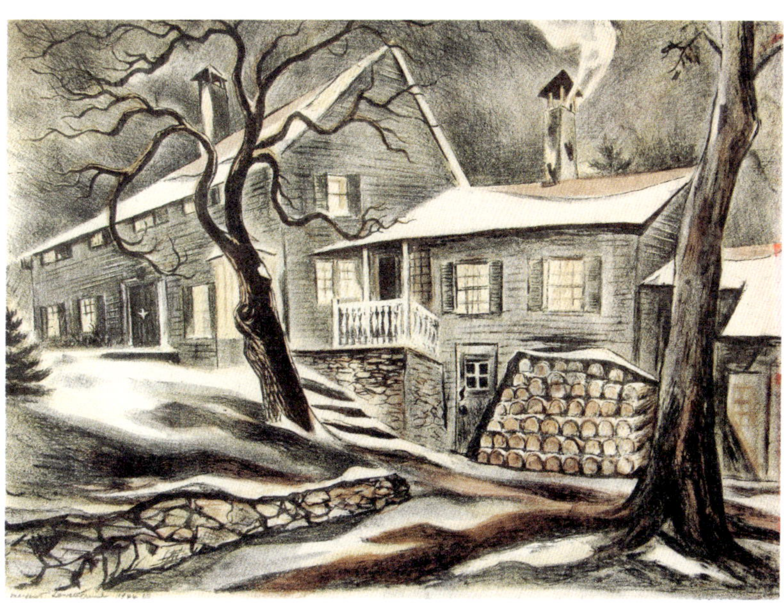

Margaret Lowengrund, *Woodstock Family Home*, 1944. Lithograph, sheet: 11 ¾ × 16 ¼ in.

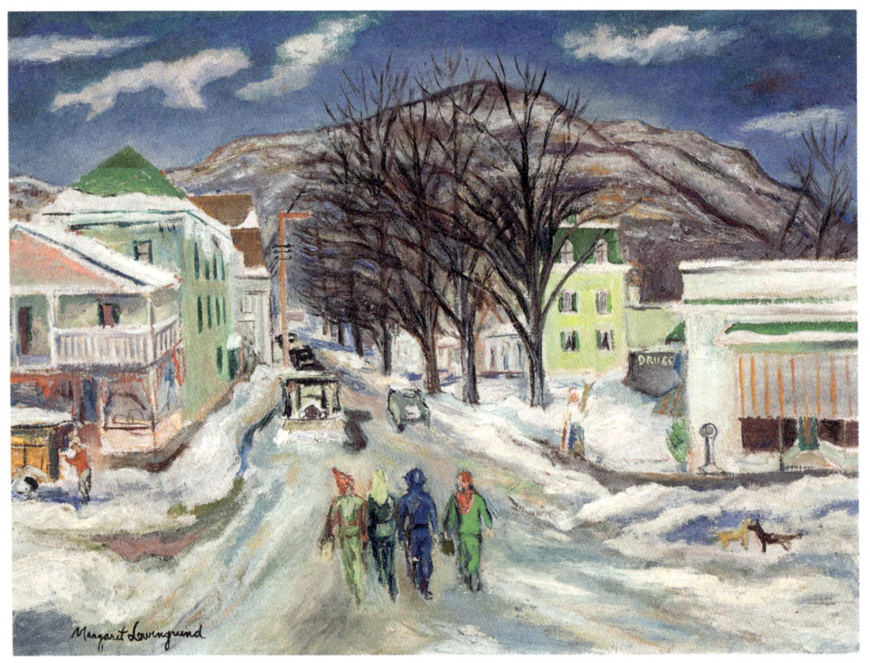

Margaret Lowengrund, *Woodstock in Winter*, ca. 1940s.
Oil on canvas, 22 × 30 in.

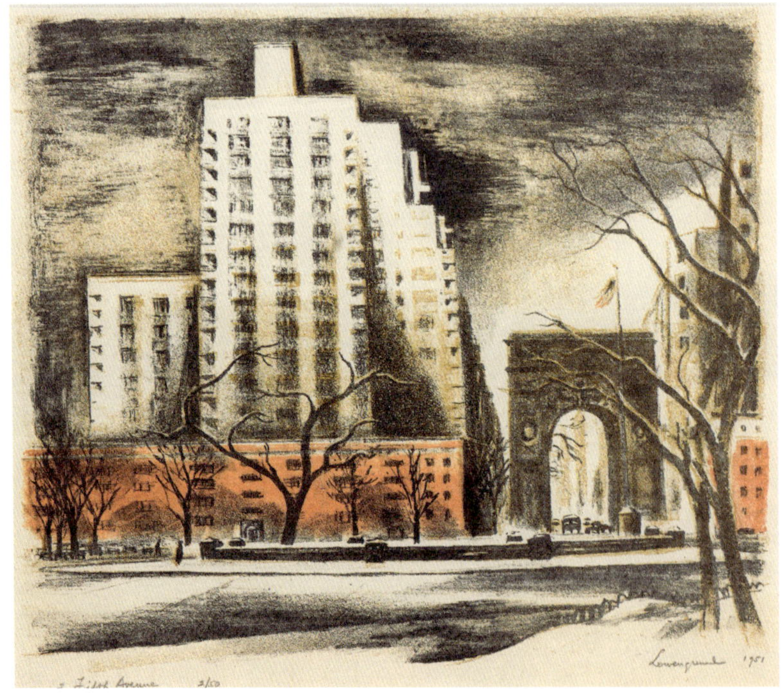

Margaret Lowengrund, *2 Fifth Avenue*, 1951.
Lithograph, edition of 50, image: 13½ x 16 in.

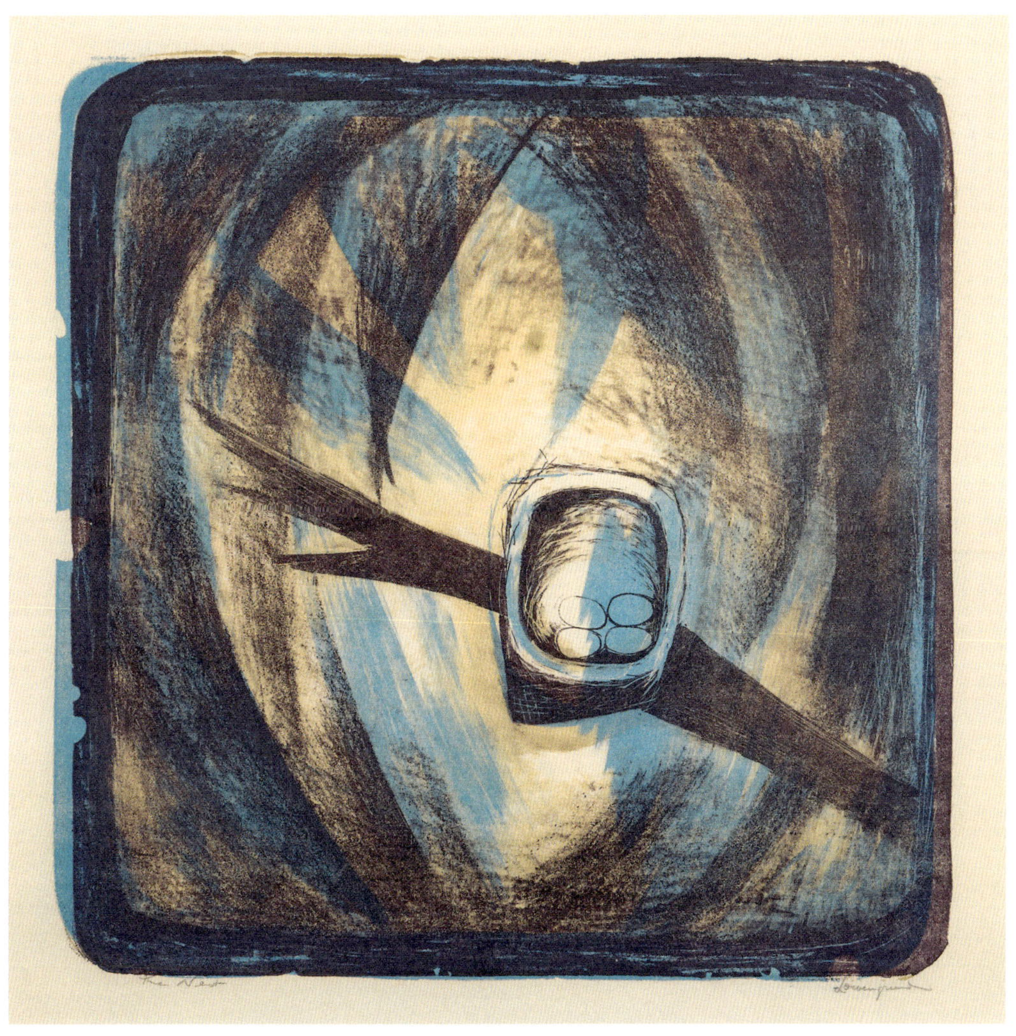

Margaret Lowengrund, *The Nest*, 1953. Lithograph, edition of 20, image: 16 × 16 in.

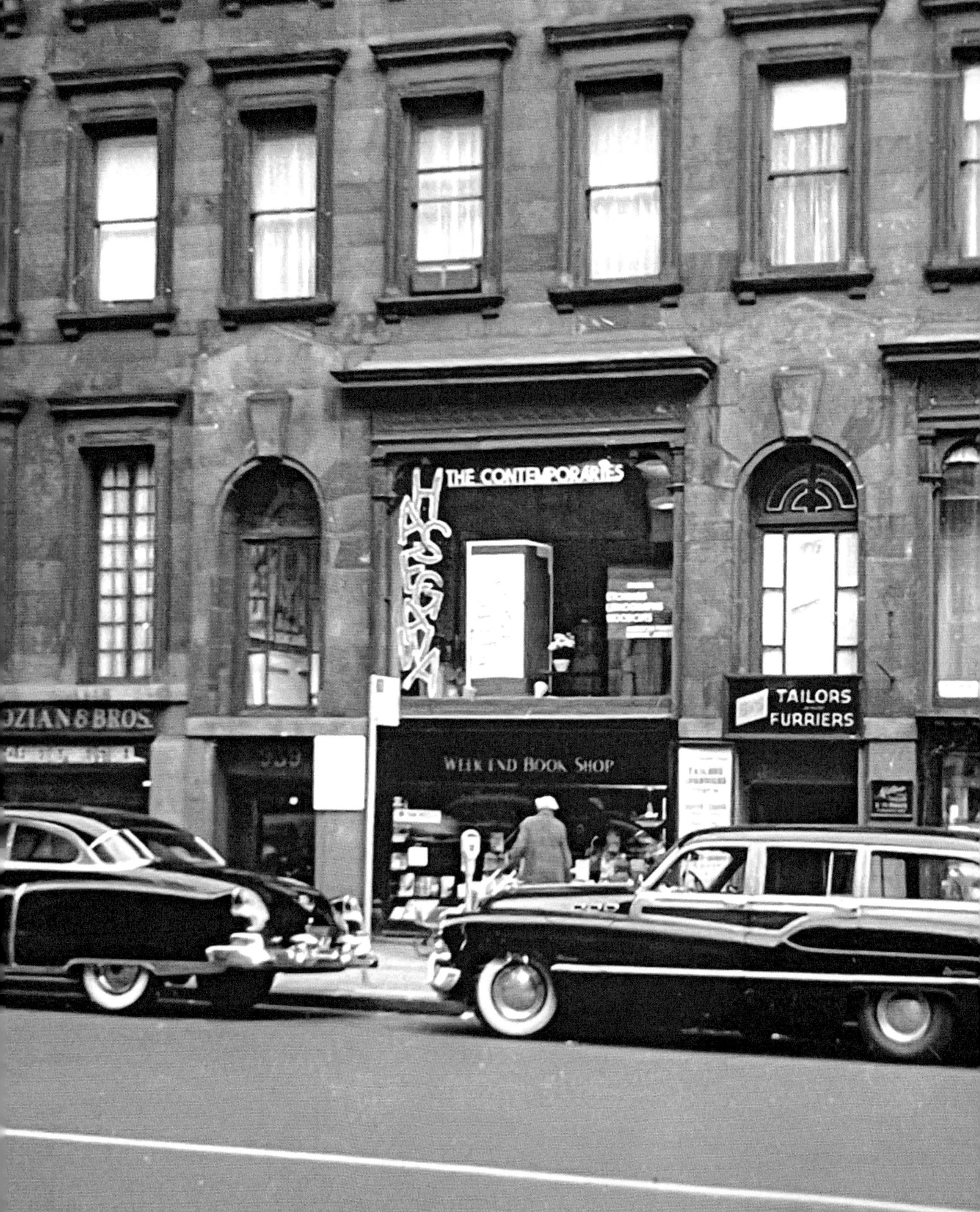
THE CONTEMPORARIES
WEEK END BOOK SHOP
TAILORS
FURRIERS

FUSING PRINTMAKING, COMMERCE, AND EDUCATION: THE CONTEMPORARIES AND PRATT GRAPHIC ART CENTER

Christina Weyl

"A taxi ride uptown in 1951 started The Contemporaries," Margaret Lowengrund once explained.[1] Traveling along Madison Avenue, she noticed a gallery moving out of the second-floor space at 959 Madison Avenue at Seventy-Fifth Street (Fig. 1). Acting quickly, she "asked the cab driver to hold the clock, jumped out, managed to corner the landlord, [and] signed the lease then and there."[2] The dumbbell-shaped space had a room in the back where Lowengrund moved her own lithography press and other equipment, creating an active printmaking workshop; in the front room, which had a large window facing Madison Avenue, Lowengrund organized a gallery which offered, according to the window signage, "original etchings, lithographs, woodcuts [by] America's finest graphic artists." Although her "taxi ride" story conveys spontaneity, Lowengrund's actions were well planned and deliberate. As a longtime observer of and participant in the art scene as an artist, lithographer, and critic, Lowengrund intimately understood the currents of postwar printmaking and its market. She sought to disrupt the status quo with The Contemporaries: its unconventional, hybrid structure was the first institution in the United States to fuse production, exhibition, and sales of prints under one roof. Her efforts were a harbinger of the seismic changes that reshaped postwar printmaking, ushering in the wave of collaborative printmaking workshops of the 1960s.

During the period covered in this essay—1951 to 1966—The Contemporaries steadily evolved: moving spaces, adding faculty, starting initiatives, and most radically, becoming an extension of the Pratt Institute in 1956 shortly before Lowengrund's untimely death. (The new entity had many names; for simplicity, this essay uses Pratt Graphic Art Center or PGAC.) While mapping this institutional history, the ensuing discussion tracks the ways Lowengrund and her successors at PGAC framed and supported contemporary printmaking. Across these fifteen years, the meaning of "contemporary printmaking" shifted based on such factors as the physical organization of the workshop and gallery, the demands of funders, and larger currents in the postwar art world. The institutional programming and goals of The Contemporaries and PGAC adapted and expanded accordingly: Lowengrund's founding concept of the hybrid and co-located workshop-gallery morphed into

Fig. 1 Exterior of The Contemporaries at 959 Madison Avenue during Hasegawa Saburō's exhibition, 1954

a modified hybrid, with physically separate but closely allied spaces. As PGAC evolved, the model of contemporary printmaking workshop changed yet again to prioritize education and professionalization.

Through these sizable changes, however, The Contemporaries and PGAC remained true to Lowengrund's vision of building appreciation and support for contemporary printmaking. She once stated that her dream in opening The Contemporaries was "to bring about a renaissance of graphic arts in this country."[3] Passionately and enthusiastically, Lowengrund and her successors advocated for printmaking as an indispensable and valuable creative medium for all contemporary artists, and they endeavored to dispel myths, provide access to all artists, and educate the public about prints.

The Contemporaries: A Hybrid Workshop-Gallery (1951–55)

The November 15, 1951 issue of *Art Digest* carried a short write-up and advertisement announcing the opening of Margaret Lowengrund's unique establishment billed as the "first combined workshop-school and exhibiting gallery."[4] Though not yet called The Contemporaries—the appellation came soon after—this hybrid space had well-articulated goals. The workshop would provide facilities and technical guidance from a knowledgeable printer for "professionals and students to experiment in otherwise prohibitive media at the least possible cost."[5] The gallery would "function informally" and "show contemporary work in all media," including graphic art, painting, and sculpture.[6]

The strength of Lowengrund's enterprise was in the synergy of creative energy and commercial sales. By fusing these functions in one location, Lowengrund built a powerful center which drew a diverse audience. In addition to serving artists who wanted to make and sell prints, The Contemporaries provided a vibrant venue for artists to connect with one other as well as with museum curators, critics, designers, architects, and collectors. Dore Ashton, a critic married to The Contemporaries' staffer Adja Yunkers, remarked on this unique aspect of the hybrid workshop-gallery, writing that it served as "a liaison between printmakers and the general public" and presented visitors with "a cross-current of printmaking throughout the country."[7] The gallery's visitors' register substantiates Ashton's observations, capturing quite the "who's who" of the midcentury print field along with gallerygoers.[8]

Over these first four years, Lowengrund refined The Contemporaries' goals to strengthen its support for contemporary printmaking. For the sake of clarity, the history below separates discussion of workshop and gallery, even though these entities occupied the same space and their initiatives were mutually reinforcing.

The Workshop

Lowengrund had big goals for the workshop at 959 Madison Avenue, despite its shoestring budget, small size—by one account, "crowded" with four people—and limitations of its facilities: graining of lithographic stones happened in the bathroom sink, and there was inadequate ventilation for etching acids.[9] Although the back workroom had an etching press and setup for screen printing, lithography was given primacy, reflecting Lowengrund's long-standing passion for the medium. In founding The Contemporaries, Lowengrund was manifesting ideas she had written about as an art critic in the years leading up to 1951, revealing her awareness that lithography was ripe for expansion in the United States.[10]

Lowengrund had long recognized the importance of building a balanced, collaborative relationship between artists and printers. In one particularly telling

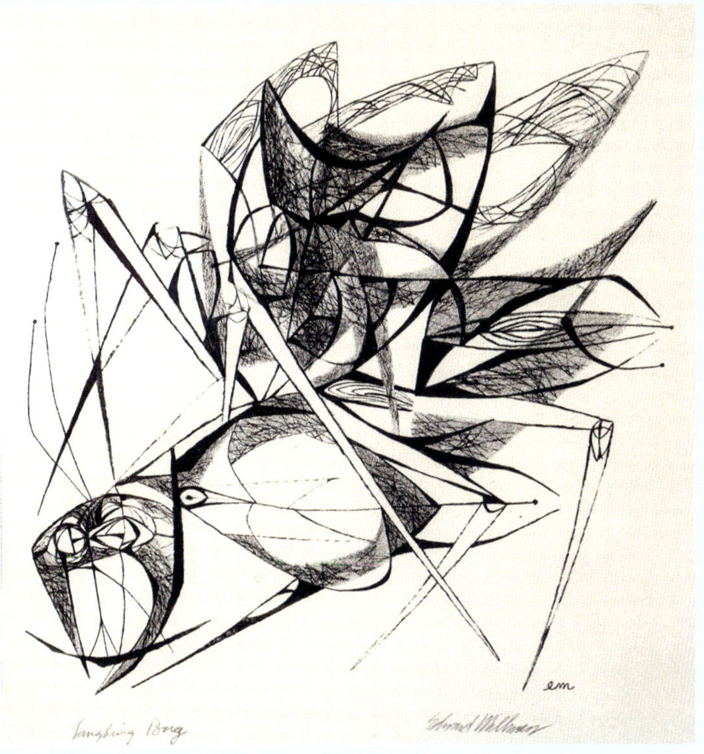

Fig. 2 Edward Millman, *Laughing Bug*, 1952. Lithograph, image: 13 ½ × 13 ½ in.; sheet: 20 × 15 in.

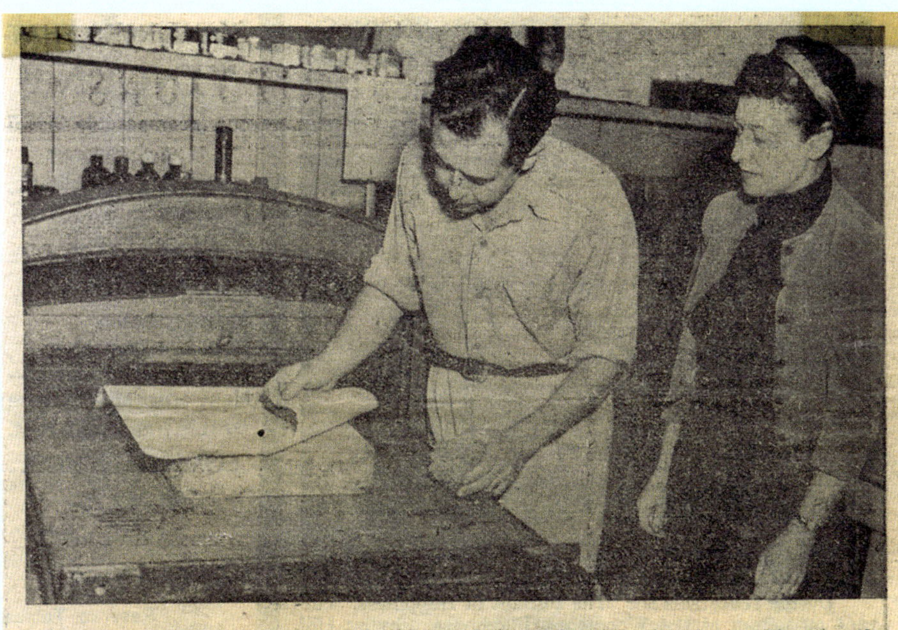

Shown with Miss Lowengrund is Edward Millman of Woodstock, working on the Bonus Print for this year which is given to sustaining members of the Woodstock Artists Association. The prints were made in the Graphic Workshop. (They will be available Saturday for distribution.)

Fig. 3 Margaret Lowengrund and Edward Millman printing *Laughing Bug*, reproduced in an unidentified newspaper, ca. July 1952

review from 1947, she lamented that three exhibitions featuring European lithography showed "the American school of lithography as yet unborn" and exposed the "limitation of good printers" in the United States.[11] She took particular aim at George Miller, who had been printing artists' editions—including her own!—since roughly 1917, deriding his dictatorial manner and his adherence to what she called his "brittle [school] of stilted mannerism."[12] In a 1948 review of the Metropolitan Museum of Art's major lithography exhibition, another pithy editorial comment foreshadows the intervention Lowengrund would make at The Contemporaries. Her words are worth quoting at length:

> *The plea . . . is for more painters to reach out in lithography and more printers to experiment, so that the field in this country is no longer left to the stereotyped printer who refuses to recognize the needs of the artist for free expression, in his zeal to make perfect reproductions. The school of stilted cross-hatching, however "safe" to multiply without risking a printer's ire, should be terminated in this country in favor of a surge of warm-blooded expression in a medium which knows few limitations.*[13]

Three years later, Lowengrund acted on her words, establishing a space where artists who had no experience could learn lithography's fundamentals from professional staff and build a lifelong appreciation for the medium's potential. With her writing and actions, Lowengrund identified problems that her friend June Wayne cited a decade later in her application to the Ford Foundation for funding her founding of the Tamarind Lithography Workshop.[14]

Lowengrund served as the workshop's first professional printer.[15] One of Lowengrund's first collaborations was with artist Edward Millman, for whom she printed a handful of editions, including *Laughing Bug* (1952), the "bonus print" given to members of the Woodstock Artists Association (WAA) in Woodstock, New York (Fig. 2). Contrary to the gendered staging for a local news photograph, in which Lowengrund demurely watches Millman peeling the paper off the stone (Fig. 3), she labored tirelessly on his editions. Millman used a subtle wash for one stone, which Lowengrund etched several times—"[watching] over it like a mother cat," she explained—to prevent the marking from disappearing.[16] Interestingly, Lowengrund had not originally planned to edition Millman's stones single-handedly, but the (male) printer she had hired admitted "he did not have the strength," nor did he think it possible to maintain the subtle wash in a projected edition of 150.[17]

Lowengrund eventually hired and trained other artists to serve as printers, thus freeing her time to manage other aspects of The Contemporaries. Michael Ponce de León became her first printer during the summer of 1952, when the workshop operated seasonally out of WAA's basement.[18] Famously, the barely trained Ponce de León printed the sculptor David Smith's first stone—proofing it with beer instead of water—after only one day's worth of instruction from Lowengrund.[19] Despite a stern lecture from Lowengrund about his brazenness, Ponce de León remained on staff at The Contemporaries and PGAC, but his true passion was high-relief intaglio.

The workshop's seasonal relocation to Woodstock for three summers (1952–54) was key to building momentum. Lowengrund had a presence in this bustling artists' colony since the mid-1930s, and she leveraged her connections with Ulster County newspapers to get coverage for The Contemporaries' activities in New York during "the season" and Woodstock during the summers. Lowengrund stressed how the New York space had "quite a Woodstock flavor" with many Woodstockers stopping by to make prints, exhibit work, and see exhibitions.[20] During its early years,

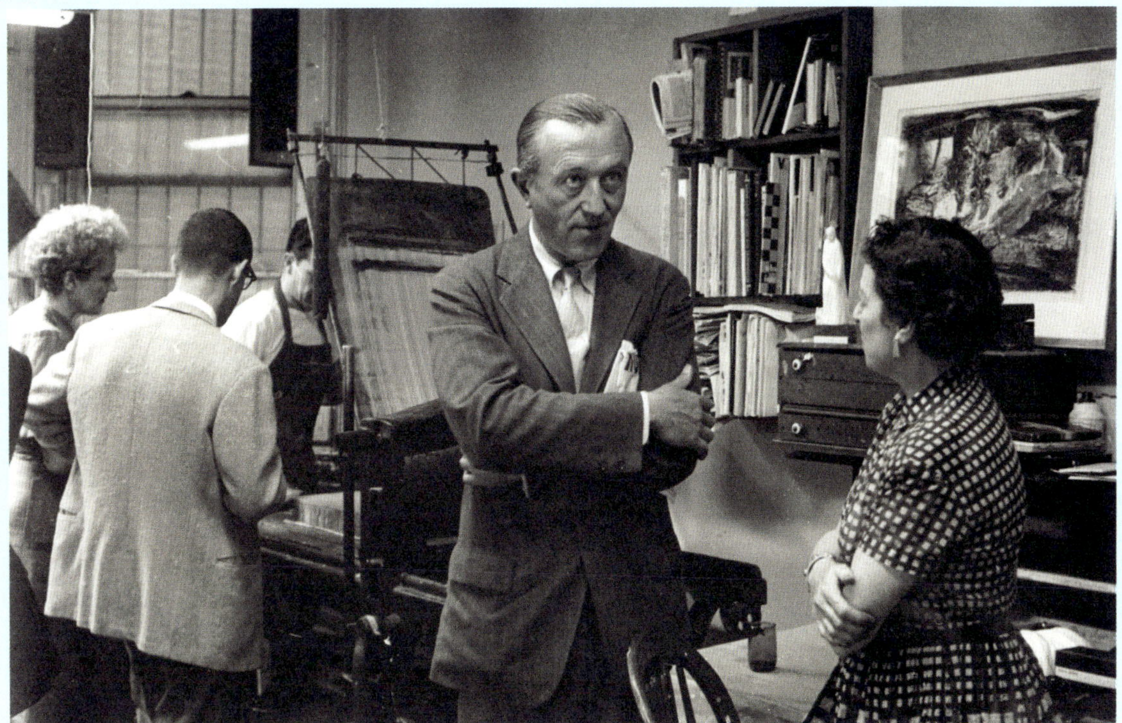

Fig. 4 Lithography demonstration at The Contemporaries, 959 Madison Avenue, ca. 1953. Pictured: Michael Ponce de León (at press); Sari Dienes (next to press); Lowengrund at far right with unidentified person. Photo by Robert Delson

The Contemporaries increased support for contemporary printmaking through such mingling between professionals and newcomers.

With each new season in Manhattan, Lowengrund advocated more powerfully for contemporary printmaking through an expanding mission, and adding staff was key. She hired John Muench in fall 1952 to serve as a professional lithographer, and she advertised additional classes in etching with Ponce de León, woodcut with Adja Yunkers, and serigraphy and "combined media" with Worden Day.[21] By 1954, Seong Moy joined as an additional woodcut instructor.

The workshop's support for contemporary printmaking coalesced around three functions: access, education, and professional services. By outfitting The Contemporaries with a range of tools and equipment, Lowengrund facilitated the ability of contemporary artists—regardless of their specialization as painters, sculptors, or printmakers—to learn and experiment with all forms of printmaking. She met artists at their level, with beginners receiving "special attention" and advanced students "encouraged in experimental phases."[22] As she had been trained, Lowengrund insisted that artists learn all steps behind the creation of a print so that they appreciated each medium's possibilities.[23] Lowengrund realized, however, that not all artists wanted to labor to create an edition, and therefore The Contemporaries offered contract printing at competitive rates.[24] Her workshop further distinguished its editioning services with the staff's ability to execute color processes—particularly color lithography. Reginald Neal, for example, who worked for The Contemporaries during its final summer in Woodstock in 1954, was a leading proponent in advancing color lithography.[25]

The workshop's educational function eventually expanded. Demonstrations became routine with periodic "open houses" where the public could watch the making of a print alongside artists, curators, and critics (Fig. 4). Staff also gave demonstrations at universities, often to complement an exhibition circulated by The Contemporaries.[26] With this public-facing work, Lowengrund and her staff were on the leading edge of efforts in the United States to educate the public about contemporary printmaking.

The Gallery

The gallery program at 959 Madison Avenue began with modest ambitions which developed into a robust calendar of exhibitions. The Contemporaries changed shows roughly every three weeks. Between 1951 and 1957, when Lowengrund sold the gallery just before her death, The Contemporaries hosted over one hundred exhibitions featuring more than 250 artists.[27] At first, Lowengrund ran the gallery herself; by 1953, she had at least one staff member.[28]

How Lowengrund defined "contemporary"—this word that anchored her hybrid space—drove her gallery's mission, and as before, her critical writings provide a helpful foundation. In early 1948, Lowengrund covered the controversy surrounding Boston's Institute of Modern Art's rebranding as the Institute of Contemporary Art (ICA). Proclaimed via provocative manifesto, ICA signaled its expansion beyond the Museum of Modern Art's (MoMA) narrow definition of "modern" as European and avant-garde. This institutional rift reflected debates percolating across the country at midcentury, and Lowengrund distilled the controversy to her readers by framing "contemporary" as the overlap in a Venn diagram of modernist styles. "Modern art," she explained, "is a trend which departed from tradition almost a hundred years back. Contemporary art includes all art of our time, including all forms of modernism which are still produced and all styles of the academic as well."[29] She carried this definition forward in her exhibition reviews, once differentiating between modern and contemporary artists in MoMA's *Master Prints* (1949), which featured prints spanning sixty-five years.[30] Lowengrund found the contemporary group most stimulating, and these artists comprised some of the earliest exhibitors at The Contemporaries.

The Contemporaries' early exhibition program explicitly favored group exhibitions over solo shows because Lowengrund believed the collective display of excellent prints would raise the profile of contemporary printmaking.[31] These multiartist exhibitions featured process (*Evolution of a Contemporary Lithograph*), pairings of artists' prints and work in other media (*Painters and Their Prints*), thematic shows (*Large Prints*, *Black and White*), or spotlights on international or regional artists (*Graphic Britain*, *Midwest Artists*, *Scandinavian Graphics*, *Modern Japanese Prints*). Lowengrund also hosted traveling group shows, including the Cincinnati Art Museum's Third International Biennial of Color Lithography and the Color Print Society's annual exhibition.

Lowengrund's major contribution was the semiregular roundup she organized of the best contemporary prints. Beginning with *52 Prints of the Year* (1952), Lowengrund mounted three additional shows called *Graphic Outlook* (1954, 1955, 1957). These ambitious exhibitions presented a cross section of contemporary graphic arts in a manner commensurate with the postwar print annuals held in the United States at museums and print clubs. Furthermore, they surpassed what some critics perceived as the stale offerings of conservative printmaking organizations such as the Society of American Graphic Artists.[32] Lowengrund even organized a traveling circuit for *Graphic Outlook '55*, thus expanding the reach of

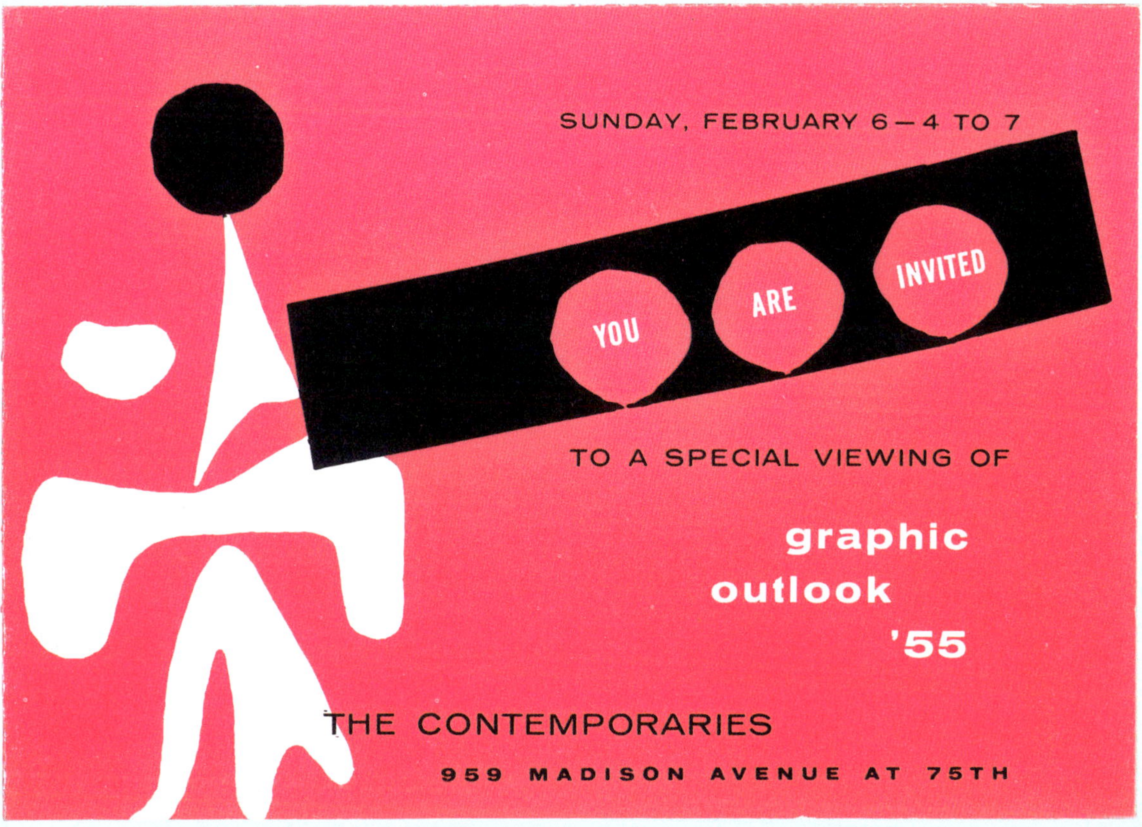

Fig. 5 Invitation for *A Special Viewing of Graphic Outlook '55*, The Contemporaries, 1955

contemporary printmaking to new audiences (Fig. 5). She touted the final *Graphic Outlook* (1957) as the "first international" iteration, a move that mirrored global trends of postwar printmaking, particularly the recently organized Ljubljana Biennial of Graphic Arts.[33]

The gallery distinguished itself through its commitment to exhibiting a wide array of contemporary printmaking, ranging from realism to nonobjective styles executed either in color or black and white.[34] Lowengrund once explained that the gallery's "policy will be inflexible as to quality; its taste catholic enough to include the works of artists of all schools of expression."[35] By offering a diverse cross section of contemporary printmaking, Lowengrund targeted the growing segment of middle-class collectors who sought original artwork at moderate prices.[36] In 1956, Lowengrund launched the "Collector's Print," a print-of-the-month series marketed to "the discriminating collector" with the price capped at fifty dollars and the edition size limited to forty.[37] The Contemporaries also consigned prints through MoMA's Art Lending Service, which allowed museum members to rent artwork before purchasing.[38] Midcentury artists recognized how substantially Lowengrund grew the market for contemporary prints and lamented the loss when, in 1957, the gallery's new owner distanced The Contemporaries from printmaking.[39]

Lowengrund could not cover the rent with moderately priced prints, and she supplemented revenue with higher-margin sales of sculptures. In fact, the gallery's program of "solo" shows often involved pairing a graphic artist and a sculptor. There were sometimes formal connections, but often the two artists did not know one another.[40] When Lowengrund moved the gallery in September 1955, she cemented this alliance by rebranding The Contemporaries as a "Gallery of Sculpture and Graphic Art." The inaugural exhibition at 992 Madison Avenue, entitled *Today: An Exhibition of Sculpture and Graphic Art*, included sculpture by major names such as Richard Lippold, Seymour Lipton, Noguchi Isamu, and David Smith.[41] At points, Lowengrund had important sculpture on consignment, including Smith's *Agricola V* (1952), and she sold to significant collectors such as Joseph Hirshhorn.[42]

Expanding Ambitions (1955–57)

Two changes fundamentally reshaped The Contemporaries between 1955 and 1957: first, its relocation from 959 Madison Avenue and reconfiguration of the workshop and gallery into two physically separate but allied spaces; and second, the merger of The Contemporaries' workshop with Pratt Institute, coupled with a major grant from the Rockefeller Foundation. Through this expansion, the mission remained true to Lowengrund's founding vision to foster appreciation of printmaking among artists—both experienced and novice—through classes and professional services and to engage the public through education, exhibitions, and sales. Sadly, Lowengrund did not live to shepherd the renamed Pratt-Contemporaries Graphic Art Centre through its first three-year grant from the Rockefeller Foundation. Fritz Eichenberg, the workshop's codirector and chair of Pratt's Graphic Arts Department, and other workshop staff worked tirelessly to carry on Lowengrund's legacy.

The Rockefeller Foundation first learned of Lowengrund's studio and gallery during the summer of 1954, around the time she was confronting the imminent demolition of the building at 959 Madison Avenue and was seeking funding to support the relocation of her hybrid venture. Meeting Lowengrund in February 1955 before the move, the foundation staff was impressed by her passion and accomplishments, but they immediately raised red flags because of The Contemporaries' unusual commingling of commerce and education.[43] Although Lowengrund had considered incorporating the workshop as a nonprofit, she never followed through on this plan.[44] The foundation's staff repeatedly told her it could not consider offering a grant to The Contemporaries unless she applied for this tax status and formally separated the gallery from the workshop.[45]

This stipulation put Lowengrund in an awkward situation; the symbiotic relationship was essential to The Contemporaries' finances and to supporting workshop activity and gallery exhibitions. In a formal proposal to the foundation dated mid-December 1955, Lowengrund emphasized that she hoped an expanded graphic art center would bring about a "national, total renaissance of graphic arts . . . without making a single concession to commercialism, without lowering standards or compromising artistic integrity."[46] Ironically, the feature that most distinguished The Contemporaries—its hybrid nature—became an impediment to its growth.

The razing of 959 Madison Avenue in summer 1955 pushed Lowengrund to envision The Contemporaries' future without Rockefeller support. The gallery reopened at 992 Madison Avenue as The Contemporaries Gallery of Sculpture and Graphic Art in much larger, ground-floor accommodations (Fig. 6).[47] The Contemporaries Graphic Art Centre opened three blocks away at 1343–45 Third Avenue in a second-floor studio that could accommodate thirty students and had presses for etching, woodcut, and lithography, along with approximately one hundred lithograph stones of various sizes (Fig. 7).[48] While physically separated, the two entities were very much intertwined: they shared a graphic identity with

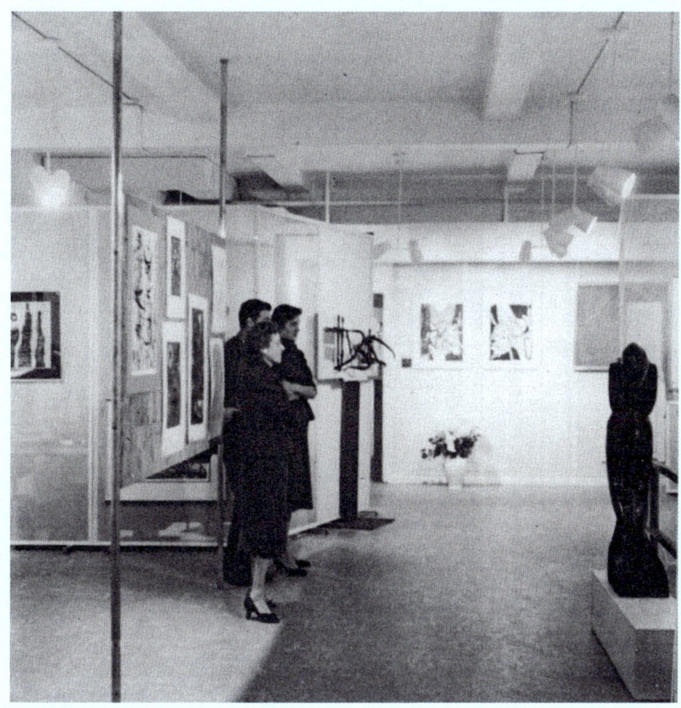

Fig. 6 Lowengrund and others at 992 Madison Avenue, ca. 1955–57

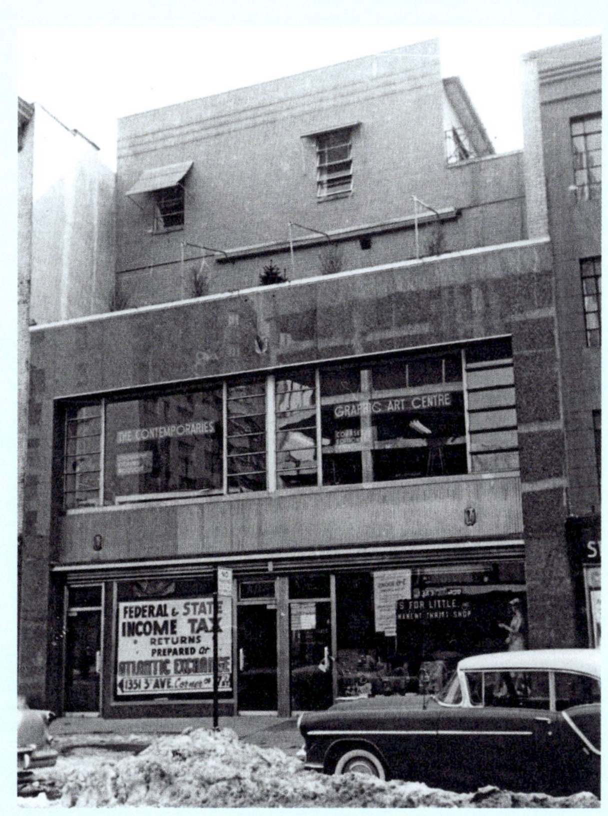

Fig. 7 Exterior of The Contemporaries Graphic Art Centre at 1343–45 Third Avenue, ca. 1955–56

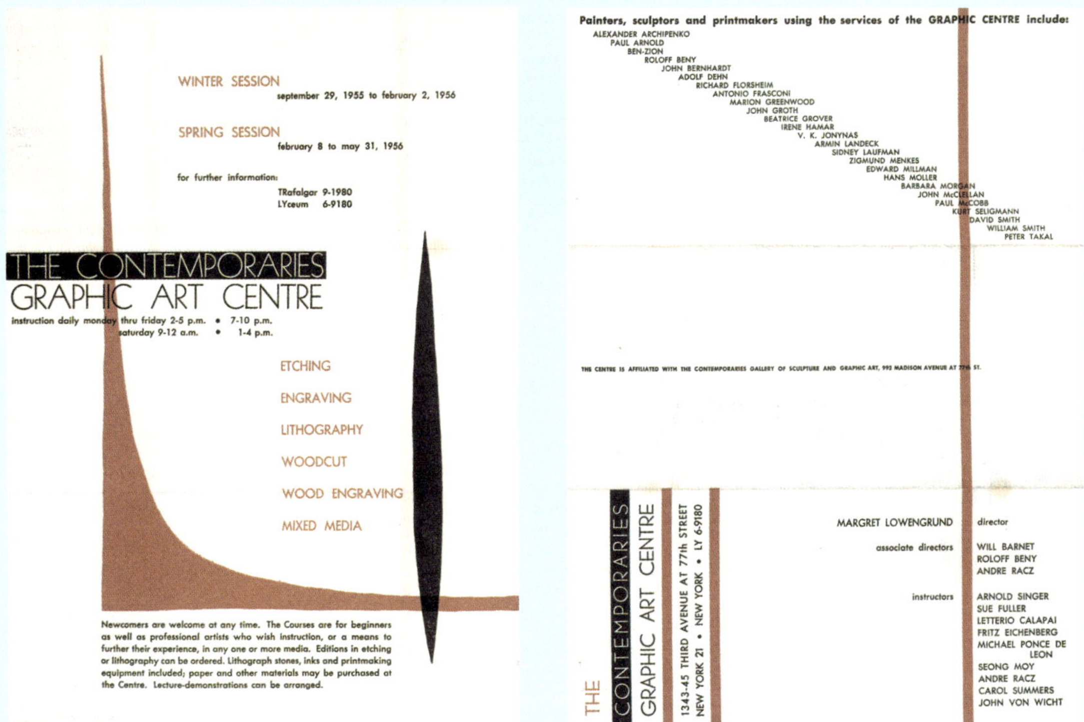

Fig. 8 Brochure (recto and verso) announcing the opening of The Contemporaries Graphic Art Centre, 1955

matching letterhead set in Futura typeface, and the workshop often listed the gallery's phone number alongside its own.

Lowengrund enlisted others to support the expanded gallery and workshop. She hired Carl Lundy in 1956 to serve as the gallery's director. At the Graphic Art Centre, three associate directors—Will Barnet, Roloff Beny, and André Racz—managed the workshop, but this triumvirate quickly fell apart (Fig. 8). Lowengrund hoped to hire Reginald Neal or Gabor Peterdi, feeling either would bring the "necessary flair ... to make the Art Center a dynamic place."[49] The Rockefeller Foundation ultimately facilitated a different solution: the merger of The Contemporaries Graphic Art Centre with Pratt Institute.[50]

The pairing of Pratt and The Contemporaries was kismet. Fritz Eichenberg had been plotting to open a graphic arts workshop since joining the faculty at Pratt in 1948, cobbling together whatever equipment he could find in dusty basements. Lowengrund approached Eichenberg about a potential merger just as he became department chair in 1956, and he jumped at the opportunity.[51] In a memo to Pratt's president, Francis Horn, Eichenberg enumerated the many synergies of a union. Besides Pratt being behind other universities in establishing a printmaking program, Eichenberg felt an alliance would expand classes to new students at the graduate level and give the Brooklyn-based school a toehold in Manhattan. He also saw advantages in allying with The Contemporaries' gallery, since its traveling exhibitions and connections with architects, decorators, and art directors would publicize the merged workshop.[52]

After lengthy negotiations over the spring and summer, all parties reached a successful agreement in August 1956. The Rockefeller Foundation funded the combined Pratt-Contemporaries Graphic Art Centre at $50,000, with tapered

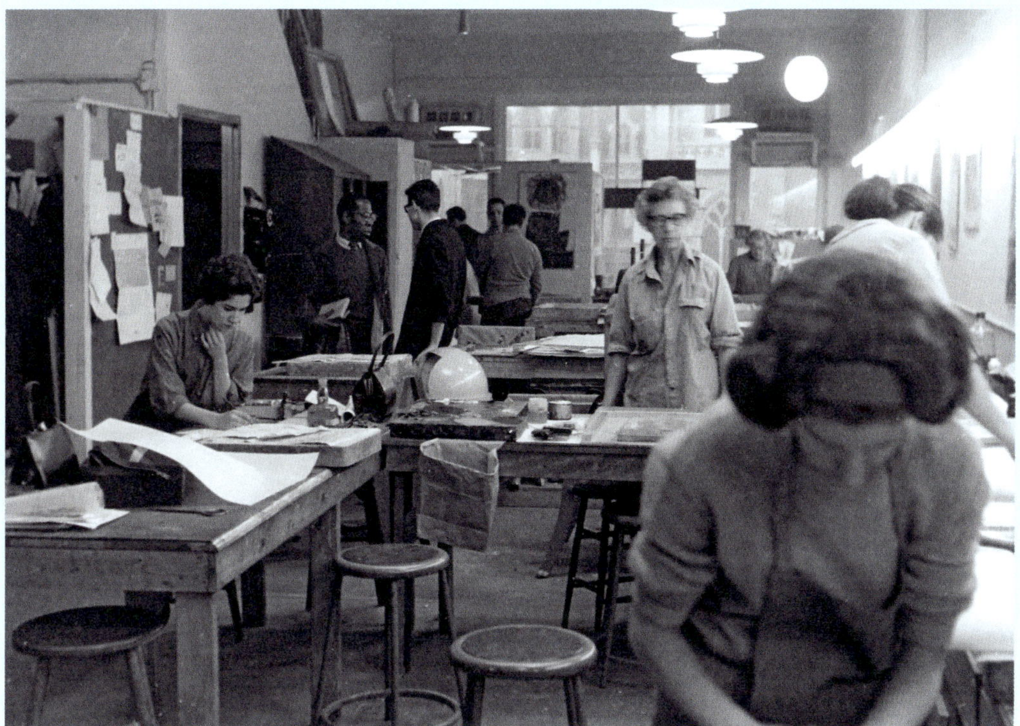

Fig. 9 Pratt Graphic Art Center at 795 Broadway, ca. 1959

annual grants spread over three years with the intention of making the Centre self-supporting.[53] Lowengrund and Eichenberg planned for tuition and professional services, such as editioning, to backstop deficits in the Centre's estimated annual operating budget of $30,000.[54] As stated in the August memorandum, the Centre had three goals still focused on access, education, and professional services: to be a "combined school and workshop" providing classes two days per week in all printmaking media at the "graduate level," with classes open to qualified artists and college graduates; to serve professional artists as a center for experimentation and edition printing; and to organize and expand traveling and local exhibitions, both in the United States and abroad.[55]

After the official merger on October 15, 1956, Lowengrund was hospitalized in January and underwent an operation for cancer.[56] By February, she was back at work. Unfortunately, she only had a limited window of time to make her mark on the Pratt-Contemporaries Graphic Art Centre because she relapsed and was too ill by September to continue her duties. Lowengrund died on November 19, 1957 at the age of fifty-five. It is impossible to project how the Centre would have evolved differently under Lowengrund's continued involvement. From the brief glimpses that archival documents afford, Lowengrund remained steadfast in her resolve to inspire an appreciation for printmaking through the activities of the newly merged Centre. A report she penned in June 1957 for the Rockefeller Foundation—probably Lowengrund's last piece of significant writing—demonstrates how deeply committed she remained to supporting contemporary printmaking until the very end of her life.[57]

Grappling with the illness and death of its founder, Pratt-Contemporaries Graphic Art Centre entered a period of crisis as it transitioned from The Contemporaries' hybrid model toward a new educational paradigm. While the Centre's core functions remained consistent, their prioritization shifted based on financial pressures and the Centre's need to distinguish itself in the quickly evolving landscape of postwar printmaking. Eichenberg, who became the Centre's sole director, faced immediate challenges on multiple fronts. Lowengrund's spotty attendance had led to friction among the staff.[58] Funding remained an issue as Rockefeller support tapered and the Centre did not realize commensurate gains from tuition and editioning. Eichenberg considered measures such as staff cuts or moving to less expensive quarters and, at times, feared the Centre could never become self-supporting.[59] The central issue, however, involved the Centre's identity and whether it should function as a school or a professional center—or, whether it could accommodate both purposes (Fig. 9).

In 1958 and 1959, the Centre's stakeholders—Eichenberg, the Rockefeller Foundation, and the Centre's Advisory Board—debated its mission and offered various solutions. The major concern centered around the balance of amateurs—allegedly all female "dilletantes"—who filled the daytime classes and professional artists who utilized the Centre in the evenings.[60] Commingling between these populations was deemed a major detraction for the professionals, who gave the Centre its clout. Gabor Peterdi suggested hosting "pro-nights," mirroring the arrangement fostered at Atelier 17, the avant-garde printmaking studio located in New York City until 1955; Una Johnson, curator of prints at the Brooklyn Museum, proposed a division of the physical space so that professionals would be walled off from amateurs.[61]

Eichenberg adeptly navigated the Centre through its first three rocky and financially strained years as an extension of Pratt Institute. Based on Eichenberg's resolve and interviews with the advisory board, the Rockefeller Foundation made a second and final grant of $60,000, again tapered over three years, which was contingent on Pratt's pledge to cover any shortfalls. Eichenberg also negotiated an additional sum to relocate to larger quarters at 795 Broadway. This move in September 1959 inaugurated a new era, and Eichenberg rechristened the workshop as Pratt Graphic Art Center (PGAC).[62]

Like Lowengrund, Eichenberg recognized the necessity of tuition and edition printing for PGAC's financial health. With 2,000 square feet, 795 Broadway provided space for more classes. PGAC's enrollment numbers are difficult to parse, but annual enrollment more than doubled between the end of the Center's second year at 1343 Third Avenue (June 1958) and the conclusion of its third year at 795 Broadway (June 1962). Growing from eighty-four to 175 students, tuition income rose from $6,561 in 1959 to $13,250 in 1962.[63] By PGAC's eighth anniversary in 1964, the count stood at two hundred student-artists.[64]

PGAC excelled in attracting an international mix of artists who were curious to explore the potentials of printmaking. To facilitate this exchange, Eichenberg raised $6,750 over four years from the Ingram-Merrill Foundation, and these funds provided scholarships for artists from countries across Europe, Latin America, and Africa, as well as India, South Korea, and New Zealand.[65] Eichenberg took great pride in welcoming international students—all told, sixty-one artists from twenty-eight countries—calling the resulting global exchange "a love fest."[66]

Edition printing for professional artists—particularly in lithography—represented another lucrative income stream, and momentum grew over time.[67]

By June 1958, nine artists engaged the Center to print nineteen editions.[68] By PGAC's eighth anniversary in 1964, Eichenberg reported that seventy-five artists were taking advantage of editioning services annually.[69] Furthermore, PGAC produced editions for magazines, galleries, and museums.[70] Arnold Singer remained the primary contract printer until 1966 and was joined in 1957 by Andrew Stasik, who assumed an increasingly large administrative role at PGAC. Visiting printers were often in residence at PGAC. Notably, the Ford Foundation's grant to June Wayne for Tamarind Lithography Workshop included an earmark of $21,000 for PGAC to bring international printers to New York City.[71] Several came through the Ford grant: from Germany, Christian Kruck; from England, Henry Cliffe; from Italy, Emiliano Sorini; from Japan, Izumi Shigeru; from France, Gérard Patris; and from the Netherlands, Ben Burns.[72] Eichenberg also brought guest instructors to PGAC through additional funding from the Rockefeller Foundation, which had an interest in facilitating cultural exchange between the United States, Latin America, and Japan.

PGAC raised its profile through commissioned editions and work produced by professional artists, which were often sold to benefit the Center. PGAC held its first benefit sale, which showcased over one hundred artists, in early 1963 at its third location at 831 Broadway.[73] The Associated American Artists (AAA) hosted a much-expanded benefit sale at its Fifth Avenue showroom the following winter, which had a rotating display of over 750 prints by three hundred artists.[74] PGAC maintained a strong relationship with AAA, to which it consigned prints from 1960 onward.

PGAC's close association with AAA suggests a flaw in the Rockefeller Foundation's insistence on breaking up Lowengrund's hybrid model. Now exclusively an educational and professional workshop, PGAC depended on robust sales and philanthropy to fund its operations.[75] The meager results of PGAC's initial membership drive in 1963—fifteen dollars in exchange for a subscription to the Center's magazine, *Artist's Proof*, or a limited-edition print—were deemed not worth the staff's time.[76] Changing tack, PGAC instead fundraised by selling editions by faculty, staff, and students, either singly or through portfolios; there were two such "member portfolios" issued in 1963 and 1966, in addition to the earlier *11 Prints by 11 Printmakers* (1961). Ironically, Lowengrund's novel alliance of workshop and gallery might have provided a better long-term situation for PGAC, which was constantly hustling for sales, private donations, and foundational support. Throughout the 1960s, the bourgeoning number of printshops located in the United States—many helmed by individuals who were inexperienced in commercial sales—tested different models for selling and distributing their editions, including partnering with publishers, cultivating networks of dealers and galleries, and establishing subscription programs. By the 1970s, some printshops resurrected The Contemporaries' hybrid model, embracing combined production and sales.[77]

Once firmly established, PGAC's exhibition program excelled in raising awareness about the growing global community of contemporary printmakers. The handful of shows mounted on Third Avenue were intermittent and lacked clear direction; besides a memorial exhibition for Lowengrund, there was a smattering of instructor showcases and group exhibitions. The Riverside Museum, located on Manhattan's Upper West Side, hosted PGAC's first proper survey (February 1959), but the show reflected PGAC's uneven quality in these early years.[78] When PGAC moved to 795 Broadway, and later 831 Broadway (Fig. 10), it finally had dedicated areas to hang shows, turbocharging PGAC's exhibition program. Initially, these shows featured PGAC faculty and staff, visiting printers, and guest instructors and were often linked to demonstrations or lectures.[79] Yearly "roundup" shows

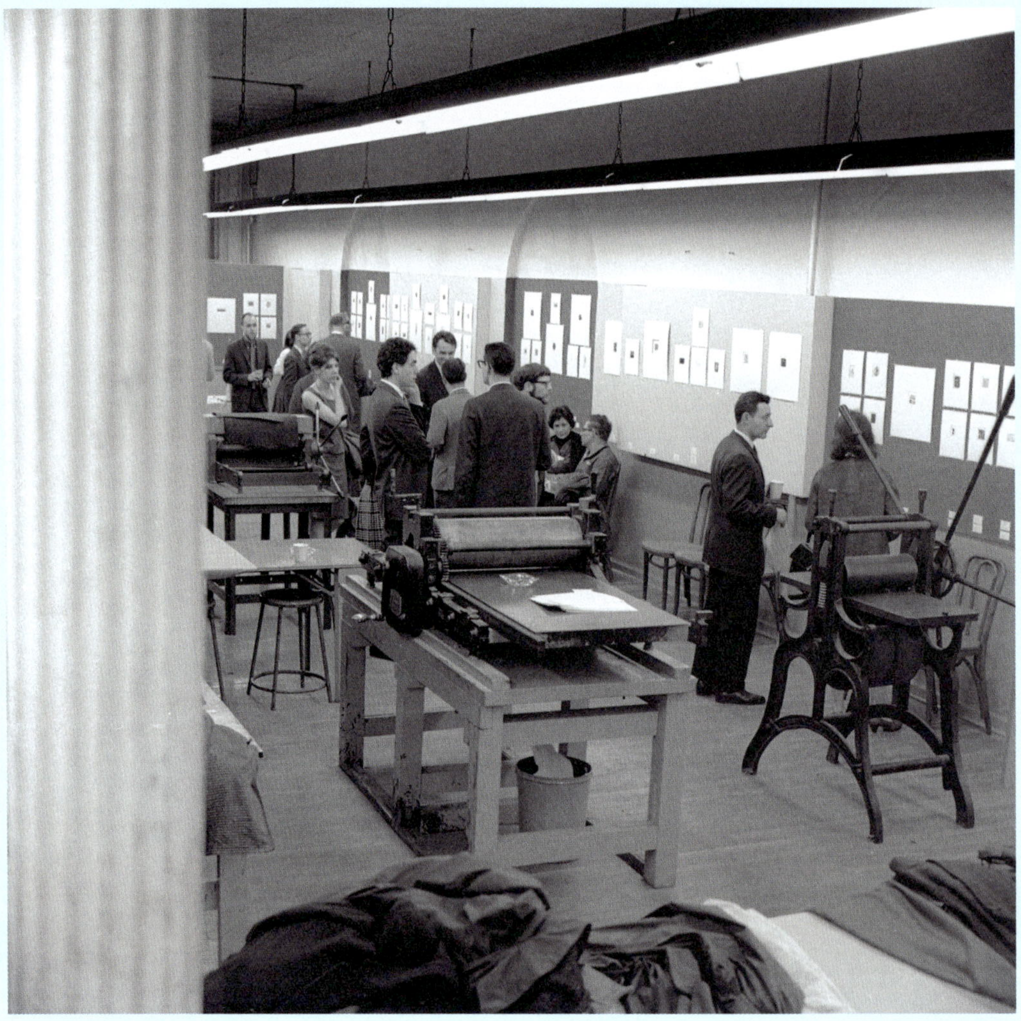

Fig. 10 Installation view of *First International Miniature Print Show*, at PGAC, 831 Broadway, 1964

continued—at larger public spaces like AAA or the lobby galleries of the Lever House or Pan Am Building—and brought the interested public into dialogue with contemporary printmaking.

The most consequential aspect of PGAC's exhibitions program, however, was its novel spotlight on international artists and printmaking centers, which introduced the New York arts community to contemporary printmaking from Germany, Hong Kong, Taiwan, Canada, England, Japan, Holland, Bulgaria, Yugoslavia, Poland, Romania, and Nigeria. Before 1966, PGAC traveled as many as fifteen of its exhibitions to museums across the United States and Canada, either through direct loans or through the assistance of arts organizations dedicated to circulating exhibitions.[80]

With *Artist's Proof*, the semiannual magazine PGAC launched in 1961, the Center captured many of its activities—visiting artists, exhibitions, lectures—and covered international happenings in the print world. Eichenberg knew this "house organ" served doubly as the Center's most effective tool for self-promotion and as a resource that connected the increasingly global community of printmakers, curators, and print enthusiasts.[81]

Margaret Lowengrund's consistent and well-informed efforts set into motion major changes that disrupted the field of printmaking. Her legacy extends from The Contemporaries through PGAC, but also beyond to the printer-publishers founded during the 1960s. Lowengrund would have heartily approved of PGAC's international focus, its community-building efforts, and outreach to bring new artists to printmaking. Certainly, PGAC maintained The Contemporaries' openness to working with any contemporary artist, regardless of style. This point is perhaps best illustrated in *100 Contemporary Prints* (1964), an exhibition at the Jewish Museum featuring PGAC artists. In addition to the "old guard" who frequented The Contemporaries and exhibited often at the gallery before 1957, the show also introduced several emerging tendencies in postwar art, including pop and conceptual prints by artists from the United States, Latin America, and Europe. For thirty years until its closing in 1986, PGAC welcomed all artists who were curious to try their hand at printmaking. By the end of his tenure as director, Eichenberg established an equilibrium, balancing the Center's mission as a school and professional center, once writing that PGAC was both "a first-aid station assisting young artists in situations new to them" and "an experimental station for professionals who are trying to solve some special technical problems."[82]

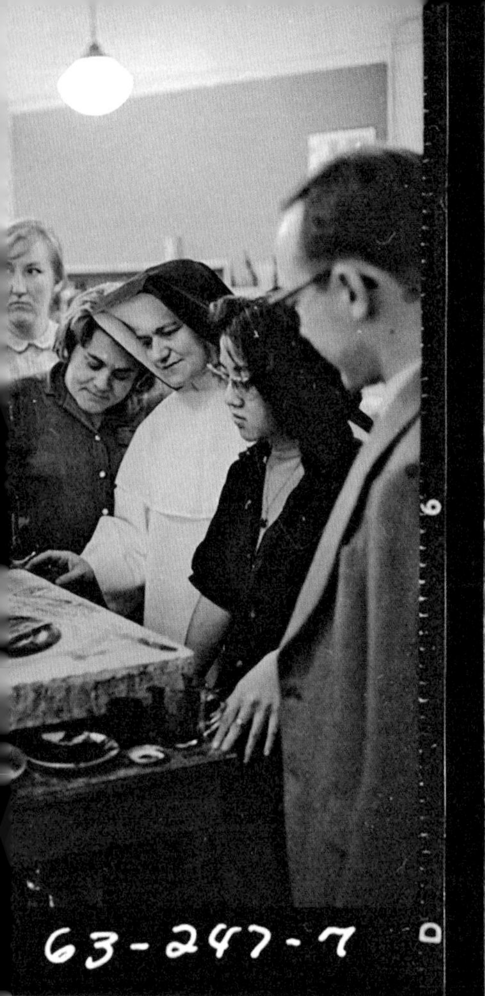

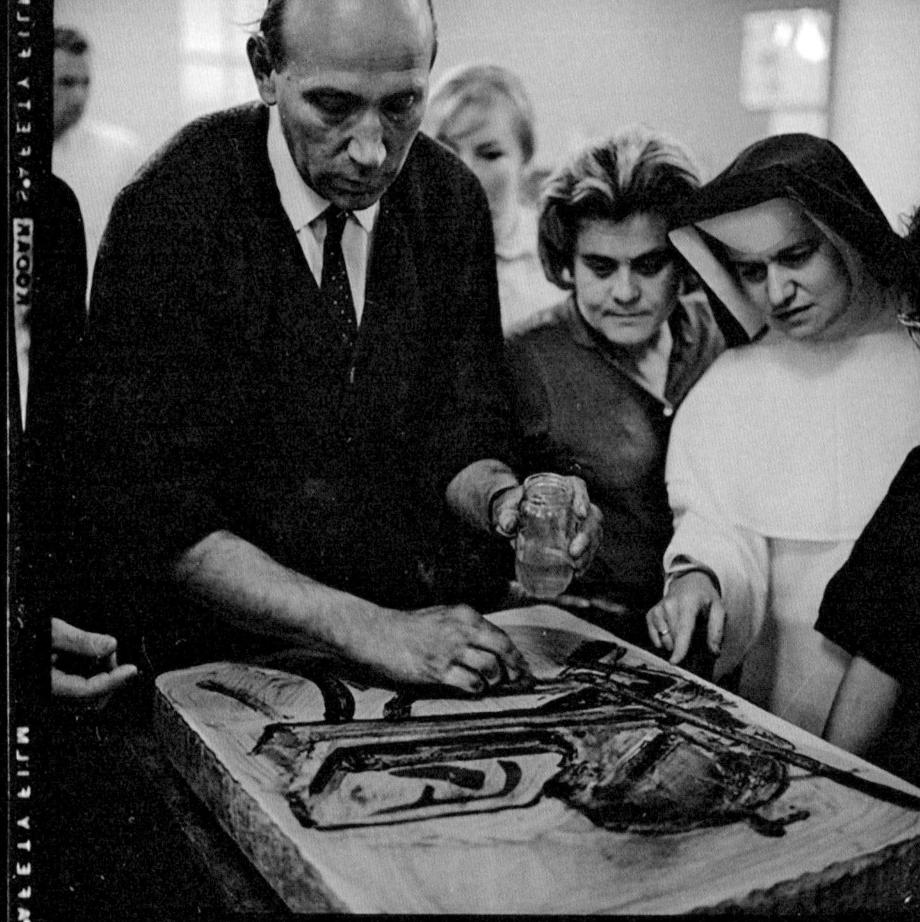

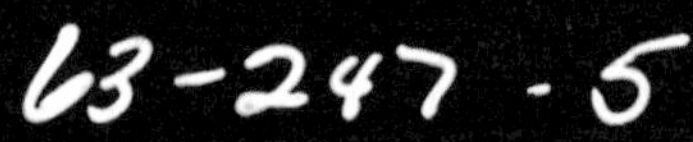

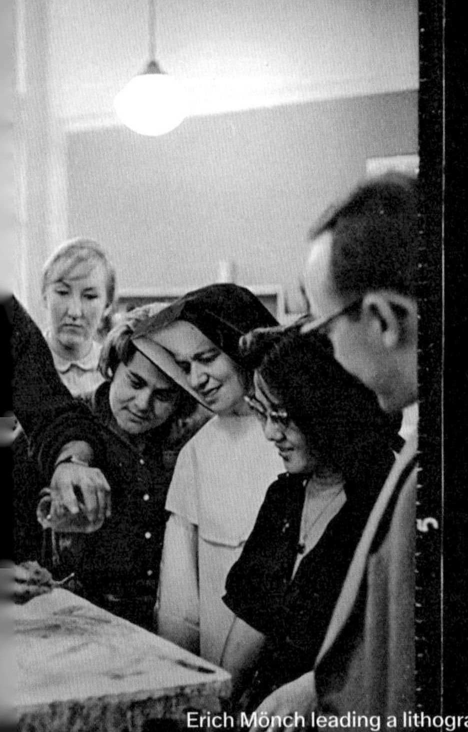

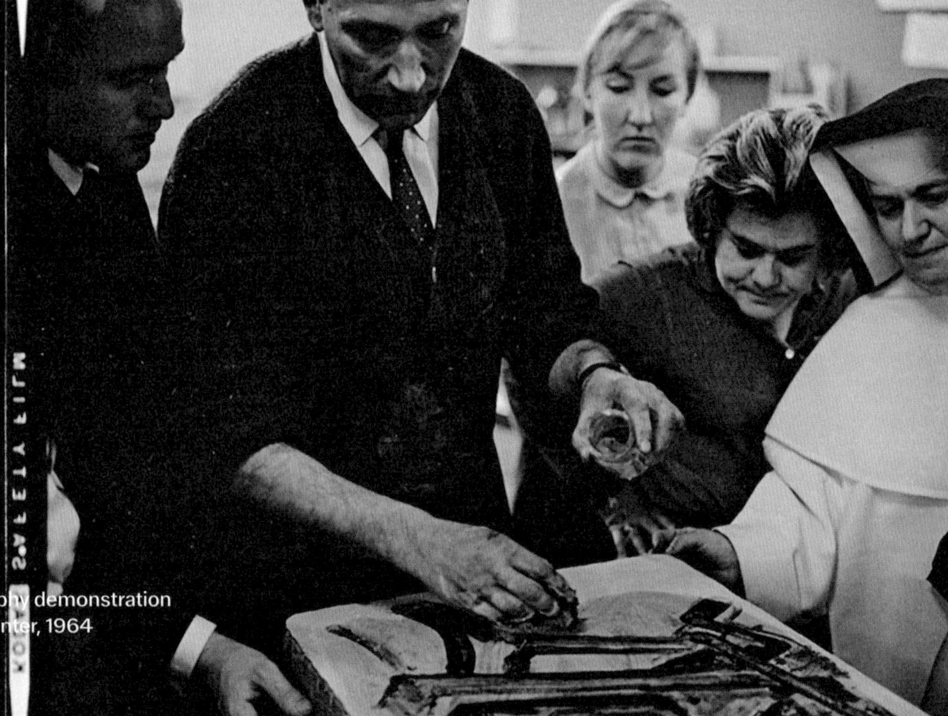

Erich Mönch leading a lithography demonstration
at Pratt Graphic Art Center, 1964

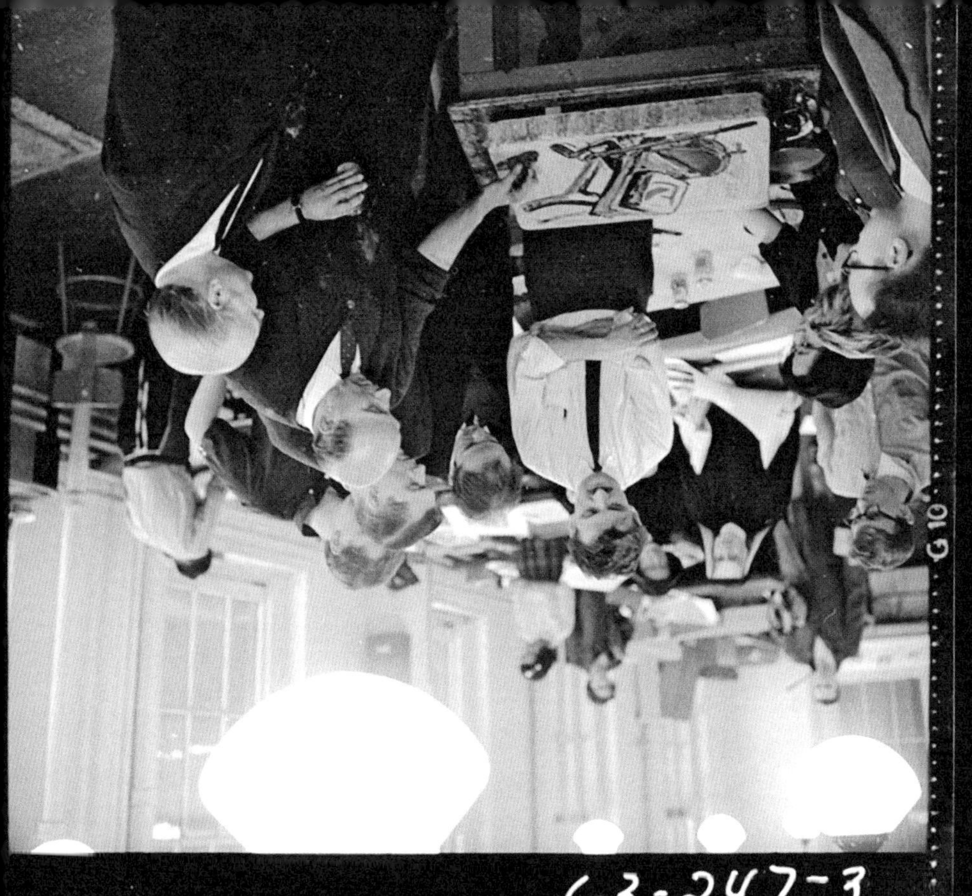

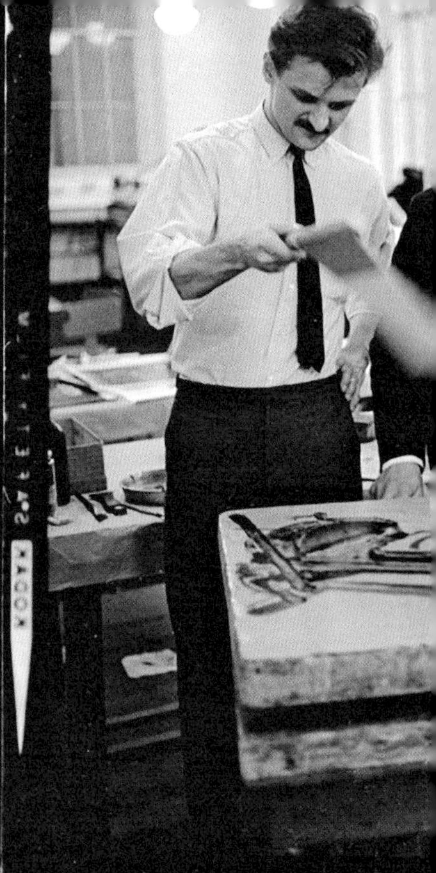

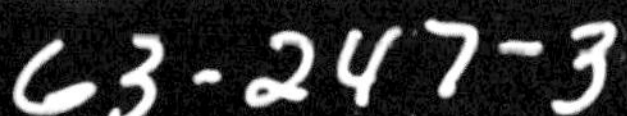
63-247-3

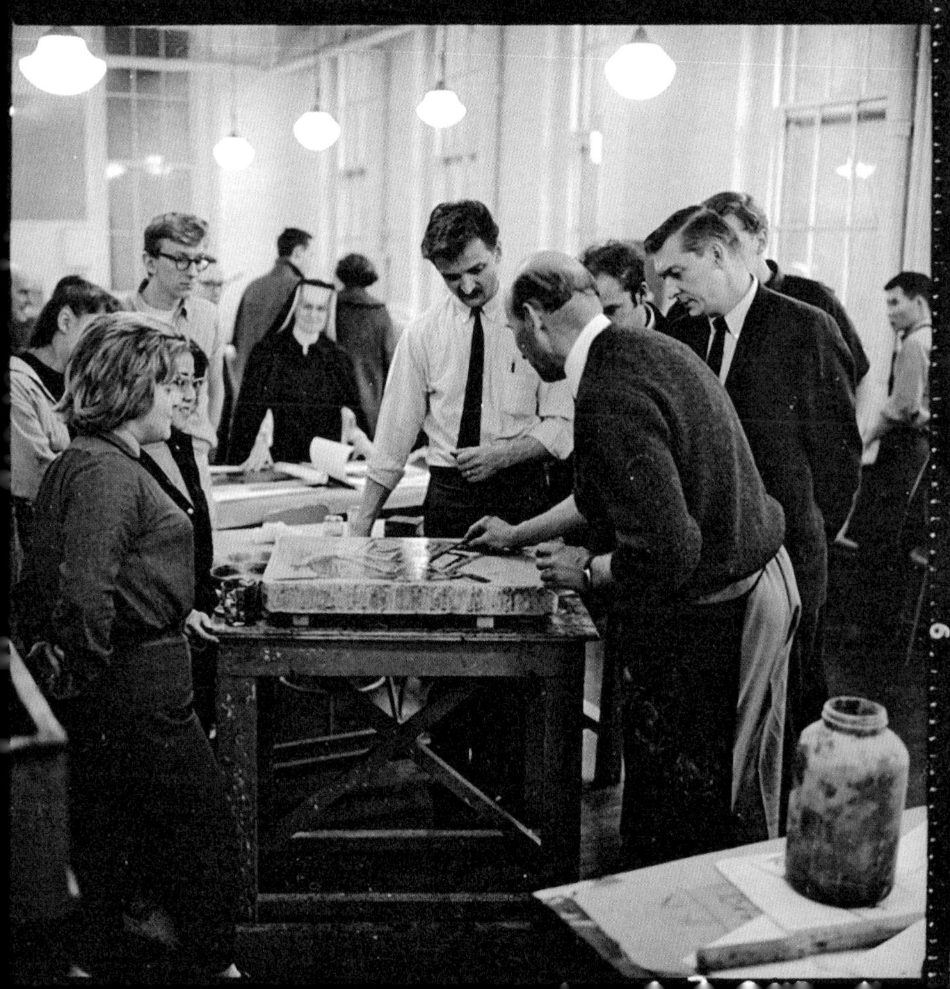

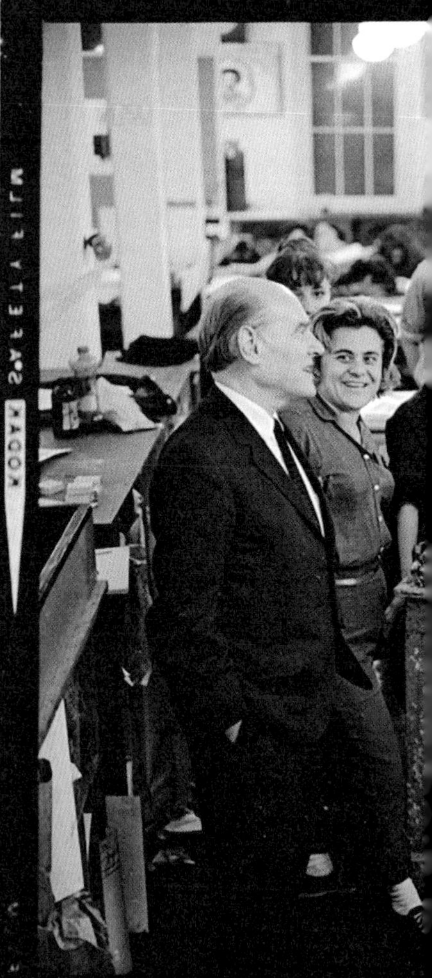

THE IMPRINT OF AN ARTIST, WITNESS, AND ADVOCATE

Ellen J. Benjamin

Although remembered primarily as a printmaker and founder of The Contemporaries, Margaret Lowengrund had an early and extended engagement as a writer and prolific illustrator for newspapers, magazines, and books. Besides offering regular income and a public outlet for her creativity, Lowengrund's work in these contexts aligned talents she spent a lifetime balancing: expressing her views through published commentary and portraying her insights through the creation of art. This essay provides the first comprehensive overview of her extensive but little-known work in the field and explores Lowengrund's efforts as an artist-advocate who had a keen eye for the range of human experience from the highbrow world of museums and cultured elites to the plight of laborers and the working-class city dweller. That she was persistent in raising her voice, despite pressure to do otherwise, is central to assessing her work as a printmaker.

In 1923, when she was in her early twenties, Lowengrund was hired by Philadelphia's *Evening Public Ledger*, her hometown newspaper. She contributed a semiregular feature with sketches of local scenic interests and conversational write-ups regarding the area's people, traditions, and history.[1] Titled "Just Little Sketches 'Round Our Town," Lowengrund's column depicted all corners of the city. Far-flung and thoroughgoing explorations, coupled with a vivid imagination, allowed her to spot what might otherwise go unobserved or put out of mind. A folksy quality dominated her vignettes and images, which readers appreciated for their straightforward charm and humor as well as for the parables they evoked.[2]

Street scenes offered an abundance of material from which Lowengrund built stories chroncling Philadelphia's famous inhabitants and latest immigrants while her headlines captured in pithy phrases the varied sights she portrayed. In one article titled "The Old Scissors Man at Fifteenth and Cherry," she recounted how the "tinkle of the little bell hanging precariously at the side of the old wooden machine" signaled the approach of an "apostle of industrious perseverance" (Fig. 1).[3] She depicted the man with the pushcart who, according to her description, "can speak little English, but well understands the meaning of 'job.'" "A Willing's Alley Serenade" brought to readers' ears the thrill that comes when "unexpectedly and with irreproachable judgment," the one-armed power musician "bursts with melody."[4] Lowengrund placed herself in a window listening to the hand organ below, as the player stood in the "shadow of the buildings in those winding and criss-crossing passages of streets."[5] She made it easy for readers to conjure the place, the man, and the sound.

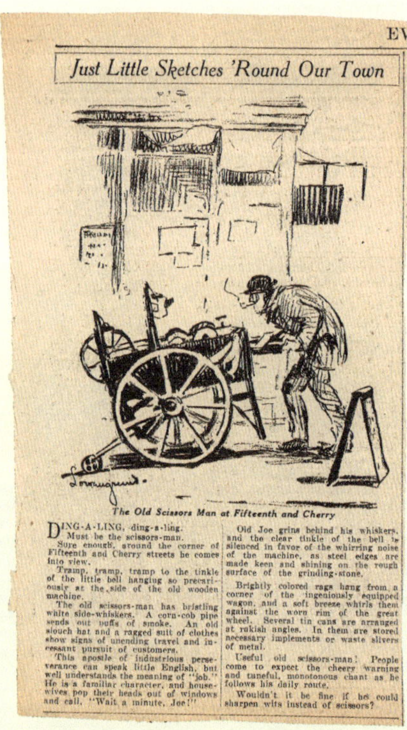

Just Little Sketches 'Round Our Town

The Old Scissors Man at Fifteenth and Cherry

DING-A-LING, ding-a-ling.
Must be the scissors-man.

Sure enough, around the corner of Fifteenth and Cherry streets he comes into view.

Tramp, tramp, tramp to the tinkle of the little bell hanging so precariously at the side of the old wooden machine.

The old scissors-man has bristling white side-whiskers. A corn-cob pipe sends out puffs of smoke. An old slouch hat and a ragged suit of clothes show signs of unending travel and incessant pursuit of customers.

This apostle of industrious perseverance can speak little English, but well understands the meaning of "job." He is a familiar character, and housewives pop their heads out of windows and call, "Wait a minute, Joe!"

Old Joe grins behind his whiskers, and the clear tinkle of the bell is silenced in favor of the whirring noise of the machine, as steel edges are made keen and shining on the rough surface of the grinding-stone.

Brightly colored rags hang from a corner of the ingeniously equipped wagon, and a soft breeze whirls them against the worn rim of the great wheel. Several tin cans are arranged at rakish angles. In them are stored necessary implements or waste slivers of metal.

Useful old scissors-man! People come to expect the cheery warning and tuneful, monotonous chant as he follows his daily route.

Wouldn't it be fine if he could sharpen wits instead of scissors?

Fig. 1 Margaret Lowengrund, "The Old Scissors Man at Fifteenth and Cherry," in the Philadelphia *Evening Public Ledger*, 1923

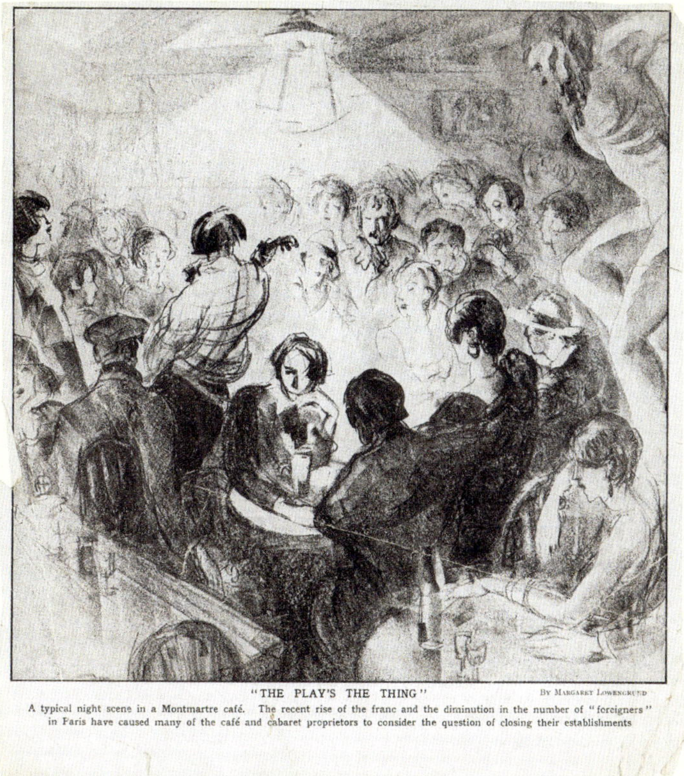

Fig. 2 Margaret Lowengrund, "The Play's the Thing," in the London *Bystander*, 1927

Lowengrund favored features about local institutions—including reporting on criminal court cases and less desirable areas of her hometown—and was particularly fascinated by architecture. One sees in this early work the genesis of Lowengrund's gravitation to constructed environments as a source for social commentary regarding the power of a metropolis to oppress and overwhelm its residents.

When Lowengrund moved to New York City for training at the Art Students League, she continued her pursuit of sharing social commentary, publishing nearly 250 illustrated columns for the *New York Evening Post* between 1924 and 1925 under the title "Little Sketches About Town." Her topics ranged from the familiar to the obscure, including "Alex, the Hot Dog Man," "The All-New York Horseshoe Squad," "The Bulletin Board at Pennsylvania Station," "Campaigning on Wall Street," "The Chinese Slaughter House," "Democrats at the Waldorf-Astoria," "Early Hours in the Subway," and "The Grave of an Amiable Child."[6]

In November 1927 both newspapers carried splashy feature articles about Lowengrund upon her return from an eighteen-month sojourn working and studying abroad. They noted her recent accomplishments and honors: one of their readers' favorite contributors was now a bona fide artist.[7]

For the rest of her life Lowengrund built on these credentials and found employment with newspapers attracted to her popularity in Philadelphia and New York. She contributed to the *Graphic*, *Daily Express*, and *Bystander* while in London during 1927 and also illustrated for French periodicals, "drawing the interiors of some of the worst dives in Paris" while reportedly having "a grand time" (Fig. 2).[8] Her infatuation with journalism was so sufficiently consuming that, during a second attempt at marriage in 1929, she tied the knot with reporter Joseph Lilly—though her commitment to her career took precedence, and the two later divorced.

Demonstrating characteristic independence and love of adventure, in 1933 Lowengrund was on the move again, having been commissioned by the Royal Netherlands and the Grace Lines to serve as a resident artist aboard their cruise ships for the purpose of developing illustrations about her journey

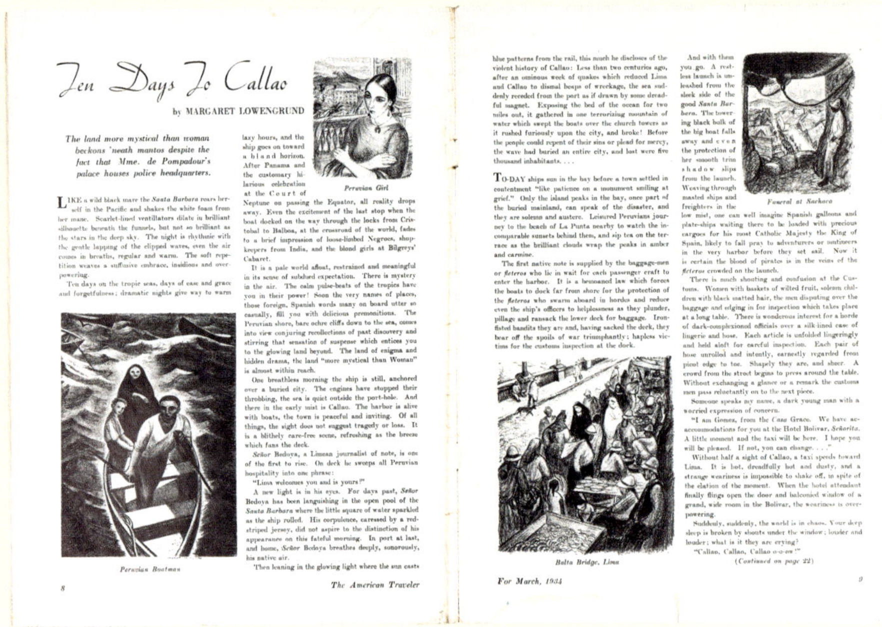

Ten Days To Callao

by MARGARET LOWENGRUND

The land more mystical than woman beckons 'neath mantos despite the fact that Mme. de Pompadour's palace houses police headquarters.

LIKE a wild black mare the *Santa Barbara* rears herself in the Pacific and shakes the white foam from her mane. Scarlet-lined ventillators dilate in brilliant silhouette beneath the funnels, but not so brilliant as the stars in the deep sky. The night is rhythmic with the gentle lapping of the clipped waves, even the air comes in breaths, regular and warm. The soft repetition weaves a suffusive embrace, insidious and overpowering.

Ten days on the tropic seas, days of ease and grace and forgetfulness; dramatic nights give way to warm lazy hours, and the ship goes on toward a bland horizon. After Panama and the customary hilarious celebration at the Court of Neptune on passing the Equator, all reality drops away. Even the excitement of the last stop when the boat docked on the way through the locks from Cristobal to Balboa, at the crossroad of the world, fades to a brief impression of loose-limbed Negroes, shopkeepers from India, and the blond girls at Bilgreys' Cabaret.

Peruvian Girl

It is a pale world afloat, restrained and meaningful in its sense of subdued expectation. There is mystery in the air. The calm pulse-beats of the tropics have you in their power! Soon the very names of places, those foreign, Spanish words many on board utter so casually, fill you with delicious premonitions. The Peruvian shore, bare ochre cliffs down to the sea, comes into view conjuring recollections of past discovery and stirring that sensation of suspense which entices you to the glowing land beyond. The land of enigma and hidden drama, the land "more mystical than Woman" is almost within reach.

One breathless morning the ship is still, anchored over a buried city. The engines have stopped their throbbing, the sea is quiet outside the port-hole. And there in the early mist is Callao. The harbor is alive with boats, the town is peaceful and inviting. Of all things, the sight does not suggest tragedy or loss. It is a blithely care-free scene, refreshing as the breeze which fans the deck.

Señor Bedoya, a Limean journalist of note, is one of the first to rise. On deck he sweeps all Peruvian hospitality into one phrase:

"Lima welcomes you and is yours!"

A new light is in his eyes. For days past, *Señor* Bedoya has been languishing in the open pool of the *Santa Barbara* where the little square of water sparkled as the ship rolled. His corpulence, caressed by a red-striped jersey, did not aspire to the distinction of his appearance on this fateful morning. In port at last, and home, *Señor* Bedoya breathes deeply, sonorously, his native air.

Then leaning in the glowing light where the sun casts blue patterns from the rail, this much he discloses of the violent history of Callao: Less than two centuries ago, after an ominous week of quakes which reduced Lima and Callao to dismal heaps of wreckage, the sea suddenly receded from the port as if drawn by some dreadful magnet. Exposing the bed of the ocean for two miles out, it gathered in one terrorizing mountain of water which swept the boats over the church towers as it rushed furiously upon the city, and broke! Before the people could repent of their sins or plead for mercy, the wave had buried an entire city, and lost were five thousand inhabitants. . . .

Peruvian Boatmen

TO-DAY ships sun in the bay before a town settled in contentment "like patience on a monument smiling at grief." Only the island peaks in the bay, once part of the buried mainland, can speak of the disaster, and they are solemn and austere. Leisured Peruvians journey to the beach of La Punta nearby to watch the incomparable sunsets behind them, and sip tea on the terrace as the brilliant clouds wrap the peaks in amber and carmine.

The first native note is supplied by the baggage-men or *fleteros* who lie in wait for each passenger craft to enter the harbor. It is a bemoaned law which forces the boats to dock far from shore for the protection of the *fleteros* who swarm aboard in hordes and reduce even the ship's officers to helplessness as they plunder, pillage and ransack the lower deck for baggage. Iron-fisted bandits they are and, having sacked the deck, they bear off the spoils of war triumphantly; hapless victims for the customs inspection at the dock.

Balta Bridge, Lima

And with them you go. A restless launch is unleashed from the sleek side of the good *Santa Barbara*. The towering black bulk of the big boat falls away and even the protection of her smooth trim shadow slips from the launch. Weaving through masted ships and freighters in the low mist, one can well imagine Spanish galleons and plate-ships waiting there to be loaded with precious cargoes for his most Catholic Majesty the King of Spain, likely to fall pray to adventurers or mutineers in the very harbor before they set sail. Now it is certain the blood of pirates is in the veins of the *fleteros* crowded on the launch.

Funeral at Sachaca

There is much shouting and confusion at the Customs. Women with baskets of wilted fruit, solemn children with black matted hair, the men disputing over the baggage and edging in for inspection which takes place at a long table. There is wonderous interest for a horde of dark-complexioned officials over a silk-lined case of lingerie and hose. Each article is unfolded lingeringly and held aloft for careful inspection. Each pair of hose unrolled and intently, earnestly regarded from picot edge to toe. Shapely they are, and sheer. A crowd from the street begins to press around the table. Without exchanging a glance or a remark the customs men pass reluctantly on to the next piece.

Someone speaks my name, a dark young man with a worried expression of concern.

"I am Gomez, from the *Casa* Grace. We have accommodations for you at the Hotel Bolivar, *Señorita*. A little moment and the taxi will be here. I hope you will be pleased. If not, you can change. . . ."

Without half a sight of Callao, a taxi speeds toward Lima. It is hot, dreadfully hot and dusty, and a strange weariness is impossible to shake off, in spite of the elation of the moment. When the hotel attendant finally flings open the door and balconied window of a grand, wide room in the Bolivar, the weariness is overpowering.

Suddenly, suddenly, the world is in chaos. Your deep sleep is broken by shouts under the window; louder and louder; what is it they are crying?

"Callao, Callao, Callao-o-ow!"

(*Continued on page 22*)

Fig. 3 Margaret Lowengrund, "Ten Days to Callao," in *American Traveler*, 1934

and the ships' destinations. These images, including the lithograph *Top Deck* (1932, page 35), were then published in *American Traveler* accompanied by extended travelogues penned by Lowengrund and Lilly (Fig. 3).[9] While in Peru, one of Lowengrund's assignments was to paint President Sánchez Cerro's portrait, a particularly risky endeavor since during the sitting revolutionists attempted his assassination—an ambition they later fulfilled.[10]

Later in the 1930s Lowengrund created sketches featuring city neighborhoods' gritty realities of homelessness and burlesque theaters for the *New York World-Telegram*, the paper where Lowengrund's second husband worked and won a Pulitzer Prize in 1932. Illustrating a 1933 article headlined "Ellis Island—This Way Out, Political Deportations Continue," Lowengrund dramatically depicted the tide of humanity being turned away at the port of entry.[11] Five years later *Paramount News* recruited her to make a series of drawings at sedition trials of confessed Nazi spies, subsequently making a newsreel showing Lowengrund coming and going from the courthouse.[12]

The broad circulation of these pieces enhanced Lowengrund's reputation, garnering requests from book publishers seeking her talents as an illustrator. Samuel Merwin's *Rise and Fight Againe*, Fay Ingalls's *The Valley Road*, and Carl Van Doren's edition of Sinclair Lewis's *Main Street* all benefited from Lowengrund's deft hand in bringing to life small-town Americana (Fig. 4).[13]

Although committed to exploring her own creative impulses, Lowengrund pivoted in the 1940s toward writing art criticism, employing this vehicle to advance printmaking. Her columns were variously called "City Sketches" (*Kingston Evening Leader*, 1947), "Art Today" (*Ulster County Sunday News*, 1947), and "Artist at Large" (*Woodstock Weekly Window*, 1948). These venues offered opportunities to voice her opinions, air questions ("What is the reason behind the sudden popularity of art as a career?"), and pronounce what she understood as truth ("Certainly abstractionism reflects the trend and pace of today and will leave a record as clear as the realism, impressionism and even that introspective phase of surrealism which is now on the decline").[14] Lowengrund demonstrated a capacity for tempering ardor with discernment, exhibiting sound instincts about whose art merited support and what gallery-goers might appreciate.

Her engaging and acerbic style appealed to *Art Digest*, which hired Lowengrund as an associate editor (1948–49) who advertised and reviewed exhibitions in the regular column "On My Rounds" and an

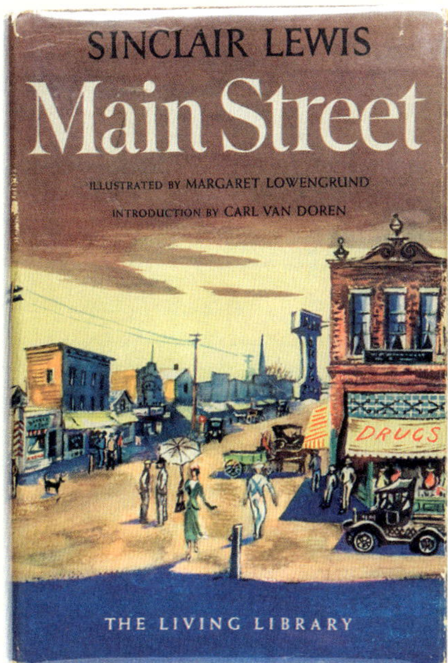

Fig. 4 Margaret Lowengrund, cover for Sinclair Lewis's *Main Street*, 1946

NEW MASSES

AUGUST 31, 1937

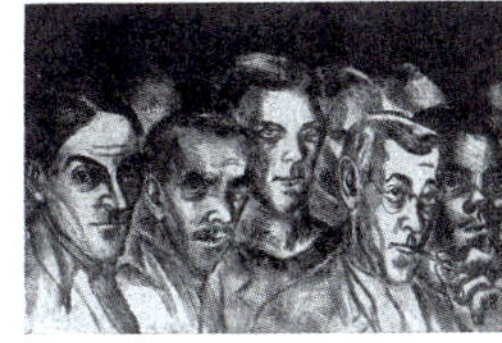

Lithograph by Margaret Lowengrund

"Give Us a Program!"

A first-term progressive, reviewing the session of Congress that has just been concluded, calls upon the people for a unified plan of action

By Congressman John T. Bernard

As I write this, the first session of the Seventy-Fifth Congress is ending in an atmosphere of confusion. In the midst of confusion it is difficult to remember that disorder must always accompany change and growth. There is growth and change in Congress today. The strong currents of political awakening which sweep the country today freshen, while they roil, the long-stagnant waters in Washington.

Party alignments, once symbolized by the aisle which divides one side of a chamber from the other, have lost their old rigidity. The aisle is no longer either a chalk mark or an unbridgeable chasm. It has become a thoroughfare, and the traffic, crossing and recrossing, is heavy.

Party labels no longer certify party loyalties. In the Senate, the Democrats Wheeler, Garner, and Copeland front for the Republicans. In the House, willing reactionaries from the majority side carry the ball for Minority Leader Snell.

Men as well as parties are having trouble making their old labels stick. Many traditional "liberals" lost that stamp of approval in the deep waters of the Court fight. They will try, of course, to paste it back on. But that they will fail is clear from one example. Senator Wheeler of Montana henceforth goes plainly marked: "Reactionary. Beware."

As important issues appear in ever sharper outline, mistakes in the labeling of individuals are revealed and rectified. Senator Nye, with his record in the munitions investigations, sold himself as a "progressive." Now Senator Nye turns out to be another case of adulterated goods. Speaking for Republic Steel, with the aid of Tom Girdler's press agent, Senator Nye attacked the National Labor Relations Board in a speech that put him among the renegades from progress.

In the House, Representative Rankin has long tried to pass as a "public-power liberal." But the label was misleading. Mr. Rankin wanted cheap power in combination with cheap labor as bait to lure runaway factories south. When the National Labor Relations Board threatened wage slavery in Tupelo by its assumption that the Wagner act meant Mississippi too, Mr. Rankin spoke up like a southern gentleman of the old school. Only his attacks on the Gavagan anti-lynching bill have equaled in venom his defense of southern workers menaced by a living wage.

Men who for years had found the designation of "conservative" eminently congenial, coasted in as "progressives" with the New Deal landslide. But the fact that in 1936 the Democratic ticket was headed by President Roosevelt worked no alchemy in these gentlemen. "New Dealer" McReynolds, chairman of the House Foreign Affairs Committee, forced through the embargo against Spain and the shameful Neutrality Act. Now he goes to bat against peaceful picketing of foreign embassies. "New Dealer" Woodrum bolted the administration leadership to marshal the reactionary forces driving for a half-billion-dollar cut in relief appropriations. There are others—too many—who traveled up to Washington wearing the New Deal tag, and who will go back home branded "not as advertised."

In addition to personal and party labels, sectional tags also begin to lose their familiar political significance. It is still true that the majority of reactionary Democrats come from the once solid South. A freshman senator, Claude Pepper of Florida, helped redeem southern honor in his maiden speech. Senator Barkley, new majority leader, unlike his predecessor, swallows the New Deal program whole, without gagging. The distance between Barkley and Joe Robinson is considerably greater than the distance which puts Kentucky north of Arkansas on the map. Senator (now Justice) Black comes from Alabama, feudal domain of landlordism, lynch law, and the Tennessee Coal & Iron Co. The fury of national and sectional reactionaries when Senator Black was nominated to the Supreme bench testifies to the validity of his liberalism. And there are plenty of tories from up north.

The split between reaction and progress, transcending party and sectional lines, appears at first to be a split between New Dealers and anti-New Dealers. But it is more complicated than that. In the House, at least, there

Fig. 5 Margaret Lowengrund, *Give Us a Program!*, in *New Masses*, August 31, 1937

occasional column titled "Field of Graphic Arts." The journal gave her a platform from which to encourage painters to explore the potential of lithography, printers to experiment with techniques that would allow artists to express themselves in an expanded range of media, and the public to appreciate both. Through this work Lowengrund was firmly placed on the national stage, where her stature continued to grow, as evidenced by *World Scope Encyclopedia* recruiting her to pen a summary about developments in the art world during 1949.[15]

But the arts community was not alone in watching her activities. Lowengrund's name was raised in testimony before Congress in 1949 in a hearing entitled "Communism in the Heart of American Art—What to Do About It." Rep. George Anthony Dondero (R-MI) proclaimed Lowengrund's articles regarding modern art to be "an attempt to glorify the vulgar, distorted, and the perverted."[16] No stranger to reactionary attempts at censorship, Lowengrund was undeterred by the inflammatory hectoring aimed at intimidating what Dondero labeled as her efforts to "laud and magnify the work of the left-wingers with whom she has associated."[17] Shortly after these hearings Peyton Boswell, editor of *Art Digest*, responded to the accusations by issuing a "plea for tolerance" that rejected the congressman's allegations and affirmed his own belief in Lowengrund's impartiality and honesty as a critic.[18]

Lowengrund sustained her efforts as an artist and advocate, utilizing the investigative skills of a journalist, the insights of a storyteller, and the instincts of an organizer to continue her long-standing commitment to documenting the public's strife and loss. In works such as such as *Breadline* (1931) and *Coal Pickers* (1936), viewers could observe the harsh realities of poverty shared by urban and rural dwellers, with the indiscernible faces of those depicted suggesting how easily audiences might be interchanged with subjects. But the beseeching eyes of unemployed workers in *Give Us a Program!* (1937), a lithograph reproduced in the left-wing magazine *New Masses*, demanded more than simply being seen—they pressed for a response (Fig. 5).[19]

These drawings, prints, and commentary bear witness to social dislocation, destitution, and the fractures created by inequalities. As an examination of Lowengrund's work makes apparent, it is a benefit for those who appreciate both art and democracy that government censorship ultimately failed. Her conceptualization of the artist's role during moments of civic and economic turmoil resonates with, and stands as a beacon for, contemporary efforts to contribute to the dialogue regarding the profound issues of our times.

VISION AND GRIT: MARGARET LOWENGRUND AND NEW YORK'S FEMALE GALLERISTS OF THE 1950S

Jillian Russo

When Margaret Lowengrund founded The Contemporaries gallery and print workshop in 1951, she became part of a postwar art scene that female gallerists and art dealers increasingly dominated. Since the early twentieth century, New York's art world offered women artist-entrepreneurs—such as Edith Halpert, owner of the Downtown Gallery, and socialites and collectors such as Peggy Guggenheim and Gertrude Vanderbilt Whitney—the opportunity to wield cultural influence and build successful careers. By the 1940s and early 1950s, the industry expanded to include a new generation of women, among them Grace Borgenicht, Martha Jackson, Betty Parsons, Marian Willard, and Virginia Zabriskie.[1] Each gallerist brought distinct interests, abilities, and approaches that distinguished their exhibition programs and fostered new developments in art in the United States. Although Lowengrund's contribution has been understudied, she built the foundations of the postwar contemporary print market among artists, collectors, and the public in the United States.

Female Gallerists and the Postwar Art Scene

In contrast to art patrons like Whitney and Guggenheim who powerfully shaped the New York art scene with the support of their immense fortunes, the new generation of women gallerists who launched businesses in the 1940s and 1950s were upper middle class and often artists themselves. Although many utilized family inheritances or the support of their spouses to finance their galleries, their ambitions were dependent on creating sustainable business models. A popular strategy was presenting a mix of modern and contemporary art.[2]

Grace Borgenicht and Virginia Zabriskie were among the leading gallerists whose curatorial programs emphasized modern art, while still including contemporary artists. In 1951, Borgenicht, a painter, established her eponymous gallery on Fifty-Seventh Street, following up her experience working in Chris Ritter's Laurel Gallery. Borgenicht represented a diverse array of modernists from the United States including Milton Avery, Ilya Bolotowsky, and Gertrude Greene, as well as contemporary artists Jimmy Ernst, José de Rivera, Reuben Kadish, and Wolf Kahn. Borgenicht was inspired to start the gallery because she recognized the paltry level of support for artists from the United States in museums and commercial galleries.[3] Borgenicht later recalled that she needed tremendous self-confidence to run the gallery, which took a number of years to achieve financial stability.[4]

Following a similar model, Zabriskie, who had degrees in art history from New York University, founded Zabriskie Gallery in 1954. Early exhibitions—including *The City 1900–1930* (1957), *The Eight* (1958), *A Decade of American Cubism* (1958) and *Collage in America* (1958–59)—provided surveys of key movements that defined modernism. Zabriskie Gallery also represented a roster of contemporary artists. Although Zabriskie had no prior business experience, she attributed her sustained success to her emphasis on the gallery's commercial function, noting: "You've got to remember you are a retail store. You must bring attention to and make money for your artists."[5]

Marian Willard, Martha Jackson, and Betty Parsons established galleries that focused on avant-garde contemporary art, placing it in context with modernism. Influenced by the writings of Carl Jung, the practice of Zen Buddhism, and the work of Paul Klee, Willard opened her gallery in 1940, with a specialization in abstraction and surrealism. She was instrumental in introducing audiences in the United States to the work of Dorothy Dehner, Richard Pousette-Dart, David Smith, and West Coast artists Morris Graves and Mark Tobey. Willard recalled that her business relied on a niche group of loyal collectors.[6]

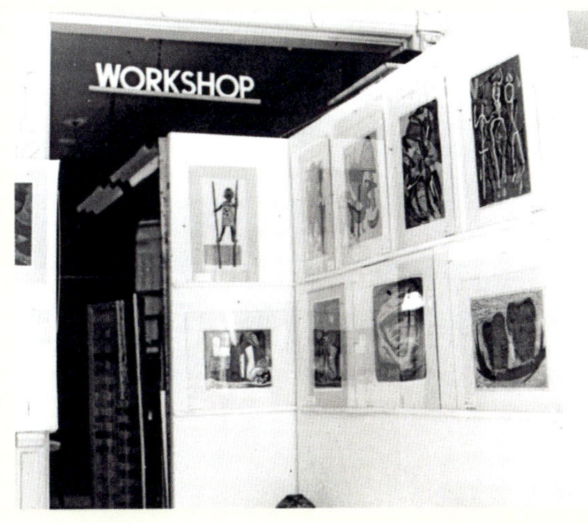

Fig. 1 Interior of The Contemporaries at 959 Madison Avenue, ca. 1952–55. Photo by Robert Delson

Martha Jackson opened her gallery in 1953 and developed an exhibition program that juxtaposed postwar art from Europe and the United States alongside emerging artists like the Gutai Group and stylistic trends like Neo-Dada. Jackson later reflected on her pioneering efforts to organize "this great agglomeration of art . . . and the young artists and develop them in a business way," laboring always "to use the gallery as an example of how art dealing should be carried on in the best way."[7] Artist and collector Betty Parsons opened her Fifty-Seventh Street gallery in 1946 with an eye toward experimental and unconventional work. Known for representing Jackson Pollock, she also advanced the careers of many women artists including Helen Frankenthaler, Judith Godwin, and Hedda Sterne. Summarizing the experience of visiting the Parsons Gallery, art critic Lawrence Campbell wrote: "A visitor . . . is immediately struck by a mood unlike that of a commercial art gallery. It is more like an artist's cooperative."[8] Both Parsons and Jackson pioneered the white-box gallery, often hanging paintings without frames, hosting performances, and creating a cultural gathering space for artists, collectors, and the public.

The Founding of The Contemporaries

Margaret Lowengrund's decision to create a hybrid workshop-gallery aligned with the model of the gallery as a creative space embraced by Parsons and Jackson. An experienced artist and printmaker, Lowengrund understood the limited resources available to artists who wanted to explore new approaches to printmaking. Her print studio allowed artists to experiment affordably with new techniques, while the adjacent sales gallery supported the operation financially and built a market for prints.

Rather than entering the established gallery scene on Fifty-Seventh Street, Lowengrund situated The Contemporaries at 959 Madison Avenue at Seventy-Fifth Street. While Fifty-Seventh Street was the major hub of the New York art world, galleries were beginning to migrate uptown. In 1949 Parke-Bernet Galleries auction house opened at 980 Madison Avenue at Seventy-Sixth Street, and the following year Eleanor Saidenberg, Pablo Picasso's representative in the United States, established her gallery at 10 East Seventy-Seventh Street. In a 1949 article for *World Scope Encyclopedia*, Lowengrund describes her anticipation that "this new location might easily become the nucleus of a new art center."[9] Lowengrund's decision to open The Contemporaries within this vanguard neighborhood underscores her vision of the gallery as an avant-garde initiative. Furthermore, the location enabled her to develop a print market with less direct competition from midtown galleries and to take advantage of quotidian commercial activity on Madison Avenue's commercial strip—the gallery was located above a bookstore and next to a tailor and furrier.

While Lowengrund's decision to create a gallery and workshop entirely devoted to prints was bold, she built upon the foundations of other galleries catering to print collectors. When she established The Contemporaries, several New York galleries specialized in selling modern prints by artists from Europe and the United States. Weyhe Gallery, a gallery and bookstore located at 794 Lexington Avenue, supported the careers of modernists including Max Weber, Rockwell Kent, Wanda Gág, and William Gropper through the production of affordable prints and portfolios.[10] Another combination bookshop and gallery, Wittenborn Schultz (38 East Fifty-Seventh Street), featured Georges Braque, Picasso, and Max Beckmann, as well as contemporary artists active in the United States.

Two significant forerunners to The Contemporaries were the Serigraph Galleries (later Melzer Gallery), a cooperative nonprofit directed by Doris Melzer, and Associated American Artists (AAA), a print publisher and gallery renowned for its affordably priced etchings and lithographs. Founded

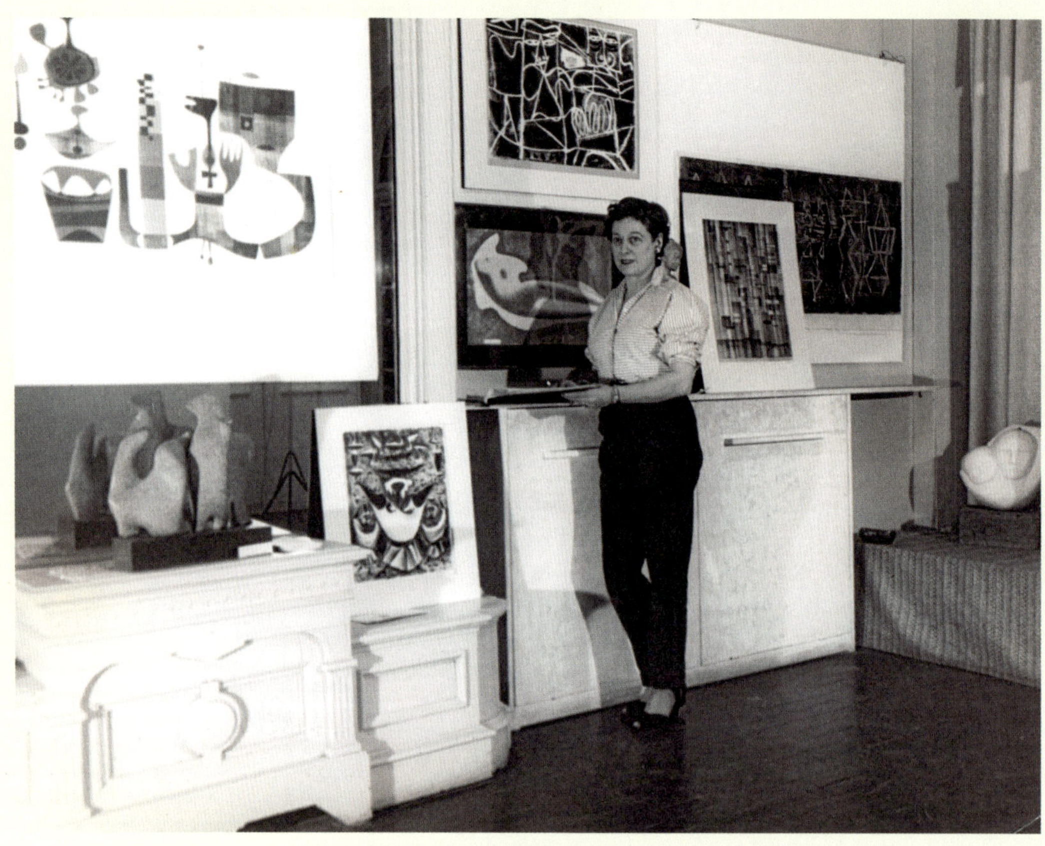

Fig. 2 Margaret Lowengrund inside The Contemporaries at 959 Madison Avenue, ca. 1952–55. Gelatin silver print. Photo by Maurice Berezov

in 1940, Serigraph Galleries at 38 West Fifty-Seventh Street was an active space, hosting film screenings, demonstrations, and other artist-oriented events centered around promoting the screenprint, but it did not include a formal workshop. Reeves Lewenthal established AAA in 1934 as a challenge to the traditional "gallery system."[11] His enterprise was incredibly successful in selling prints to middle-class consumers through direct mail order, in partnership with department stores, and at AAA's gallery at 711 Fifth Avenue. Lowengrund offered a counterpoint to AAA's model, targeting serious collectors by showcasing innovative contemporary prints and integrating their presentation in the gallery with an allied workshop that embraced experimentation.

Although only a few photographs of Lowengrund's gallery at 959 Madison Avenue remain, the images document a modernist, quirky, but well-designed interior (Fig. 1). The mixed-use building had a brownstone facade with both residential apartments and retail space on the ground and second floors. Lowengrund renovated her second-floor space, adding storage cabinets and shelves to display matted prints. She also added a V-shaped decorative screen to create an office area for her desk and movable walls to allow for flexible exhibition design.

A striking photograph by Maurice Berezov, taken between 1952 and 1955, depicts Lowengrund as a stylish and authoritative gallerist (Fig. 2). Wearing tailored trousers and a formfitting collared blouse, she poses rather seductively against the modernist cabinets, a collection of prints and sculpture artfully installed behind her. Berezov's image evokes Louis Faurer's photograph of Edith Halpert in the Downtown Gallery, which appeared in *Life* magazine in 1952 (Fig. 3). Although Faurer's image featured Downtown Gallery artists holding their artwork in the background, Halpert and Lowengrund are both holding a commanding gaze focused directly at the viewer. As Berezov's photograph illustrates, prints were

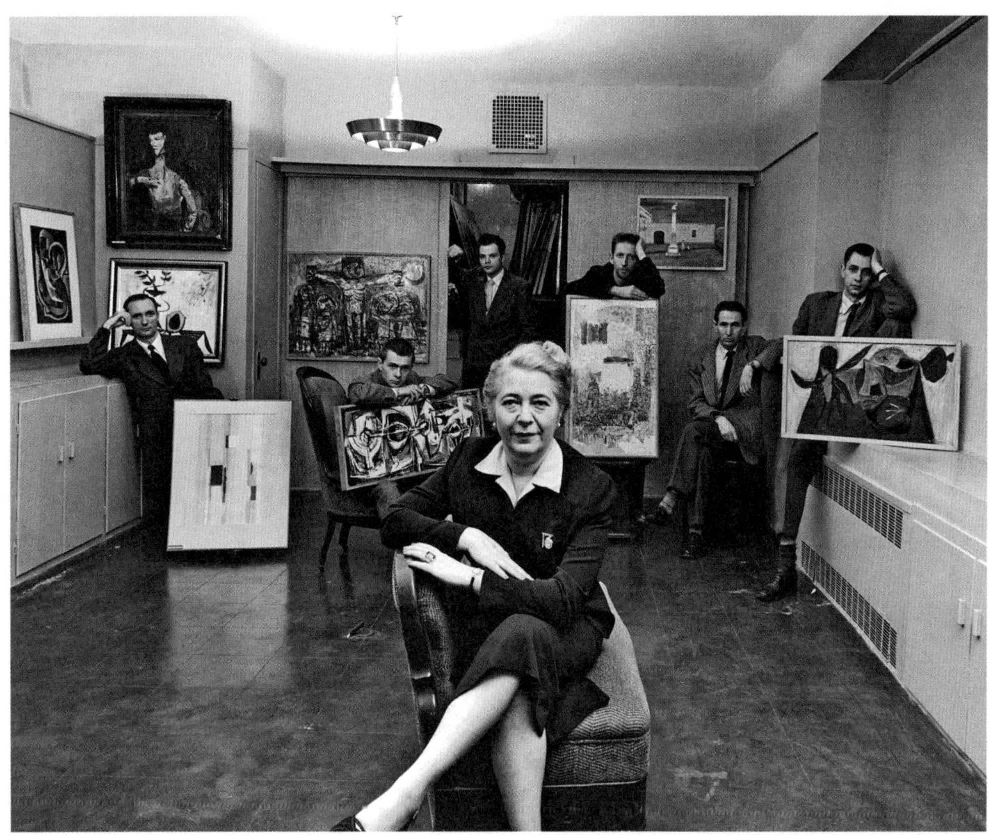

Fig. 3 Edith Gregor Halpert photographed for *Life*, 1952. Photo by Louis Faurer

treated like paintings—in some cases hung unframed, displayed in salon-style groupings, or as solitary pieces—commanding an entire wall.

At 959 Madison Avenue, Lowengrund developed an exhibition program that was in dialogue with the combination of contemporary and modern art shown by Borgenicht, Jackson, and Zabriskie. The Contemporaries' second exhibition, *Painters and Their Prints* (January–February 1952), featured works by several artists affiliated with 7 Painter-Printmakers, a collective Lowengrund had spearheaded in 1950, including Will Barnet, Sue Fuller, Hans Moller, and John Von Wicht as well as renowned contemporary painters who worked in the print medium such as Milton Avery, Werner Drewes, Rico Lebrun, Seong Moy, and Kurt Seligmann. While Lowengrund represented their graphic work, many of the artists were affiliated with other galleries for their painting. Seong Moy, for example, exhibited with Betty Parsons, Milton Avery with Grace Borgenicht, and Werner Drewes with Kleemann Gallery.

The Contemporaries Gallery of Sculpture and Graphic Art

In the fall of 1955, when 959 Madison Avenue was slated for demolition, Lowengrund separated the gallery and workshop, leasing a large exhibition space at 992 Madison Avenue, directly across from Parke-Bernet, as well as a studio space at 1343 Third Avenue. The new gallery, which she renamed The Contemporaries Gallery of Sculpture and Graphic Art, allowed for more substantial exhibitions and a greater focus on sculpture. Situated on the ground floor, the new space had large window displays facing Madison Avenue and Seventy-Seventh Street.[12]

To create a streamlined interior, Lowengrund hired Robert Delson, a photographer who had designed art centers for the Federal Art Project throughout Florida during the 1930s (Fig. 4).[13] Delson's sketches and plans for The Contemporaries as well as photographs of the gallery reveal his use of screens and wall panels mounted on metal supports. These

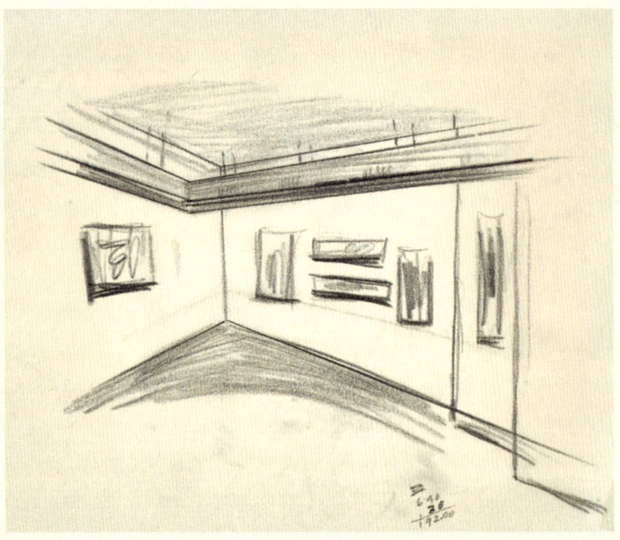

Fig. 4 Robert Delson, *The Contemporaries, New York*, sketch for the interior at 992 Madison Avenue, 1955. Graphite on tracing paper, 9⅛ × 12 in.

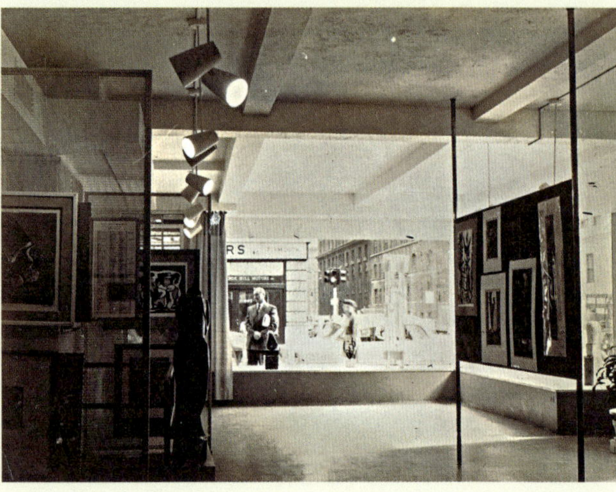

Fig. 5 Installation view of *Today: An Exhibition of Sculpture and Graphic Art* at The Contemporaries, 992 Madison Avenue, September 1955. Gelatin silver print. Photo by Robert Delson

lightweight dividers were used to define distinct spaces, such as a seating area/viewing room, and to provide additional wall space (Fig. 5). The result was a more modular aesthetic reflective of the international style. A critic remarked on the aesthetic of the gallery by concluding: "As artistically conceived as any of the works themselves is the structure of the gallery with its flood of natural light, its streamlined display features, and air of elegant restraint."[14]

Legacy of The Contemporaries

While it took vision and grit for any of the women gallery owners to succeed, Lowengrund's vision for The Contemporaries was more radical and complex than her colleagues'. All of these female gallerists understood the necessity of developing successful commercial business models that focused on sales, the cultivation of collectors, and the promotion of artists. In addition to trying to integrate commercial and nonprofit models, Lowengrund was trying to establish a high-end market for graphic arts, which did not possess the same cachet as painting and sculpture in the early 1950s. It is clear that Lowengrund influenced Martha Jackson, and likely other dealers, by foregrounding the importance of prints as a creative medium and a source of interest for new collectors. In 1965, Katherine Goodman, a director at Martha Jackson Gallery, proposed establishing a department of prints. Jackson enthusiastically supported the idea and secured a Ford Foundation grant that allowed Goodman to visit the Tamarind Lithography Workshop in Los Angeles to learn about techniques.[15] By that time, Jackson and Goodman were responding to growing interest in print media rather than developing the market, as Lowengrund had. Years earlier, through determined effort, Lowengrund blazed the path for the commercial success of contemporary prints, and her work quickly became a model for these female gallerists to follow.

IDEAL PICTURES FOR MODERN WALLS: MARGARET LOWENGRUND, THE CONTEMPORARIES, AND THE POSTWAR MIDDLE-CLASS INTERIOR

Sarah Archer

In the summer of 1953, a striking new apartment complex opened in Riverdale, New York, on an unassuming stretch of the Henry Hudson Parkway (Fig. 1). The Briar Oaks apartments were not luxurious, exactly, but they were commodious: there was a twenty-four-hour doorman, Formica countertops, picture windows, and "unusually large closets."[1] Inside the fully decorated model apartments, there were clues that signaled what kind of prospective renters the developers of Briar Oaks hoped to attract: original, affordable works of art on the walls. They had been put there by Beryl Austrian, a decorator who made her name designing the interiors of New York lobbies through her company Intramural, Inc.[2] A notice in the *New York Herald Tribune* about Briar Oaks included a list of suppliers who had provided furniture, textiles, and even plants for the model dwellings (Fig. 2). Among these was The Contemporaries, credited as having supplied "pictures."[3] Though they weren't identified as such, the pictures in question were almost certainly prints.

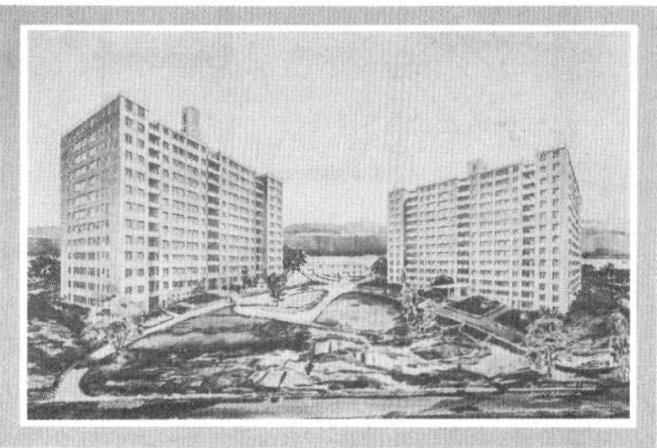

BRIAR OAKS

Just off Henry Hudson Parkway at 246th Street
RIVERDALE, NEW YORK

Fig. 1 Brochure for Briar Oaks at 4525 Henry Hudson Parkway, 1953

Apartment houses like Briar Oaks weren't glamorous, but they weren't kitschy, either. They were akin to the affordable and abundant Levittown tract houses that served as havens for the white middle class aspiring to homeownership in the postwar era: homes that were never meant to be—nor were they advertised as—steps up the ladder of sophistication or social capital. Some Levittown houses came with an Admiral TV set built into their living room walls.[4] They were solid, roomy, and did much to give the proliferating suburbs an atmosphere of staunch anti-communism and to define a way of life for the United States.

A Briar Oaks apartment didn't offer a built-in TV or a small patch of the American Dream, but it did offer middle-class renters on the outskirts of New York proximity to the city's cultural ferment and style. A January 1955 guest book from The Contemporaries includes Beryl Austrian's name, suggesting that prints remained on the decorator's radar.[5] In effect, Austrian selected works from Margaret Lowengrund's gallery to lend the Briar Oaks model residences a sense of authenticity, charm, and uniqueness. In a 1966 interview, Austrian said that lobbies were a "welcome mat for tenants and guests" that gave visitors "the total impression of the property."[6] That she was also hired to decorate model apartments suggests that her "welcome mat" theory worked wonders bewitching prospective tenants who found themselves browsing a lifestyle where the walls were a place to both share personal interests and signal sophistication—not just a place to hang one's hat.

The way the works from The Contemporaries are credited—or not credited—in the *Herald Tribune* is telling. The gallery is given credit as a "source," akin to the creator of hand-blocked wallpaper or upholstery fabric, but the individual artists who made the prints in question are not identified.[7] This gesture positioned The Contemporaries in a category closer to a craft or artisanal workshop in which a predictable final product can be reliably found rather than to a studio in which an artist might produce works that evolve in form and content over time as their vision develops. But Lowengrund does not seem to have been ambivalent about making inroads for The Contemporaries—and perhaps for printmaking more broadly—in the world of interior design. Quite the contrary, she expressed enthusiasm for the artistic possibilities that this sort of clientele might afford, implying acceptance that prints possessed a nebulous status somewhere between works of fine art, examples of skilled craft, and modern design.

As new technology proliferated in the late 1930s and 1940s, elite and popular understanding of the nature of printmaking itself evolved. If the techniques used to produce "real" prints—the unique etchings, engravings, and lithography made in The Contemporaries' workshop—were opaque to the casual observer, how were they to understand why less costly photomechanical reproductions were any different? Both limited-edition fine art prints and mass-market color prints might share space on a gallery or shop wall, appealing to a range of potential consumers and perhaps even offering different iterations of the same original image. That they sat perched along a spectrum of perceived authenticity demonstrates the significance within printmaking of proximity to the artist's touch.

This distinction even made it into contemporary social commentary: critic Russell Lynes's famed 1949 article "High-Brow, Low-Brow, Middle-Brow" provided a satirical illustrated chart that mapped the contours of social class and consumer taste in the United States according to "brows."[8] Lynes positioned a "highbrow" Pablo Picasso painting at the top, a "lowbrow" pin-up girl at the bottom, and in between, where upper- and lower-middle class consumers jockeyed for status, he posited that an attraction to "original prints" like etchings and lithographs existed in tension with the desire to buy a "color reproduction of a van Gogh or a Cézanne."[9] Like Beryl Austrian, Lynes understood that there was meaning legible in the different ways that prints are made, and that the closer a print was to an original, the more artful its production would be. Similarly, its status would be higher as a work of art and even as an object of decor.

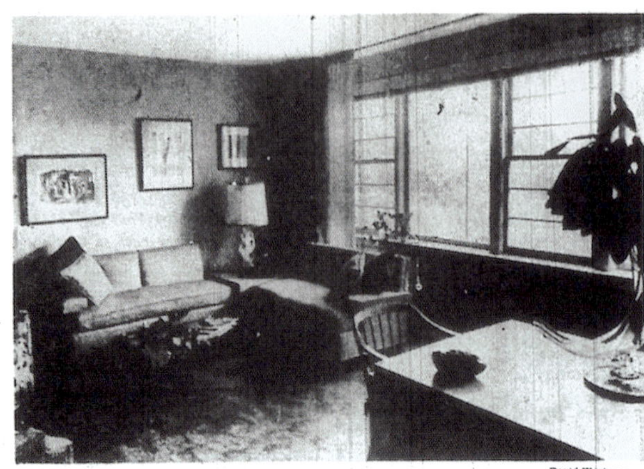

David Workman

Model suite in Briar Oaks, Fisher Brothers' apartment project in Riverdale.

This living room is in one of two apartments in Briar Oaks, the Fisher Bros. development at 4555 Henry Hudson Parkway, West, in the Riverdale section of the Bronx, which have been designed by Intramural, Inc., under the personal supervision of Beryl S. Austrian, to show both contemporary and traditional treatments. All items of furniture and acessories were chosen to be readily adaptable to any one of the appropriate rooms throughout the buildings, Mrs. Austrian said.

Suppliers who co-operated included P. Nathan Sons, furniture; Stroheim & Romann, fabrics; Simon Manges & Son, carpet; Jules Edlin, draperies; Designed for Living, accessories, and The Contemporaries, pictures, and Stanley Bernstein, plants.

Fig. 2 "Model suite in Briar Oaks, Fisher Brothers' apartment project in Riverdale," in the *New York Herald Tribune*, July 26, 1953

This was the context in which Margaret Lowengrund decided to open The Contemporaries in 1951. Because of her varied personal history as an illustrator, artist, critic, and administrator, Lowengrund was content to accept the support of any community or industry with an interest in the medium she loved. In the early 1950s, one of the biggest of these was not the art world, but the booming field of postwar interior design. This was also true in the 1930s, when Reeves Lewenthal lamented that "the gallery system is doomed. The rich collector class is dying out."[10] He was soon animated by advancing technology and a broadening audience of new homeowners as the future market for prints (Fig. 3). Lewenthal's business, Associated American Artists (AAA), provided affordable, aesthetically accessible graphics—notably by the regionalists Thomas Hart Benton, Grant Wood, and John Steuart Curry—made available to middle-class consumers across the country through mail order.[11] AAA thrived by positioning art as a design solution at a moment when interiors and entertaining were more important to the middle class than ever before. Lewenthal disseminated the idea that "orphan" wall spaces, as

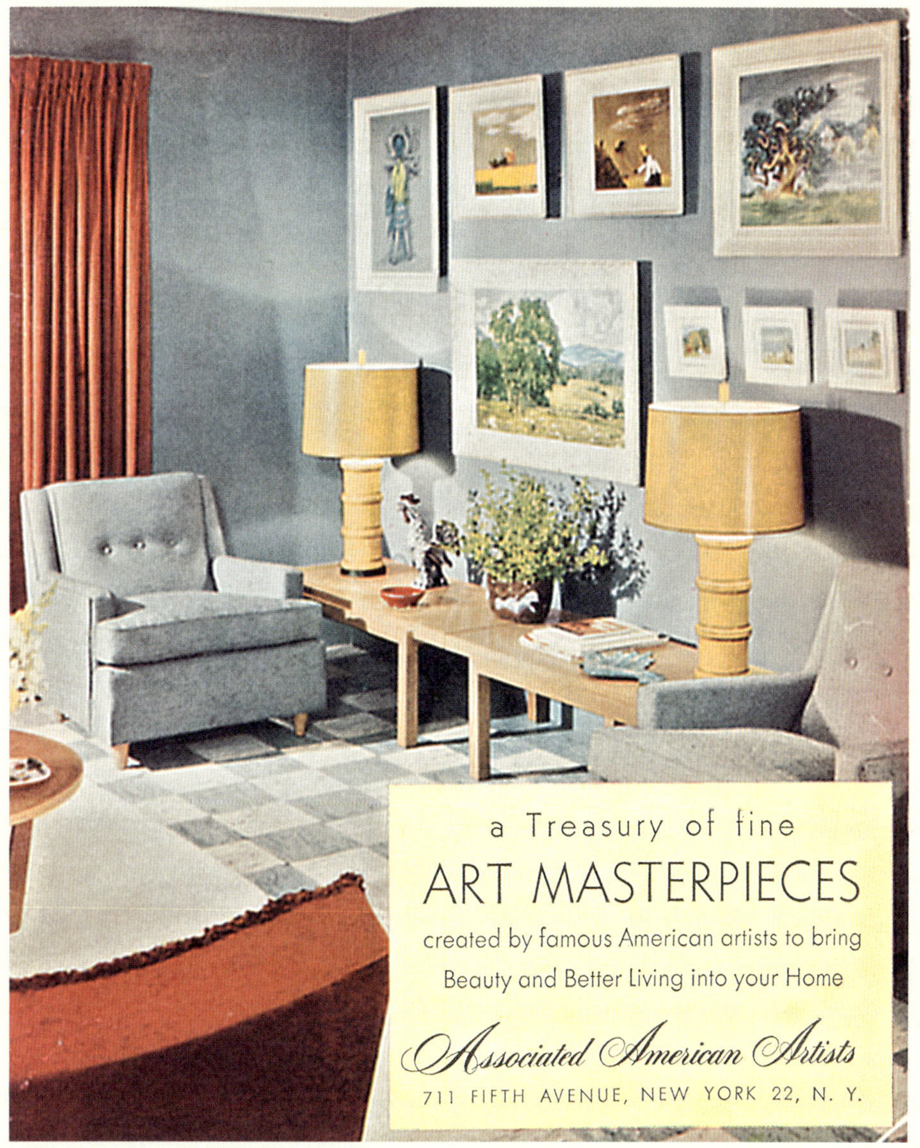

Fig. 3 Associated American Artists, cover of *A Treasury of Fine Art Masterpieces Created by Famous American Artists to Bring Beauty and Better Living into Your Home*, 1951

one AAA catalogue identified the problem, were to be avoided, and AAA's prints could help achieve decorative unity in a room.[12] Lowengrund's gallery, by contrast, was more experimental and thus closer to the constellation of art world prestige than AAA; yet she wasn't afraid to court interior designers. She realized that noncollectors with modern tastes—the prospective Briar Oaks renters and their compatriots, for instance—were eager to find distinctive pieces for their own modern walls, but were not in the market for costly works of art.

Lowengrund was intrigued by the possibilities of prints that exceeded traditional paper dimensions. Reviewing a print annual at Jacques Seligmann's gallery in *Art Digest* in 1949, she remarked on works by the Graphic Circle artist collective: "Their size very often gives them away, since most of the twelve [artists] have long since broken the average bounds of dealer's print racks and exhibition mat requirements (14 ¼ × 19 ¼, 18 × 22—or else!) and work unfettered on plates or woodblocks commensurate with their growing ideas."[13] Later, while

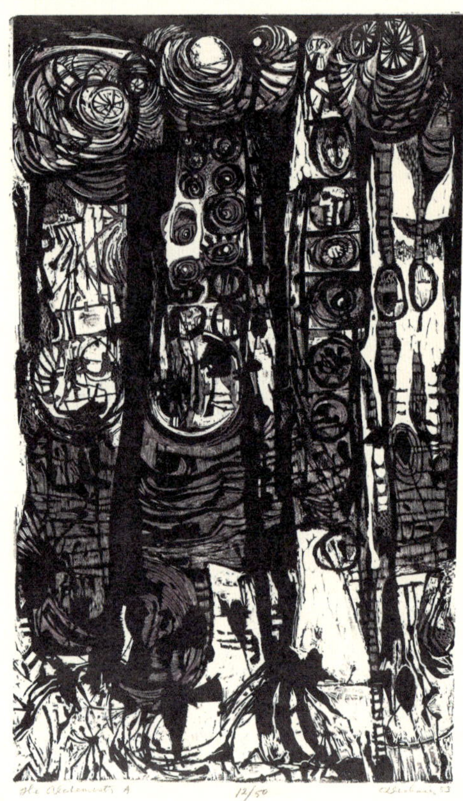

Fig. 4 Arthur Deshaies, *The Alchemists*, 1953. Wood engraving, edition of 50, image: 20 × 11 ⅞ in.; sheet: 23 ¼ × 17 ¹³⁄₁₆ in.

preparing to open the exhibition *Large Prints* at The Contemporaries in February 1952, she described new examples by Arthur Deshaies as "handsome technically," adding that she hoped to elicit interest "in their mural qualities."[14] In both instances, scale implied a mechanical rigor and an avant-garde impulse in printmaking (Fig. 4).

Larger prints also represented a formal rejection of established parameters in the medium and suggested a professional niche for the artform: custom works of art for modern walls. Arts writers gained awareness that The Contemporaries had the design world in its sights (Fig. 5). Reviewing *Graphic Originals for Modern Walls* (1953) in *Art Digest*, Dore Ashton opens with this observation: "Architects and decorators have come to recognize the practical and esthetic [*sic*] advantages of the graphic media. Their demand has brought about this exhibition of etchings, lithographs, woodcuts and serigraphs" by Karl Schrag, Louis Schanker, Sari Dienes, and Adja Yunkers, among others, "who think of their work in mural rather than cabinet terms."[15] Lowengrund's initiative was made explicit in a 1955 proposal to the Rockefeller Foundation, writing that The Contemporaries would offer:

> *[a] special service to advertising art directors, decorators and architects will enable them to commission specific works designed to fulfill a precise decorative function in their clients' offices, advertisements and homes. Hence, they can commission works of a specific dimension and—provided the artist is amenable—request execution in a certain color range.*[16]

In this scenario, the printmaker is still beholden to a theoretical client, but the creative canvas would be the expansive wall rather than a flat file. This shifts the position of a print from a small-scale curiosity to a work of art fit for a gallery space, even if the context of a corporate commission might feel uncomfortably commercial.

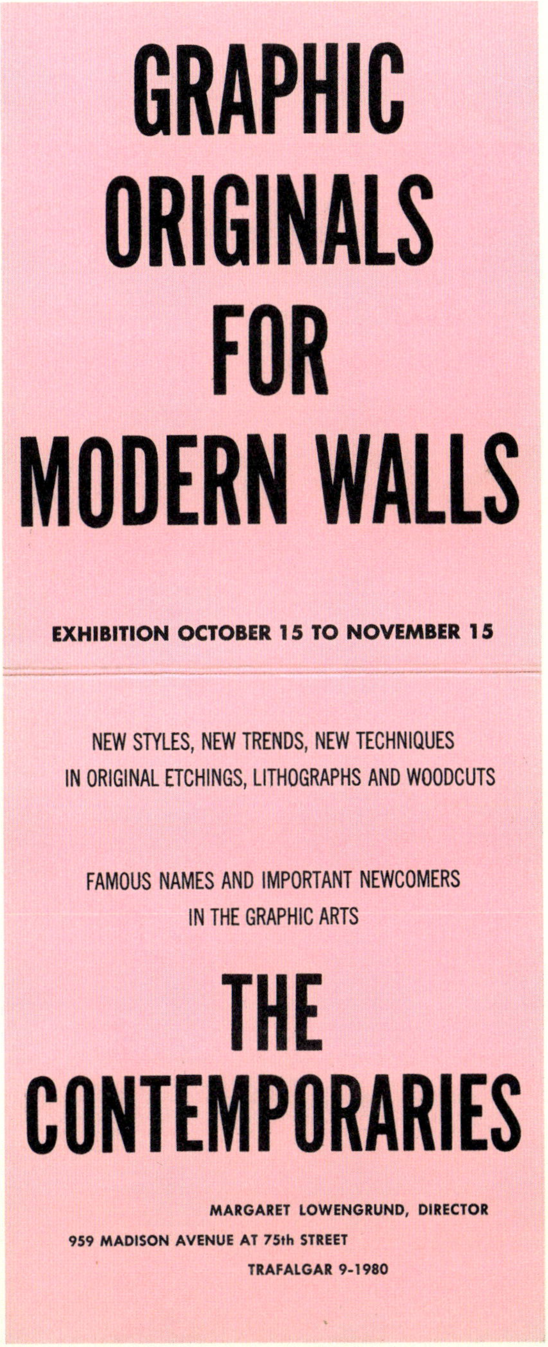

GRAPHIC ORIGINALS FOR MODERN WALLS

EXHIBITION OCTOBER 15 TO NOVEMBER 15

NEW STYLES, NEW TRENDS, NEW TECHNIQUES
IN ORIGINAL ETCHINGS, LITHOGRAPHS AND WOODCUTS

FAMOUS NAMES AND IMPORTANT NEWCOMERS
IN THE GRAPHIC ARTS

THE CONTEMPORARIES

MARGARET LOWENGRUND, DIRECTOR
959 MADISON AVENUE AT 75th STREET
TRAFALGAR 9-1980

Fig. 5 Invitation card for *Graphic Originals for Modern Walls*, 1953

That November, Lowengrund sent a version of *Graphic Originals for Modern Walls* to Vassar College, during the course of which she later gave a lecture specifically promoting modern prints—etchings, woodcuts, engravings, etc.—as works of art. In her talk, Lowengrund explained that although there was only one final composition, there were typically several proofs by the artist, and each one was "as much an individual production as a 'painted original.'"[17] A short write-up in the *Vassar Chronicle* mentions that prints from The Contemporaries were for sale at prices that students might afford, a point Lowengrund may have emphasized.[18] Pinpointing that prints, as multiples, are usually less expensive than paintings may seem obvious; but crucially, this quality of printmaking is what Lowengrund relied on to build The Contemporaries—that its products were both "real" and affordable.

Margaret Lowengrund's project of recontextualizing prints so that they could be understood as murals or "painted originals" required that she work across disciplines, toggling back and forth between the worlds of art and interior design. This also meant that she needed to convince clients that there was something essential about having an original work of art in one's home; something "real"—even if there were thirty or so works almost exactly like it. In the postwar period, the people who lived within "modern walls" faced a choice about how to make their homes and offices their own. Neither the new high-rise developments like Briar Oaks nor chilly international style office buildings could offer quarters rich in antique character, charm, or individuality. It was up to the consumer to make their living space unique, and as Lowengrund had astutely realized, her gallery and workshop, The Contemporaries, was ideally positioned to help them do so on an intimate scale. According to the 1950 AAA catalogue: renters, modernists, traditionalists, and homeowners "all have perhaps been begging for the ideal pictures."[19]

The Contemporaries

During Lowengrund's ownership of The Contemporaries between 1951 and 1957, she presented the work of more than 250 artists in almost 100 exhibitions. The Contemporaries' workshop also drew many artists who experimented with techniques on their own or collaborated with the studio's professional printers.

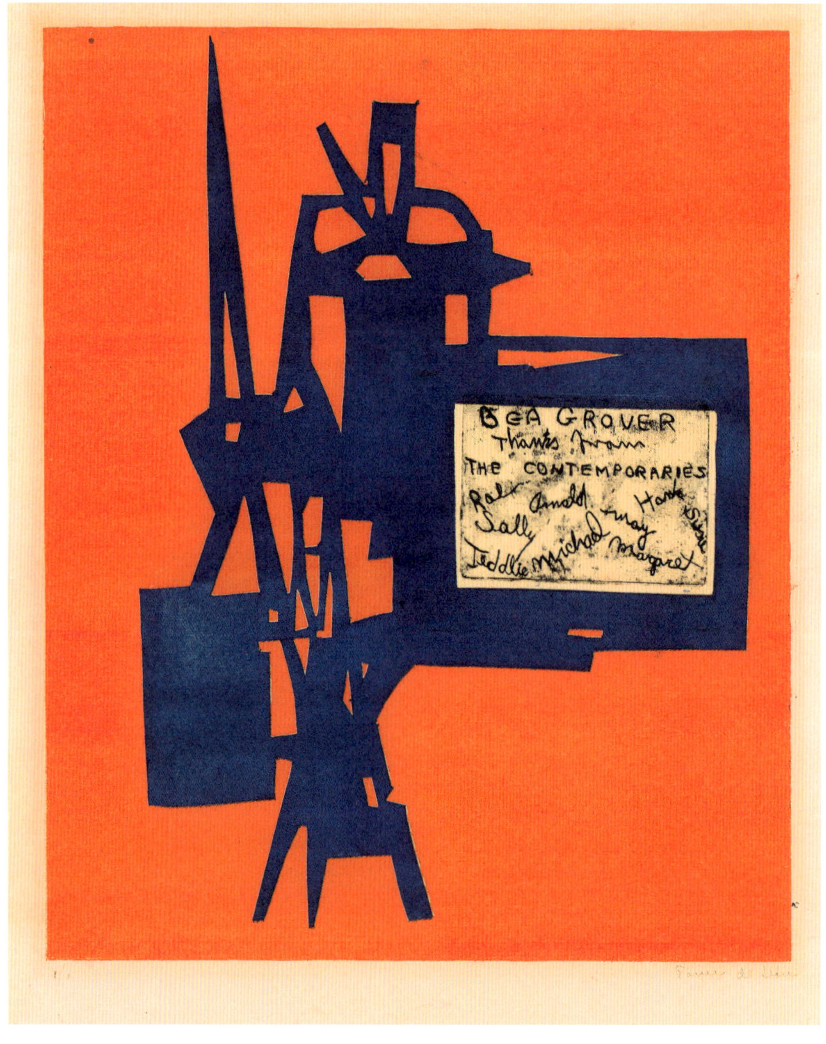

Michael Ponce de León, *Thanks from The Contemporaries*, ca. 1955.
Etching and metal relief, edition of 1, plate: 18 13⁄16 × 14 ¾ in.; sheet (irreg.): 19 15⁄16 × 16 7⁄16 in.

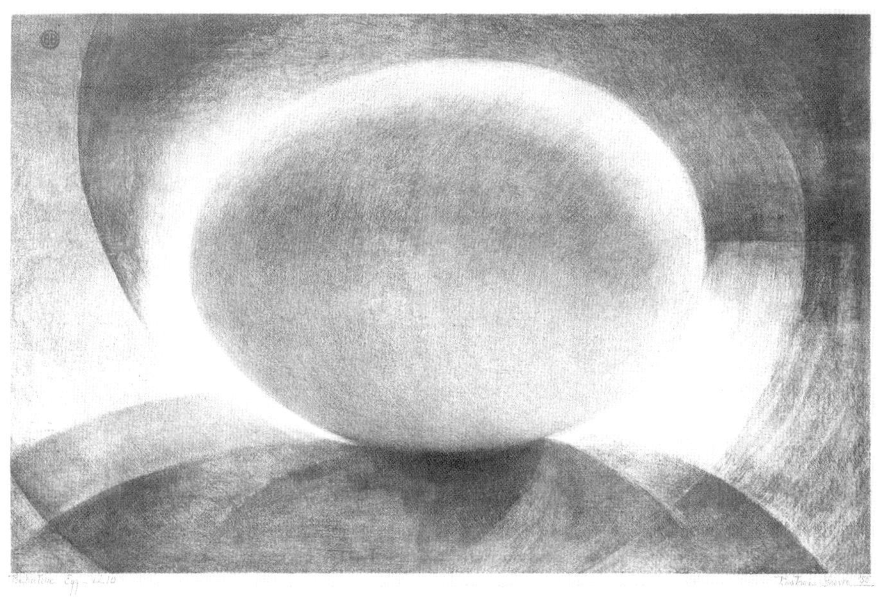

Beatrice Grover, *Prehistoric Egg*, 1955. Lithograph, edition of 10, image: 16 ½ × 25 ⅞ in.

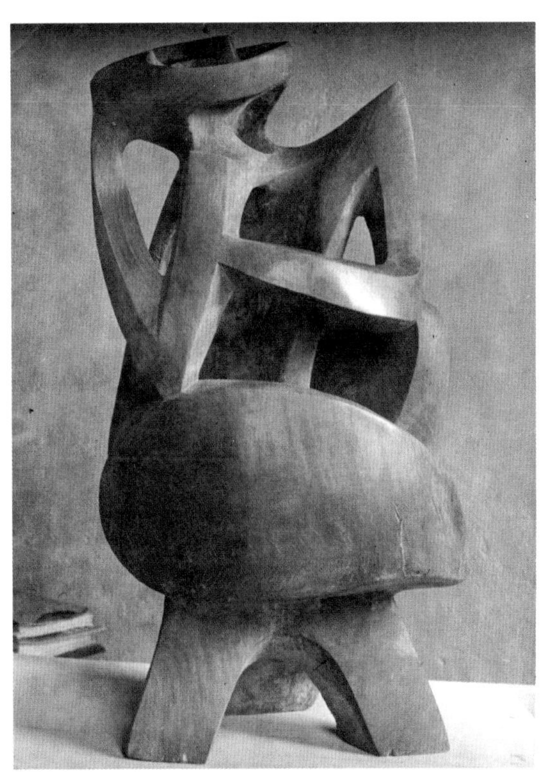

Peter Lipman-Wulf, *Man in the Moon*, 1952.
Lignum Vitae, 24 ½ × 14 × 10 ½ in.

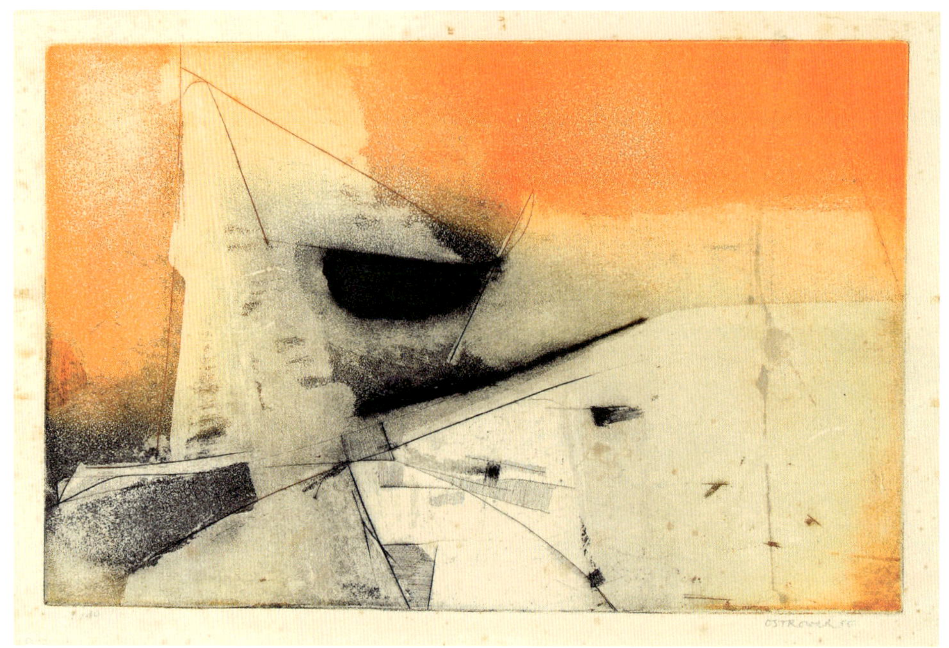

Fayga Ostrower, 5502 *[Suspension or Forma Suspensa]*, 1955.
Aquatint, engraving, and drypoint, 11 5⁄16 × 17 15⁄16 in.

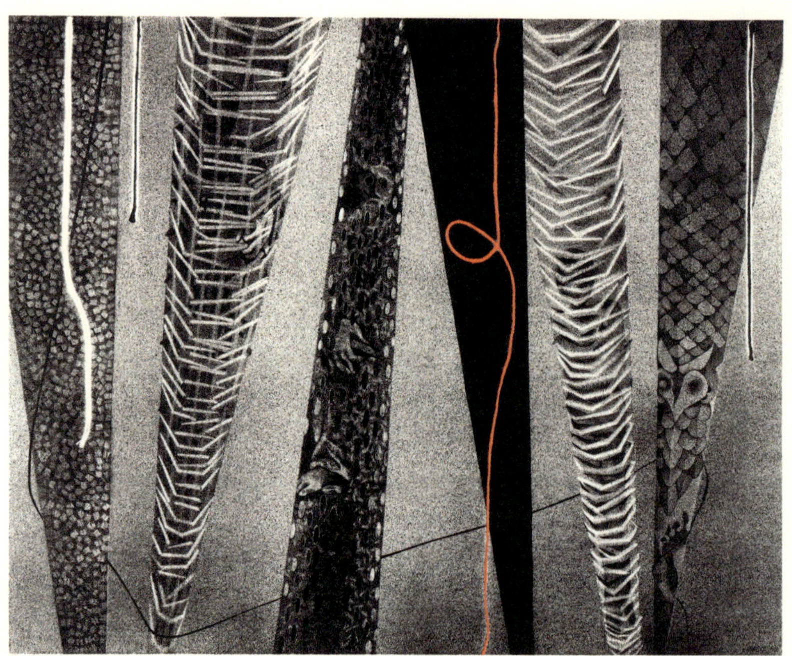

June Wayne, *The Witnesses (State II)*, 1952. Lithograph, edition of 14,
image: 22 3⁄16 × 28 15⁄16 in.; sheet: 26 × 33 7⁄8 in.

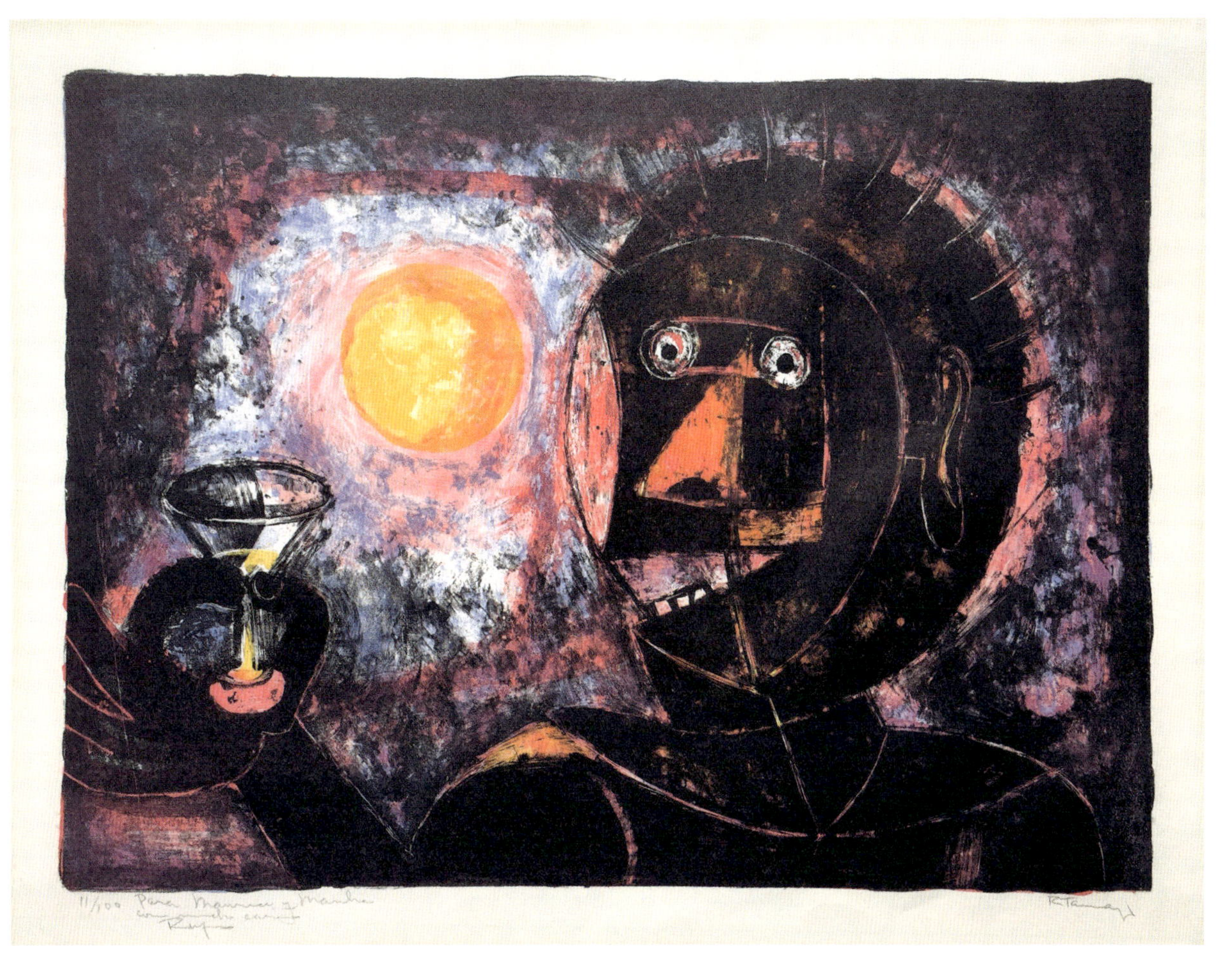

Rufino Tamayo, *El Brindis (The Toast)*, 1957. Lithograph, edition of 100, image: 15 3/16 × 20 7/8 in.; sheet: 18 × 23 3/4 in.

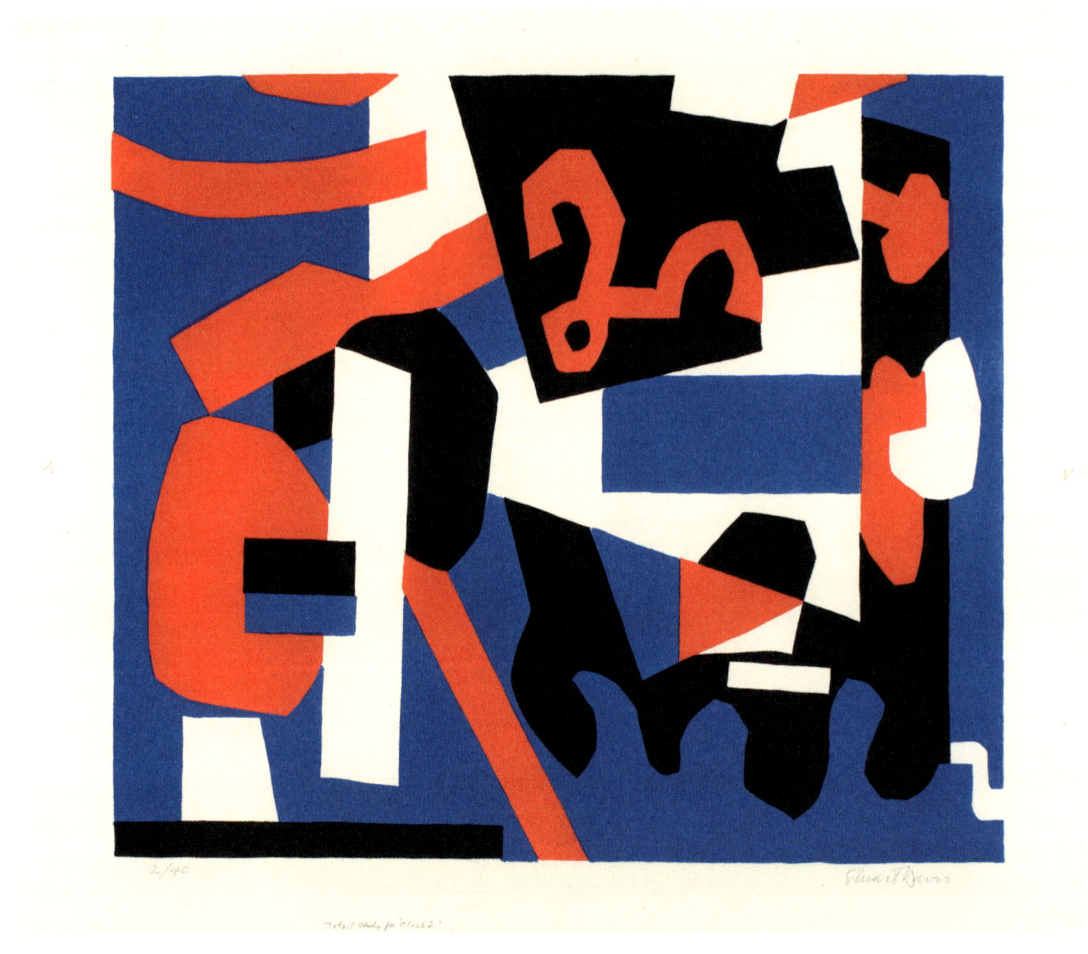

Stuart Davis, *Detail Study for Cliché*, 1957. Lithograph, edition of 40, image: 12 ½ × 14 ¾ in.; sheet: 15 3/16 × 18 3/16 in. Published by The Contemporaries, New York.

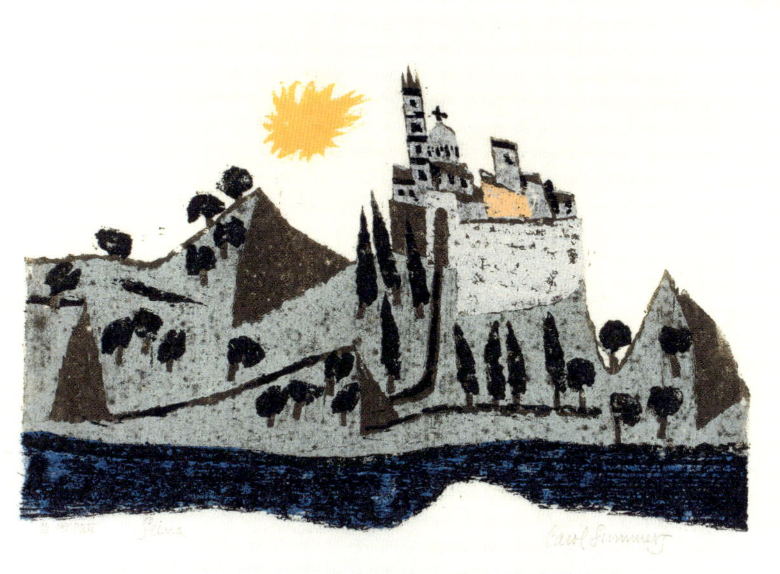

Carol Summers, *Siena*, 1955. Woodcut, edition of 30, image (irreg.): 11 ¾ × 18 ¾ in.; sheet: 15 ⅛ × 23 ½ in.

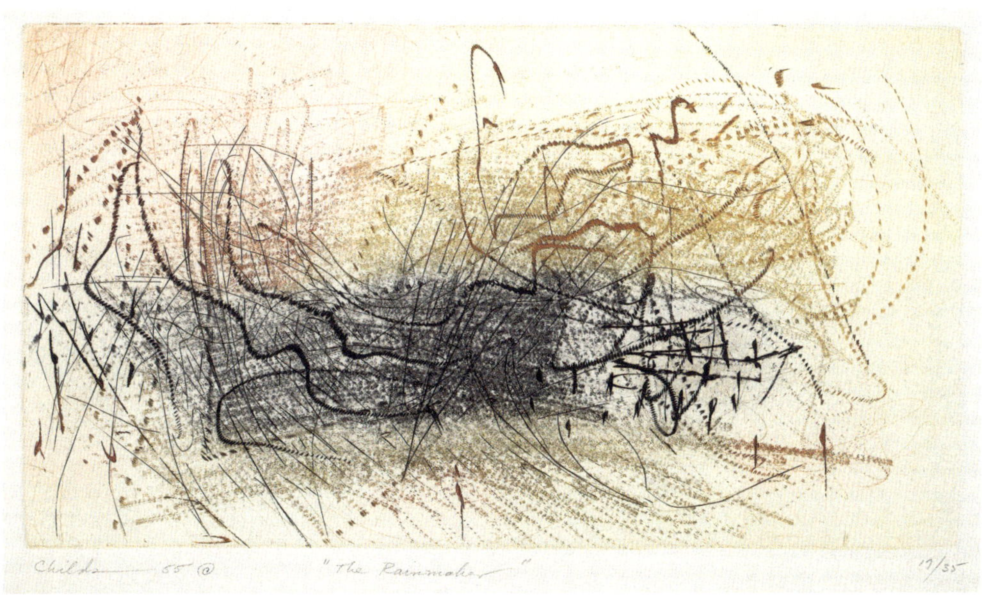

Bernard Childs, *The Rainmaker*, 1955. Etching, edition of 35, plate: 6 ⅞ × 12 11⁄16 in.; sheet: 11 ¼ × 17 13⁄16 in.

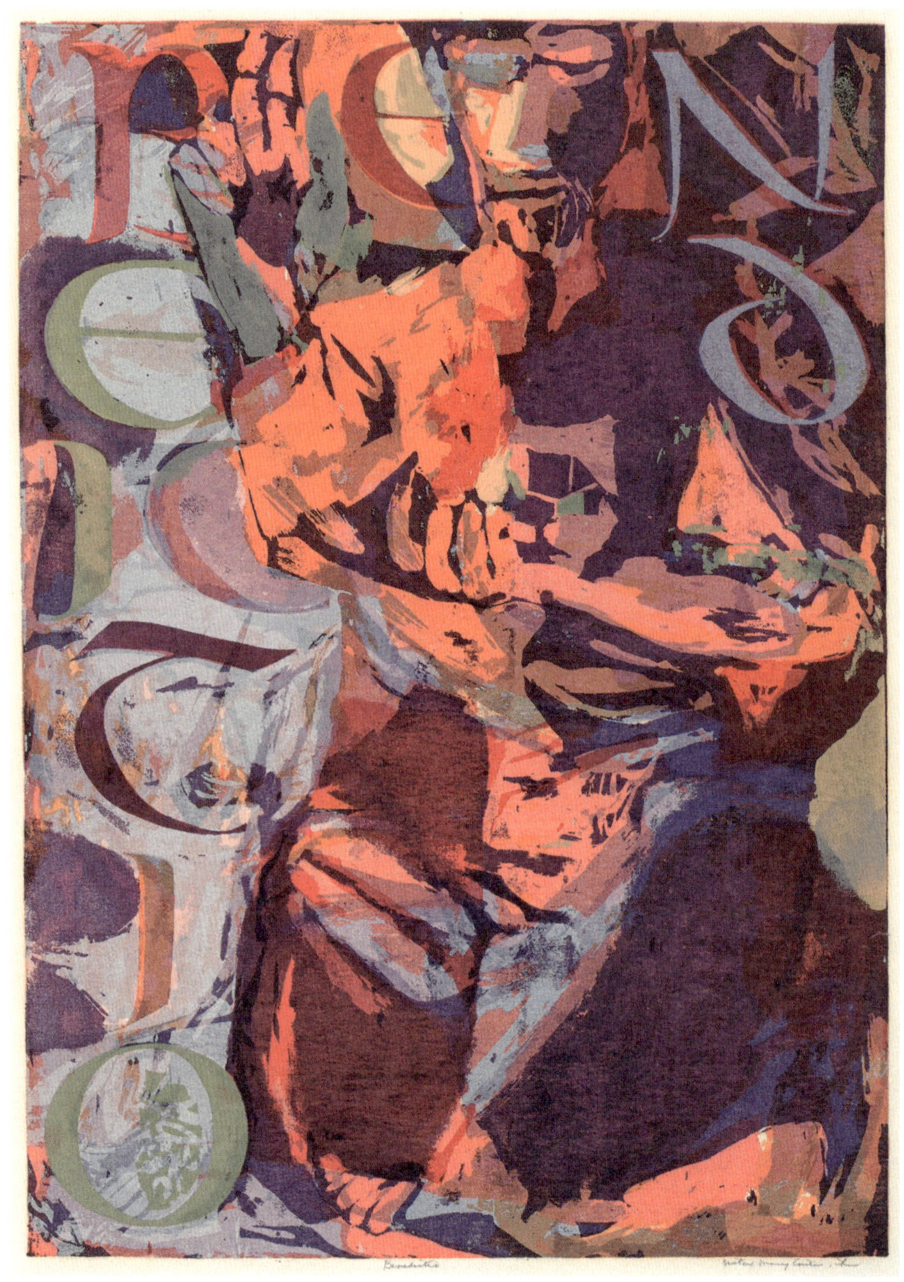

Sister Corita Kent, *Benedictio*, 1954. Screenprint, image: 21 9/16 × 15 9/16 in.; sheet: 24 3/16 × 17 11/16 in.

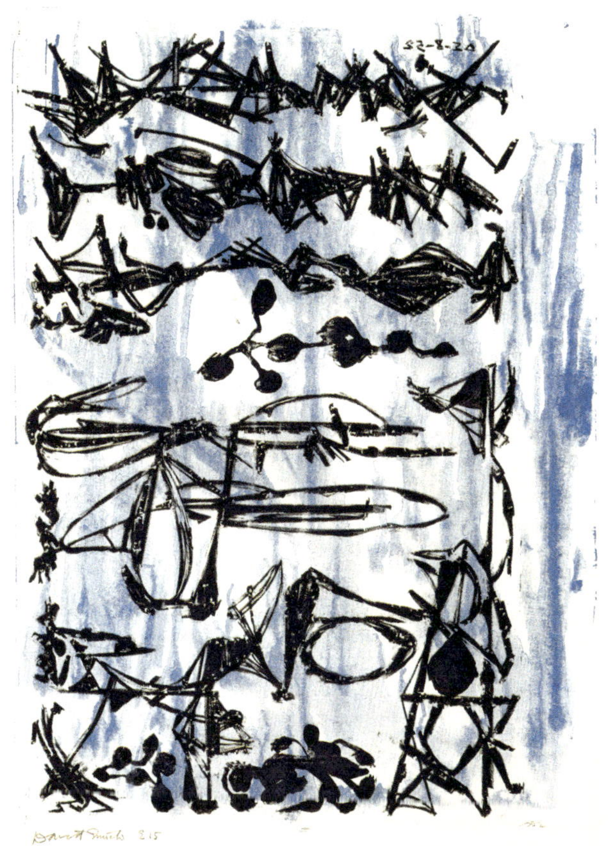

David Smith, *Untitled*, 1952. Lithograph, edition of about 17, image: 24 ¼ × 16 ⅞ in.; sheet: 26 × 21 ⅞ in.

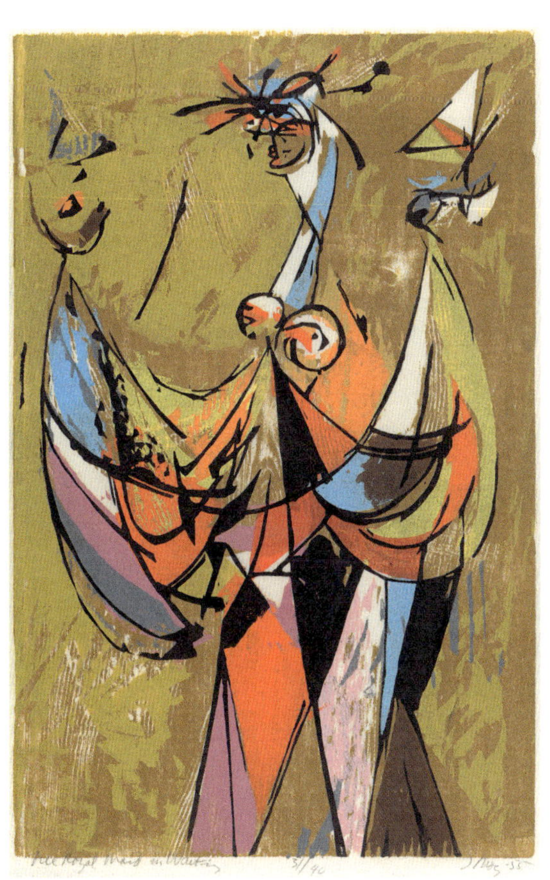

Seong Moy, *The Royal Maid in Waiting*, 1955. Woodcut, edition of 40, sheet: 18 × 11 ⅝ in.

PRINTMAKING EXCHANGES BETWEEN JAPAN AND THE UNITED STATES IN THE MID-TWENTIETH CENTURY

Noriko Kuwahara
Translated by Chiaki Ajioka

With the signing of the 1951 Treaty of Peace with Japan and the end of the Allied occupation that followed, Japanese artists began participating in international exhibitions. Many also began traveling overseas, signaling the beginning of the globalization of Japanese art. New York City, the emergent international art capital, became the most popular destination as a center of avant-garde activity. Several Japanese printmakers visited or moved to New York in the postwar period, and many became involved with Margaret Lowengrund and The Contemporaries or, later, the Pratt Graphic Art Center (PGAC), holding exhibitions, offering demonstrations, or teaching at the workshop. Their visits did not occur in a vacuum, and this essay considers these artists' activities at The Contemporaries and PGAC within the context of the United States' postwar cultural policy and the practice of printmaking in Japan at midcentury. Furthermore, it considers how The Contemporaries and PGAC contributed to raising the international profile of Japanese printmaking.

Immediately after the Pacific War, Japanese modern prints (*sōsaku hanga*)—as distinct from the familiar ukiyo-e prints—attracted the attention of some Allied occupation personnel.[1] From 1951, the artists entered their prints into international exhibitions and won important prizes. These printmakers also had local support: Tokyo's Yōseidō Gallery opened in 1953 specializing in modern prints, and the College Women's Association of Japan's annual exhibition, which launched in 1956, provided sōsaku hanga artists with additional opportunities to show and sell their works. The first Tokyo International Print Biennale (1957) declared the globalization of Japanese modernist prints. Additionally, several books introduced Japanese prints to English-speaking audiences. Oliver Statler, an accountant in the Occupation force who remained in Japan after leaving office, published *Modern Japanese Prints: An Art Reborn* (1956), which became an immediate success. James A. Michener, Statler's friend the popular novelist, further disseminated information in *Japanese Prints from the Early Masters to the Modern* (1959) and *The Modern Japanese Prints: An Appreciation* (1962).

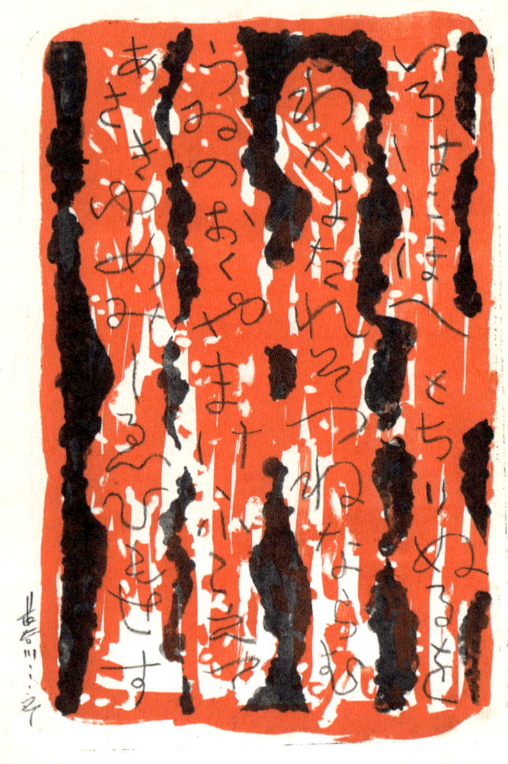

Fig. 1 Hasegawa Saburō, *Iroha*, 1954. Lithograph, image: 18 ¾ × 12 3⁄16 in.; sheet: 20 11⁄16 × 14 ¾ in.

New York became a beacon for Japanese artists as the city emerged as an exciting art center and experienced a wave of postwar *Japonisme*. The Museum of Modern Art (MoMA), for example, showcased everyday objects from

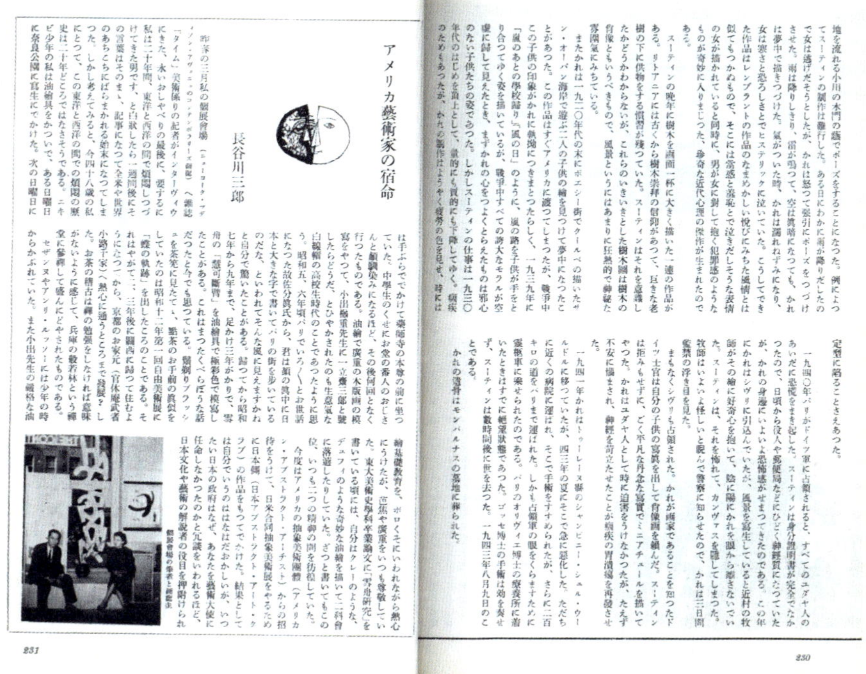

アメリカ藝術家の宿命

長谷川三郎

251

250

Fig. 2 Hasegawa Saburō and Margaret Lowengrund sitting in The Contemporaries, as reproduced in *Geijutsu Shinchō*, April 1955

Japan—pottery, baskets, and lacquer pieces—in a 1951 exhibition featuring the collection of architect Antonin Raymond and his wife Noémi Pernessin Raymond, and mounted exhibitions on traditional Japanese architecture such as *Matsukazesō* (*Japanese Exhibition House*, 1954–55), as well as *Abstract Japanese Calligraphy* (1954). D. T. Suzuki, a Zen scholar, offered Zen seminars at Columbia University. Aware of these shows and events, Japanese artists were motivated to go to New York but faced challenges in supporting themselves and finding outlets to show their work. PGAC, with its openness to international exchange, was an ideal institution where Japanese printmakers could work, teach, and exhibit.

The postwar political climate supported Japanese printmakers' travel to the United States. John D. Rockefeller III, who visited Japan in 1951 with his wife as cultural consultants to the Dulles peace settlement mission led by John Foster Dulles, committed to funding cultural exchange programs between the United States and Japan. The Rockefeller Foundation, which also supported Lowengrund and PGAC, gave significant grants to several initiatives that brought Japanese artists to the United States. These visits were considered culturally significant and conformed diplomatically to the United States' Cold War foreign policy to prevent Japan from coming under communist influence.

The Contemporaries and Japanese Printmakers (1954–57)

Margaret Lowengrund organized four Japanese print exhibitions at The Contemporaries before her death, including three solo exhibitions. Since Lowengrund generally favored group exhibitions and duo shows, it is notable that she offered exclusive solo shows to three Japanese artists.

Of the four, Hasegawa Saburō's exhibition in March 1954 is significant because Lowengrund actively sought the artist's cooperation. Hasegawa, who was Japan's leading abstract artist, was in New York in early 1954 representing Japan at the *American Abstract Artists 18th Annual Exhibition* at the Riverside Museum (March 7–28).[2] He gave a well-publicized speech at MoMA's forum "Abstract Art around the World Today" (March 16) about how abstraction accorded with Zen and Japan's traditional

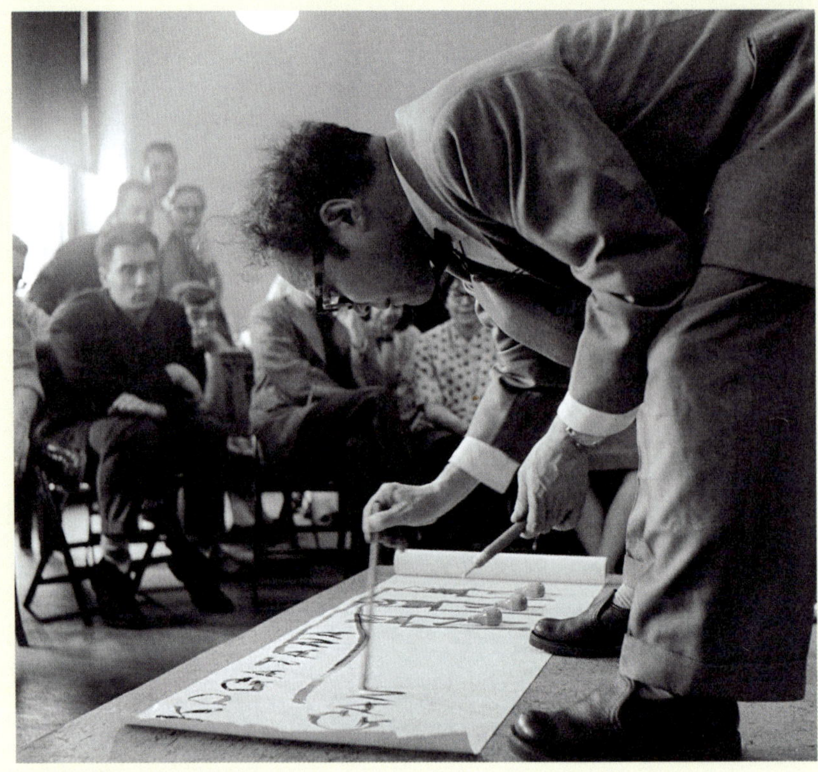

Fig. 3 Munakata Shikō demonstrating calligraphy for a PGAC-sponsored event, 1959

art.[3] His solo exhibition at The Contemporaries opened on March 21, at a moment when he was a focus of New York's art world.

Having arrived early to prepare for the Riverside Museum exhibition, Hasegawa told a friend later, he walked into The Contemporaries "by mistake" and met Lowengrund, who urged him to try his hand at lithography.[4] Hasegawa, who had stopped painting in oil around 1951 in order to focus on woodcut, rubbing, and ink painting, felt obligated by her invitation. The resulting five lithographs—including the two-color *Iroha* (The Japanese Syllabary, 1954), which features the forty-seven letters of the hiragana alphabet—appeared in his solo exhibition alongside fourteen other works (Fig. 1). A photograph, possibly taken by Hasegawa, of The Contemporaries' exterior at 959 Madison Avenue features a vertical sign with hand-cut letters of the artist's surname (page 40); while another reproduced in the magazine *Geijutsu Shinchō* documents Hasegawa and Lowengrund together inside the gallery during his exhibition (Fig. 2). It appears Lowengrund advised Hasegawa to learn lithography with the hope that he would propagate the medium in Japan, though there is no evidence he did so.[5]

Few details are known about the other exhibitions. Douglas Overton, the Japan Society's executive director, assisted Lowengrund in preparing *Modern Japanese Prints* (January 1956), for which they likely borrowed works from the Japan Society and the Philadelphia Print Club.[6] Featured artists included Yoshida Tōshi and Hodaka, sons of Yoshida Hiroshi, the internationally acclaimed woodblock printmaker active before World War II.[7] The brothers had been active overseas, but their sojourn to the United States in early 1955 did not coincide with *Modern Japanese Prints*.

The other solo exhibitions were for Saitō Kiyoshi and Wakita Kazu. Both visited the United States at the invitation of the State Department under its International Visitor Program, which provided travel fares and three months' living expenses. Saitō was increasingly recognized after winning the Japanese Prize at the first São Paulo Biennial (1951), and audiences in the United States had seen his work at a handful of exhibitions during the early 1950s.[8] During his State Department–sponsored trip in

1956, he traversed the United States, giving demonstrations and exhibiting prints. During his stay in New York (March 25–April 3, 1956), he met with John D. Rockefeller III, Douglas Overton, and Charles B. Fahs of the Rockefeller Foundation.[9] It is important to remember that, at this exact moment, Margaret Lowengrund was deeply involved in negotiations with the Rockefeller Foundation regarding a major grant for her printmaking workshop, and she may have offered to host Saitō's solo show (March 1956) to establish a good relationship with the foundation.

Wakita Kazu, known primarily as an oil painter, also exhibited at the first São Paulo Biennial and several other international exhibitions. He practiced lithography and, during his travels under the auspices of the International Visitor Program (March–June 1956), he exhibited three lithographs at the Cincinnati Art Museum's Fourth International Biennial of Contemporary Color Lithography.[10] After six months in Europe, Wakita returned to New York in December 1956 just before his works were shown at The Contemporaries in January 1957.[11] He showed oil paintings, watercolors, and lithographs, some of which were mounted as scrolls.

Lowengrund's interest in Japanese artists' prints dovetailed with her goals to exhibit the best examples of contemporary graphic art. As the postwar art world became more international, so too did Lowengrund's vision for The Contemporaries. Japanese artists, with their growing presence on the international stage, were one component of The Contemporaries' increasingly global focus.

Pratt Graphic Art Center and Japanese Printmakers (1958–1960s)

After Lowengrund's death, Japanese artists continued to frequent the newly merged Pratt-Contemporaries Graphic Art Centre located at 1343 Third Avenue, thanks largely to the support of the Japan Society and the Rockefeller Foundation. In fact, the three institutions were fairly intertwined. The Japan Society, founded to facilitate exchange between the United States and Japan, pursued its mission with funding from the Rockefeller Foundation, which also supported PGAC—as the workshop eventually became known—over its first six years (1956–61).

While Japanese artists came to the United States through various programs and invitations, the Japan Society supported their activities once

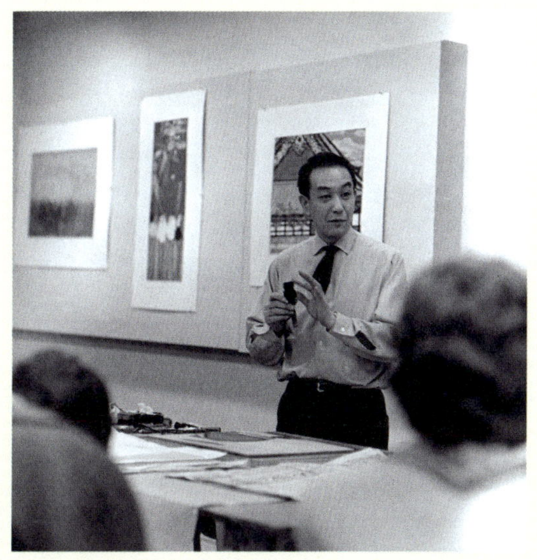

Fig. 4 Uchima Ansei teaching woodblock printing at PGAC, 1963

stateside. Recognizing the significance of Saitō's and the Yoshida family's visits, Douglas Overton wrote Charles B. Fahs seeking grants to bring three more printmakers over three years, proposing that each would spend three months in New York teaching and creating.[12]

The woodblock specialists chosen for the Japan Society's special projects—Sekino Juni'ichirō, Munakata Shikō, and Mori Yasu—all gave demonstrations and taught classes at PGAC. Sekino spent four months at PGAC (April–July 1958), teaching twice weekly. Munakata visited PGAC in April 1959, and later that spring gave demonstrations and served as a guest instructor (Fig. 3). Mori offered demonstrations from late 1960 to 1961. Since none were fluent in English, Beate Gordon of the Japan Society acted as an interpreter and guide.[13]

Outside the Japan Society's special project, still more Japanese printmakers taught at PGAC. Kobashi Yasuhide, a multi-media artist, originally traveled to New York in 1959 by invitation of Lincoln Kirstein, then general director of the New York City Ballet, to serve as a stage designer.[14] Izumi Shigeru, who specialized in lithography, came to New York in 1960, assisted by Thomas George, an artist from the United States who had exhibited at The Contemporaries in 1956. George knew Izumi while living in Japan (1956–57).[15] Kobashi and Izumi contributed to the portfolio *11 Prints by 11 Printmakers* (1961), featuring work by PGAC faculty and staff.

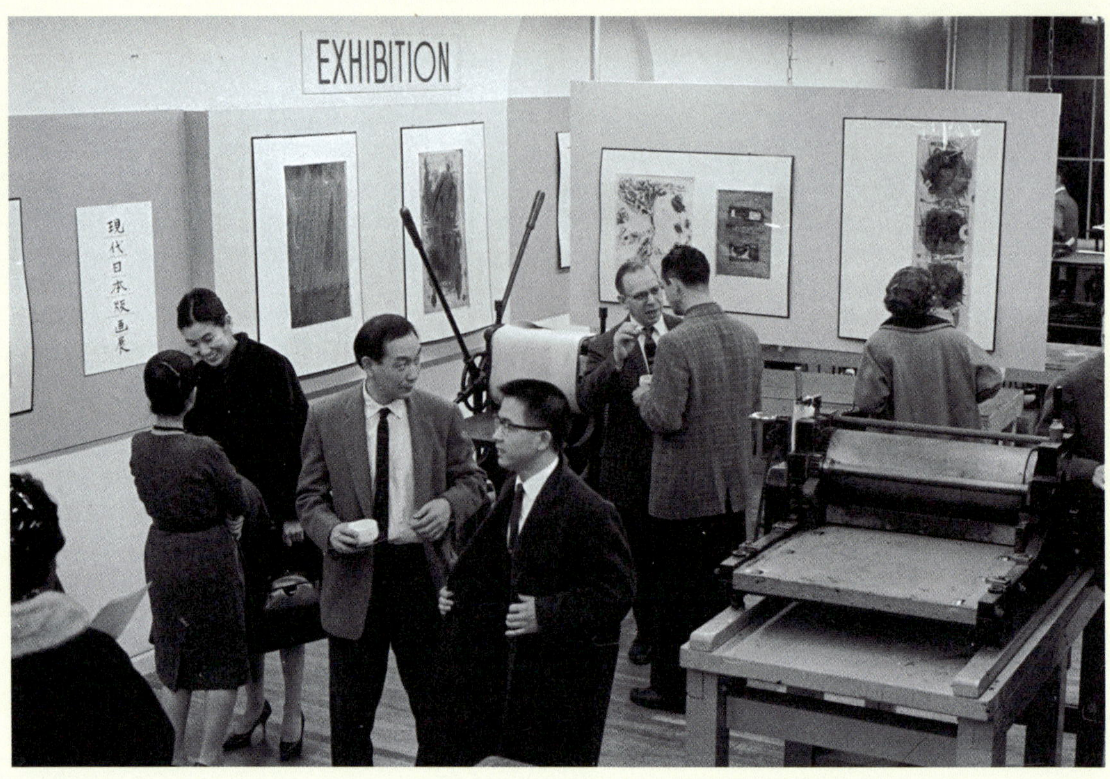

Fig. 5 Opening party for *Contemporary Japanese Prints* at PGAC, 1962

Uchima Ansei, a Japanese American printmaker, taught at PGAC from 1960 until around 1962 and sporadically thereafter.[16] Unlike others previously discussed, Uchima settled in New York City with his family. Born in Los Angeles, he moved to Japan in 1940 and returned to the United States in 1959 with his wife, the artist Toshiko. Fluent in English and Japanese, Uchima was an important liaison between the art communities in Japan and the United States. In Japan, he interpreted for Oliver Statler as he researched for *Modern Japanese Prints*. In New York, Uchima not only taught woodblock printmaking on the faculty at PGAC (Fig. 4) but also served as a liaison connecting Japanese artists with PGAC. Furthermore, he coordinated the joint exhibition of woodcut artists Yoshida Masaji and Yoshida Hodaka (1963) and an exhibition of Joryū Hanga Kyōkai (1966), the Association of Women Printmakers, of which Toshiko was a founder.[17]

Finally, Matsubara Naoko came to PGAC after having a Fulbright scholarship at Carnegie Mellon University. She became assistant to PGAC's director Fritz Eichenberg in 1965, had a small show of her woodcuts at Pratt's Brooklyn campus (October 1965), and offered her first woodcut course at PGAC in November 1966.[18]

Conclusion

The Contemporaries and PGAC, along with the Japanese artists who flocked there, contributed to building a community and marketplace for Japanese art in New York City. By the 1960s, New Yorkers were primed for survey exhibitions of sōsaku hanga, such as *Contemporary Japanese Prints* staged at PGAC in November 1962 (Fig. 5). Some of the artists discussed here traveled onward with their New York experience under their belt, while others, after returning to Japan, moved away from woodblock printmaking and began working in other media. Throughout the 1960s and 1970s Japanese modernist prints continued to gain international recognition; this globalization would not have been possible without the networks and opportunities offered at centers like The Contemporaries and PGAC.

REDEFINING CONTEMPORARY PRINT: LUIS CAMNITZER, LILIANA PORTER, AND THE NEW YORK GRAPHIC WORKSHOP

Rachel Vogel

When Luis Camnitzer first arrived in New York from Uruguay in 1962 on a Guggenheim Fellowship, he quickly gravitated toward the Pratt Graphic Art Center (PGAC), which had been recommended to him "as the best and most specialized place for printmaking."[1] PGAC provided more than studio space and equipment; as a *New York Times* article reported, it was "the only international nonprofit graphic workshop in the world," where students and professional printmakers from across the Americas, Europe, and Asia could be found "comparing notes, sharing discoveries, developing new techniques and having a wonderful time."[2] There, Camnitzer worked alongside and learned from many other Latin American artists making prints—including Iván Vial, Rodolfo Opazo, and Enrique Castro-Cid from Chile; Julio Girona from Cuba; Armando Morales from Nicaragua; Marcelo Bonevardi from Argentina; and Antonio Frasconi from Uruguay—as well as the Japanese printmakers Uchima Ansei and Munakata Shikō.[3] He returned to PGAC to complete the second half of his Guggenheim Fellowship in 1964, after spending a year in Montevideo, and it was during this stay that he was introduced to Argentinian artist Liliana Porter, who had come to work at PGAC just four days after arriving in New York.[4] She, too, was drawn to the global reach of PGAC's participants and its well-stocked facilities, which she described as "a paradise."[5] The workshop's international roster made it a welcoming space for a newcomer to the United States; Porter recounts that she "was beginning to learn English.... My first vocabulary were all the things I used at Pratt Graphics Center."[6]

The environment at PGAC encouraged both artists to hone their technical skills as well as to experiment with new techniques and styles. Camnitzer continued to work in the expressionist style he developed through his previous printmaking training in Germany, but began to take more risks with materials and scale, making increasingly larger prints.[7] Porter also extended themes from her previous bodies of work—such as her Goya-inspired depictions of the Spanish royal family that she had made in Buenos Aires prior to coming to New York—but the new prints bore the influence of the pop art Porter had recently seen at the Castelli Gallery.[8] In her 1965 *Pop Duchess of Alba*, a layer of Warhol-esque flowers in florescent spray paint produce a striking contrast to the somber etching of the duchess beneath. Both artists also began moving beyond the flat surface of the paper: Porter's print *About Geometry with Fruit* incorporates three-dimensional plastic prints into the composition, and Camnitzer began printing on plaster bandages and plastic tablecloths.[9]

Most significantly, their experiences at PGAC stimulated a broader reassessment of the medium of printmaking. In spaces dedicated to the advancement of printmaking, they determined, innovation was often framed primarily through the evolution of technique, rather than the question of aesthetic development. As Porter described, "the traditional printmaker is sometimes just an excellent technician; that is the sum total of his or her merits."[10] Camnitzer recalled how he was first introduced to the PGAC faculty: "This one prints on extra-thick hand-made paper with a self-made hydraulic press; that one engraves on plexiglass with a roto-tool; that other one burns into polyvinylic-chloride sheets; so-and-so does lithographic processes on zinc plates, etc."[11] But by the end of his tour he still had no sense of what their work actually looked like, what they were trying to accomplish, or what problems they were trying to solve. It seemed that printmaking's purpose was reduced to technical breakthroughs, but to what end?

A somewhat serendipitous encounter would provide the opportunity for the artists to pursue these investigations even further. At a 1964 exhibition of Porter's work at Van Bovenkamp Gallery, she was approached by dentist, art collector, and amateur printmaker Julian Firestone. He offered Porter free use of an electric printing press, initiating a series of events that would culminate in Porter, Camnitzer, and the Venezulean artist José Guillermo Castillo establishing their own "alternative to Pratt

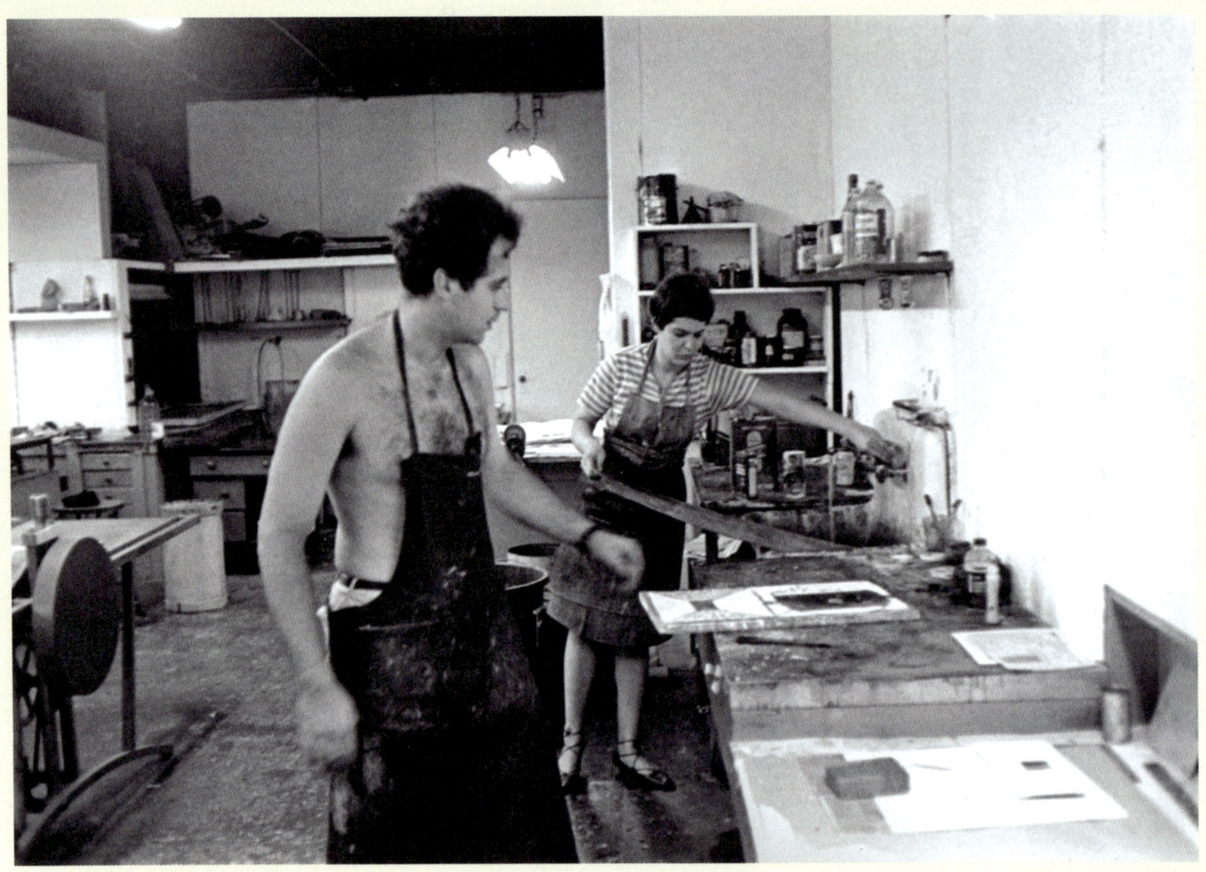

Fig. 1 Liliana Porter and Luis Camnitzer at the New York Graphic Workshop, ca. 1965. Photo by Basil Langton

Graphics [*sic*] Art Center," as Camnitzer described it, which they named the New York Graphic Workshop (NYGW) (Fig. 1).[12]

The artists began working out how one might newly approach and reinvigorate the medium of print—how one could be "conditioned but not destroyed by our techniques."[13] To this end, the group of artists developed the idea of the FANDSO—the "free assemblable nonfunctional disposable serial object."[14] The notion of FANDSO offered a conceptual, rather than technical, definition of printmaking, emphasizing the medium's capacity for producing editions and "the possibility of unlimited distribution."[15] This, the members of the NYGW radically claimed, was more important than "what happens on the printing plate."[16] In 1966, the group sent to friends and various art institutions a short manifesto outlining these beliefs tucked beneath a cookie stamped with the phrase "GREETINGS—1966—NEW YORK GRAPHIC WORKSHOP" (Fig. 2). The cookie itself was a playful demonstration of the FANDSO idea—a form of printmaking that moved beyond "paper, ink, and a printing press," that wasn't limited by two-dimensionality, and that was disposable—or edible—rather than treated as a precious commodity.[17] Ultimately, the artists of the NYGW believed their redefinition of printmaking could help erase a seemingly steadfast distinction between artists and consumers: it could "bring to everybody the opportunity to develop their own creativity," making the world of art inclusive, democratic, and participatory.[18]

The establishment of the NYGW did not end Porter and Camnitzer's involvement with PGAC. They each would occasionally produce prints there, be included in its portfolios or exhibitions—such as the 1964 exhibition *100 Contemporary Prints* held at the Jewish Museum—and Camnitzer would periodically teach classes there.[19] Moreover, the NYGW managed

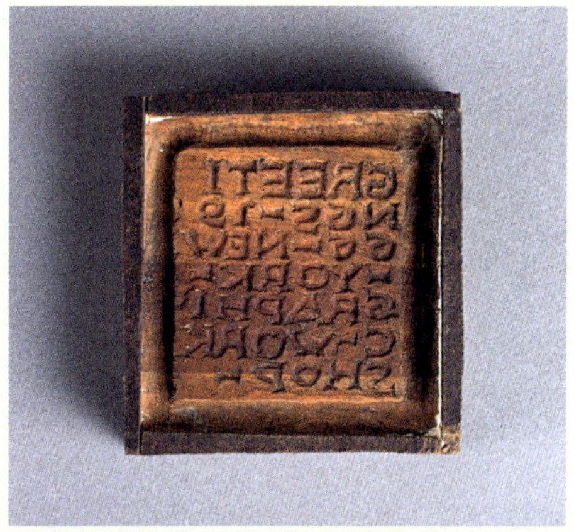

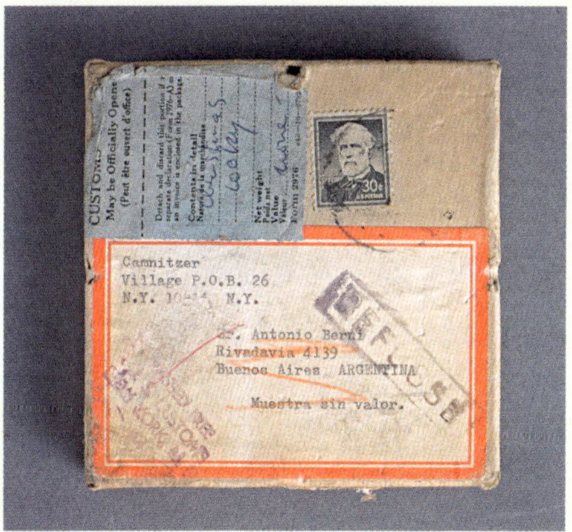

Fig. 2 Luis Camnitzer, José Guillermo Castillo, and Liliana Porter, *Manifesto Cookie*, 1966. Cookie mold and cookie in box, ⅞ × 4⅛ × 4⅛ in.

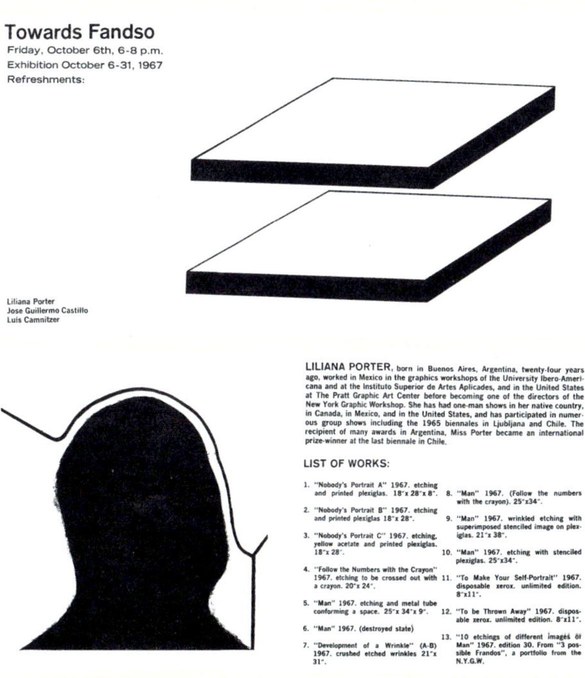

Towards Fandso
Friday, October 6th, 6-8 p.m.
Exhibition October 6-31, 1967
Refreshments:

Liliana Porter
Jose Guillermo Castillo
Luis Camnitzer

LILIANA PORTER, born in Buenos Aires, Argentina, twenty-four years ago, worked in Mexico in the graphics workshops of the University Ibero-Americana and at the Instituto Superior de Artes Aplicades, and in the United States at The Pratt Graphic Art Center before becoming one of the directors of the New York Graphic Workshop. She has had one-man shows in her native country, in Canada, in Mexico, and in the United States, and has participated in numerous group shows including the 1965 biennales in Ljubljana and Chile. The recipient of many awards in Argentina, Miss Porter became an international prize-winner at the last biennale in Chile.

LIST OF WORKS:

1. "Nobody's Portrait A" 1967. etching and printed plexiglas. 18"x 28"x 8".
2. "Nobody's Portrait B" 1967. etching and printed plexiglas 18"x 28".
3. "Nobody's Portrait C" 1967. etching, yellow acetate and printed plexiglas. 18"x 28".
4. "Follow the Numbers with the Crayon" 1967. etching to be crossed out with a crayon. 20"x 24".
5. "Man" 1967. etching and metal tube conforming a space. 25"x 34"x 9".
6. "Man" 1967. (destroyed state)
7. "Development of a Wrinkle" (A-B) 1967. crushed etched wrinkles 21"x 31".
8. "Man" 1967. (Follow the numbers with the crayon). 25"x34".
9. "Man" 1967. wrinkled etching with superimposed stenciled image on plexiglas. 21"x 38".
10. "Man" 1967. etching with stenciled plexiglas. 25"x34".
11. "To Make Your Self-Portrait" 1967. disposable xerox. unlimited edition. 8"x11".
12. "To be Thrown Away" 1967. disposable xerox. unlimited edition. 8"x11".
13. "10 etchings of different images of Man" 1967. edition 30. From "3 possible Frandos", a portfolio from the N.Y.G.W.

Fig. 3 Exhibition brochure (recto and verso) for *Towards Fandso* at Pratt Center for Contemporary Printmaking, 1967

to mobilize PGAC's publication and exhibition venues as platforms to reach publics for their new approach to printmaking. In the 1966 issue of *Artist's Proof*—PGAC's semiannual journal—Camnitzer published a short article entitled "A Redefinition of the Print." As in the NYGW's manifestos, the article encouraged printmakers to break out from their restrictive and siloed understanding of their medium by expanding their conception of printmaking's materials to include anything capable of producing multiple identical images—from "computer products" to "the reflection in a mirror."[20] By marshaling this quality of reproducibility, artists could challenge the dominant paradigm of the artwork's uniqueness, or what Walter Benjamin would call its "aura."[21]

Fritz Eichenberg, PGAC's director and the editor of *Artist's Proof,* was compelled by Camnitzer's arguments, which echo throughout his own editor's introduction to the issue. He writes repeatedly of the "new definitions" that "must be found for the contemporary print" as "the old ones are becoming increasingly obsolete."[22] Just as Camnitzer argues that printmaking must exceed its traditional two-dimensional materials, Eichenberg similarly accepts that "the word 'print' no longer exclusively implies the depositing of ink on a piece of paper."[23] The tension between the vision of printmaking the NYGW sought to escape and the one they hoped to advance was precisely the subject of Eichenberg's essay—the gap between "the rear-garde and the avant-garde, the way-in and the way-out, the traditional and the experimental."[24] By capitalizing on their existing relationship with PGAC, the NYGW was able to communicate their ideas about printmaking's potential to those most invested in the future of the medium.

In October 1967, the NYGW mounted their first major exhibition in the United States at the

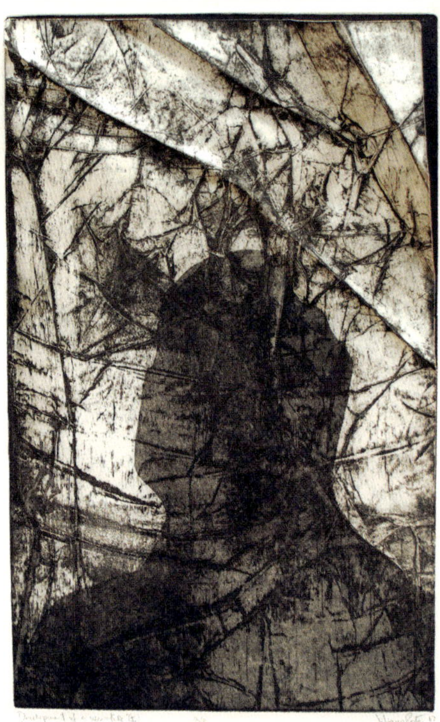

Fig. 4 Liliana Porter, *Development of a Wrinkle (I)*, 1967. Etching and wrinkled paper, plate: 27 × 17 in.

Pratt Center for Contemporary Printmaking (PCCP), as PGAC was renamed in September 1966. Titled *Towards FANDSO*, the show served as the opportunity to demonstrate how the NYGW's conceptual and theoretical approach to printmaking could manifest in new material forms (Fig. 3). Porter, Camnitzer, and Castillo's individual practices remained distinct, but each established a unique approach to the principles of FANDSO. Porter's works emphasized disposability, as seen in an unlimited edition of "disposable Xeroxes" titled *To Be Thrown Away.*[25] In several works, Porter also crumpled the paper and incorporated the motif of the wrinkle—a subject she would return to frequently over the next several years (Fig. 4). Castillo's works privileged the final term of the FANDSO acronym, "object," by screenprinting Plexiglas and vacuum-formed plastic to create interchangeable modular units that could be combined in different patterns. In doing so, Castillo extended the serial quality of printmaking into a spatial and temporal installation. Camnitzer also utilized nontraditional materials: vacuum-formed polystyrene and acetate, chrome steel cubes with photoengraved sentences (Fig. 5), and stickers with sentences printed by rubber stamps. In these latter two works, the evocative text functioned as "visual statements to be recreated in the spectator's imagination."[26] Above all, the artist sought to produce works that transformed viewers—or "consumers"—into creative individuals by involving their participation.

The following year, Camnitzer again collaborated with PCCP to curate the exhibition *Art in Editions: New Approaches* at New York University's Loeb Student Center. In addition to featuring the members of the NYGW, the show brought together a broad range of works—for example, the cast sculpture of Ernest Trova, Tom Wesselmann's vacuum-formed plastic prints, a book by Dieter Roth with hole-punched pages, Béla Julesz's computer-generated random dot stereograms, and Nam June Paik's television distortions. This grouping, as Camnitzer elaborates in the exhibition's accompanying essay, was united in their shared "editional thinking," often borrowing freely from industrial processes.[27] By juxtaposing such formally and materially disparate works, Camnitzer sought to call attention to printmaking's conceptual

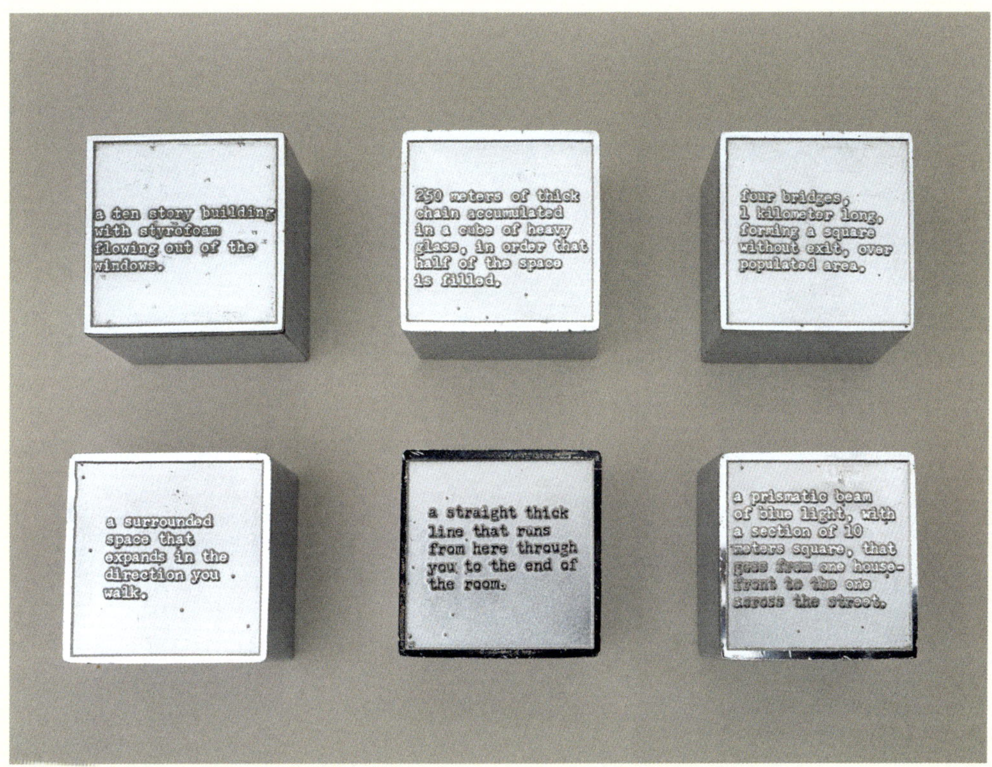

Fig. 5 Luis Camnitzer, *Sentences*, 1966. Steel, 2 × 2 × 2 in. each

affordances—seriality, multiplicity, reproduction, and permutation.

Camnitzer bookends his essay by emphasizing that the exhibition was made possible by PCCP's support, but not in the perfunctory way that one might thank sponsors and funders. Rather, the seemingly adversarial relationship between the NYGW and more traditional printmaking organizations is leveraged as part of the exhibition's argument. The fact that the idea for the exhibition came from contemporary printmakers and was sponsored by a printmaking institution, he asserts, is "symptomatic of a general feeling" that traditional printmaking lags behind its potential to meet the present moment.[28] He closes by mapping a new aspirational direction for PCCP's exhibition program—one that aligns with the NYGW's own core beliefs:

> *It is hoped that this exhibition will serve as an introduction to a cycle of shows to be organized by the Pratt Center for Contemporary Printmaking. It is an attempt to bring printmaking into a contemporary framework and to stimulate the creative possibilities of mass production as opposed to the creation of unique originals.*[29]

For the NYGW, contemporary printmaking—this ever-changing concept that had motivated PGAC's formation from Margaret Lowengrund's workshop at The Contemporaries—was not a matter of aligning the medium with stylistic developments in the broader art world, but expanding upon the specific "editional thinking" of print. Likewise, printmaking need not be defined by a set of technical procedures to be mastered, but instead could be imagined as a set of conceptual tools. How those tools might be used was precisely the question the NYGW invited artists to explore.

Pratt Graphic Art Center

After merging with the workshop at The Contemporaries in 1956, Pratt Graphic Art Center became an international meeting point for artists interested in exploring printmaking. *11 Prints by 11 Printmakers*, a portfolio published by PGAC of its staff and guest instructors and sold to benefit the Margaret Lowengrund Scholarship Fund, offers a window into the wide range of work being made at PGAC.

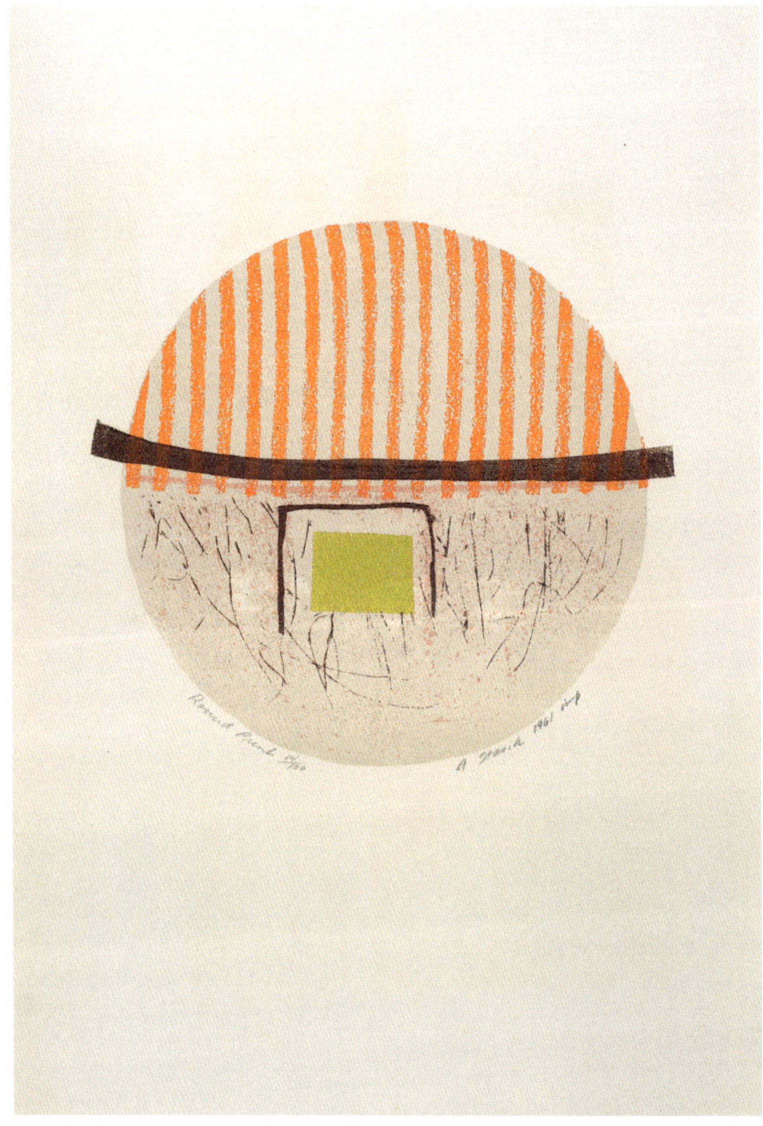

Andrew Stasik, *Round Print* from *11 Prints by 11 Printmakers*, 1961. Screenprint, edition of 100, image (irreg.): 9 7/16 × 10 5/8 in.; sheet: 19 7/8 × 14 in.

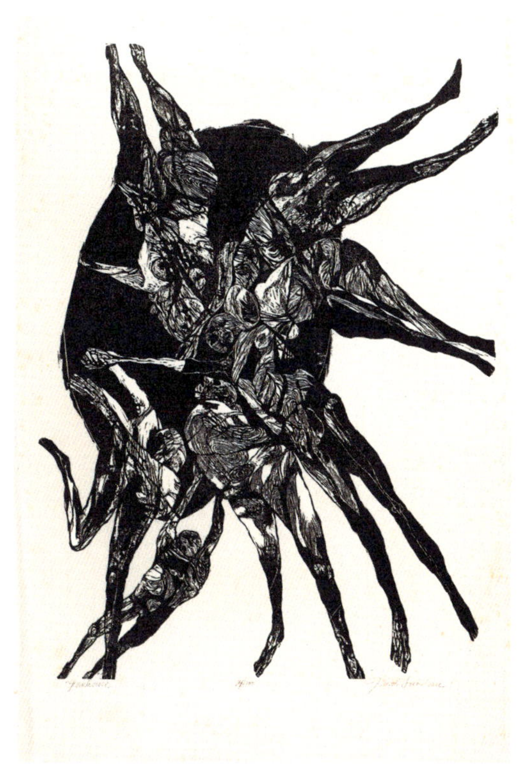

Jacob Landau, *Funhouse* from *11 Prints by 11 Printmakers*, 1961. Woodcut, edition of 100, image (irreg.): 16 7⁄16 × 12 5⁄16 in.; sheet: 20 1⁄16 × 14 in.

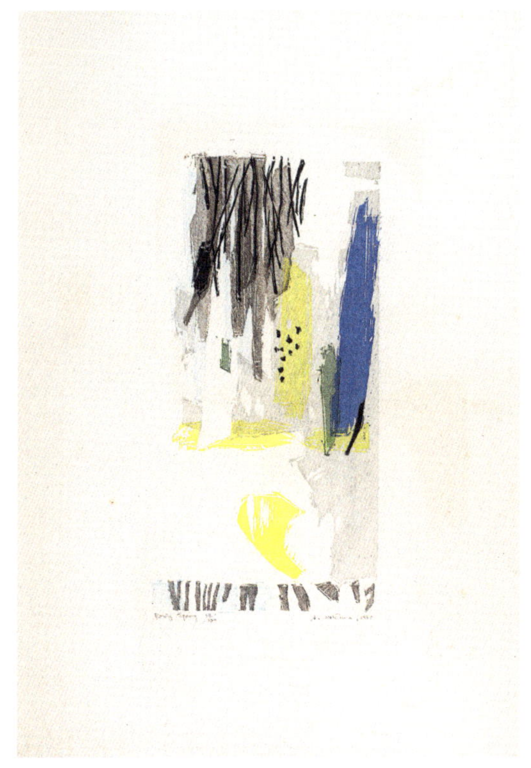

Uchima Ansei, *Early Spring* from *11 Prints by 11 Printmakers*, 1961. Woodcut, edition of 100, image (irreg.): 12 1⁄8 × 6 1⁄8 in.; sheet: 19 15⁄16 × 14 in.

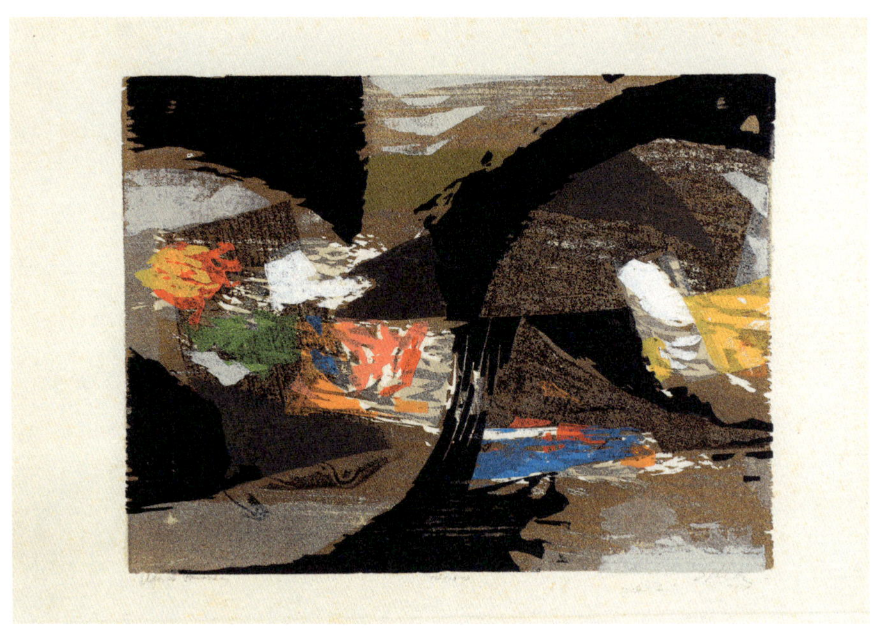

Seong Moy, *Ujon's Journey* from *11 Prints by 11 Printmakers*, 1961.
Woodcut, edition of 100, image: 11 ¼ × 15 in.; sheet: 14 × 20 ⅛ in.

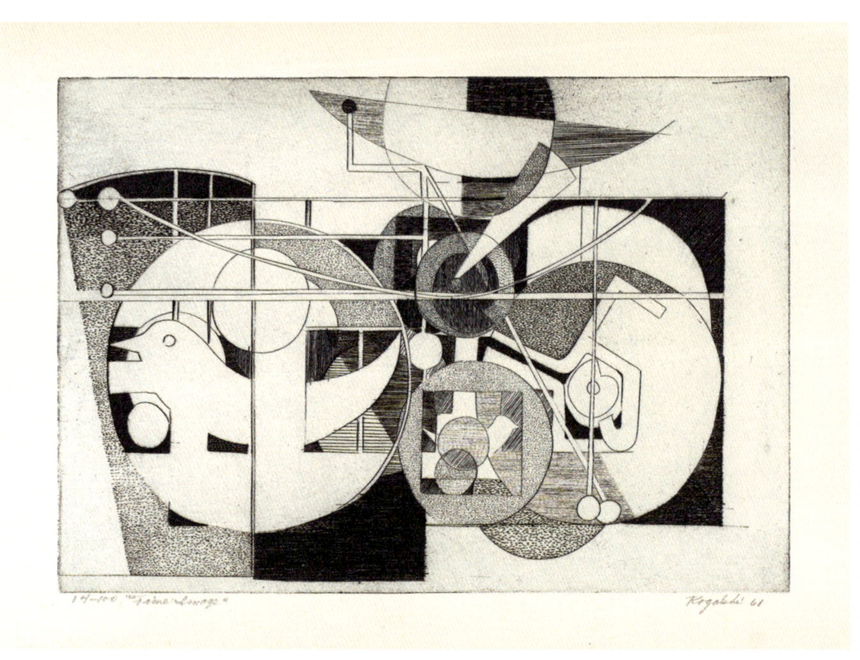

Walter Rogalski, *Time Image* from *11 Prints by 11 Printmakers*, 1961.
Engraving, edition of 100, plate: 11 7/16 × 16 ¾ in.; sheet: 14 1/16 × 19 13/16 in.

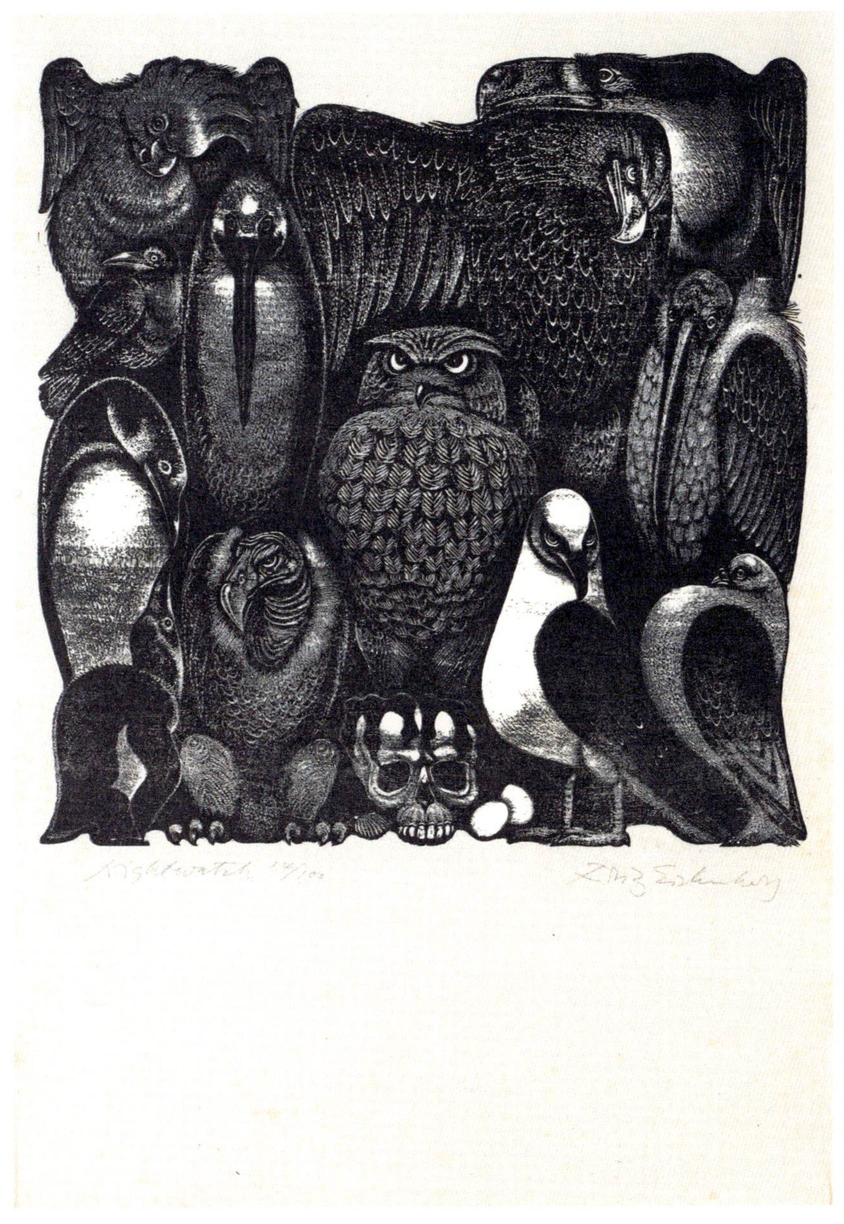

Fritz Eichenberg, *Night Watch* from *11 Prints by 11 Printmakers*, 1961. Wood engraving, edition of 100, image (irreg.): 13 × 13 in.; sheet: 20 3/8 × 14 in.

LITHOGRAPHY
studio-workshop
instruction printing
black & white color
959 MADISON AVE., New York 21
Margaret Lowengrund, director TR. 9-1980

LITHOGRAPH WORKSHOP
Special attention to beginners
Editions printed for professionals
The Contemporaries
Margaret Lowengrund, director
959 MADISON AVE., N. Y. 21 TR. 9-1980

Advertisements for The Contemporaries in *Art Digest*, 1951

1951

October
Lowengrund signals her plan to open a summer print workshop in the basement of the Woodstock Artists Association (WAA).[1]

November–December
Art Digest carries notice of The Contemporaries opening at 959 Madison Avenue as a hybrid workshop and gallery.

The Contemporaries opens to the public on December 10, 1951.

1952

January
Painters and Their Prints opens, which earned the gallery a reputation for being innovative and "provocative."[2]

Summer
The Contemporaries opens its satellite in WAA's basement, called The Graphic Workshop. Lowengrund enlists several artists to assist as printers, including Rodney Lethbridge, Karl Fortess, Albert Heckman, and Michael Ponce de León. David Smith makes six lithographs, including his iconic *Don Quixote*, which hangs alongside other contemporary prints in a survey show at WAA and later at the Woodstock Playhouse.

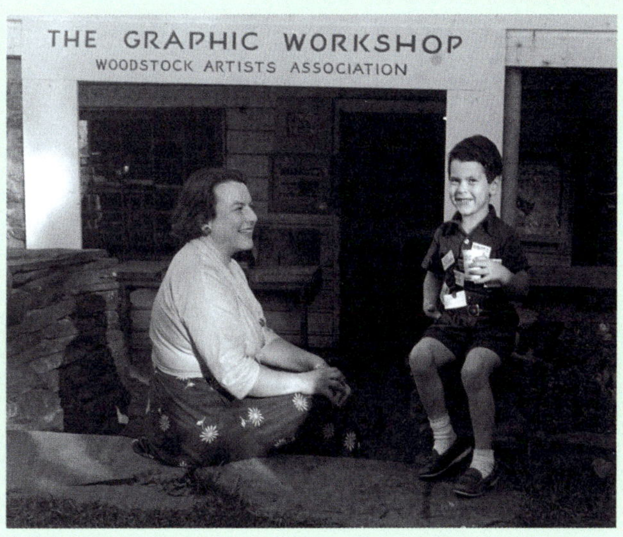

Poet Muriel Rukeyser behind the WAA with son William, summer 1952. Photo by Lee Sievan

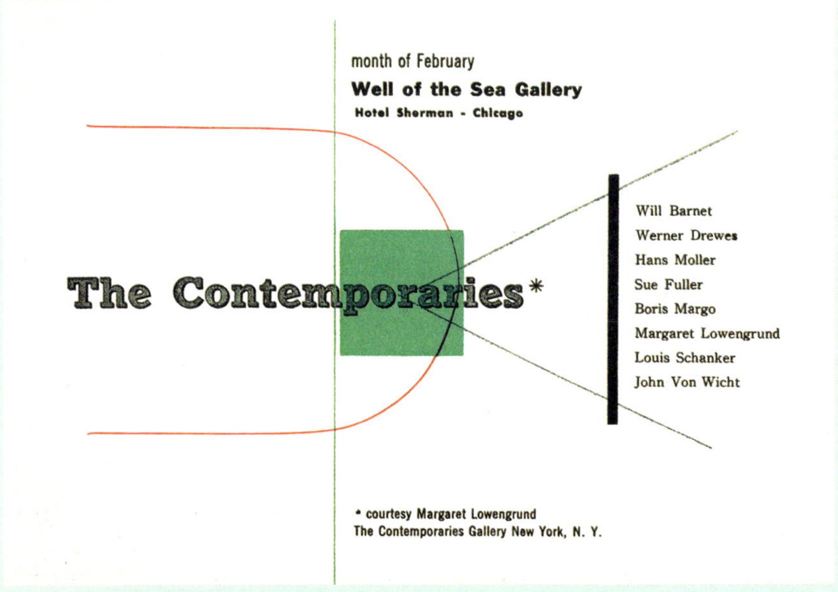

Exhibition card for *The Contemporaries* at Well of the Sea Gallery, Chicago, 1952. Designed by Frank Barr

October
John Muench, Adja Yunkers, Ponce de León, and Worden Day offer courses in their respective fields at The Contemporaries.

1953

February
Yunkers offers a demonstration of the woodcut process on February 27. Demonstrations become a regular part of the programming at The Contemporaries.

Summer
The Graphic Workshop opens for its second summer season at WAA. Ernest DeSoto and Ponce de León serve as assistants.

October
Lowengrund sends a version of *Graphic Originals for Modern Walls* to Vassar College. In conjunction, she and Ponce de León offer demonstrations in lithography and etching, respectively, and Lowengrund lectures about the creative potentials of the graphic arts.

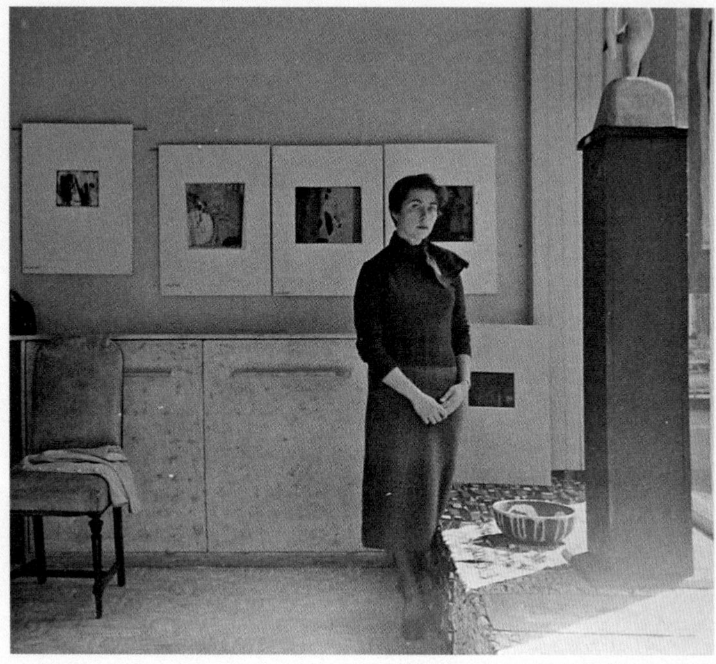

Fayga Ostrower at The Contemporaries, 959 Madison Avenue, May 1955. Photo by Robert Delson

1954

June
959 Madison Avenue is slated for demolition. Activating her network, Lowengrund begins discussions with curators, philanthropists, and other supporters about the future of The Contemporaries.[3] In the fall, Lowengrund circulates a fundraising appeal to rally support for an expanded graphic art center, which she envisions reorganizing as a nonprofit, though she never does.[4]

Summer
Reginald Neal, a noted expert in color lithography, serves as professional printmaker for The Contemporaries' final summer season in Woodstock and works with David Smith, Herman Cherry, and Adolf Dehn, among others.

1955

February
Still facing eviction and a precarious financial situation, Lowengrund meets with representatives from the Rockefeller Foundation. She emphasizes the demand for her printing services and the need for a larger workshop space.

April
Graphic Outlook '55, highlighting the strongest contemporary prints of the year, begins a nine-month national tour to Vassar College, Wichita Art Museum, Davison Art Center, Rhode Island School of Design, Allen Memorial Art Museum at Oberlin College, and City Art Museum and Washington University in St. Louis.

October
Lowengrund reopens The Contemporaries Gallery of Sculpture and Graphic Art at 992 Madison Avenue at Seventy-Seventh Street. Simultaneously, Lowengrund is recuperating from an operation after her cancer diagnosis in the spring.[5]

The Contemporaries Graphic Art Centre opens in a second-floor studio at 1343 Third Avenue, a short walk away from the gallery. The Centre remains a for-profit business with close ties to the commercial gallery, complicating ongoing discussions with Rockefeller Foundation about financial support.

November
In a continuation of special programming, the Centre screens Neal's film, *Color Lithography: An Art Medium*.

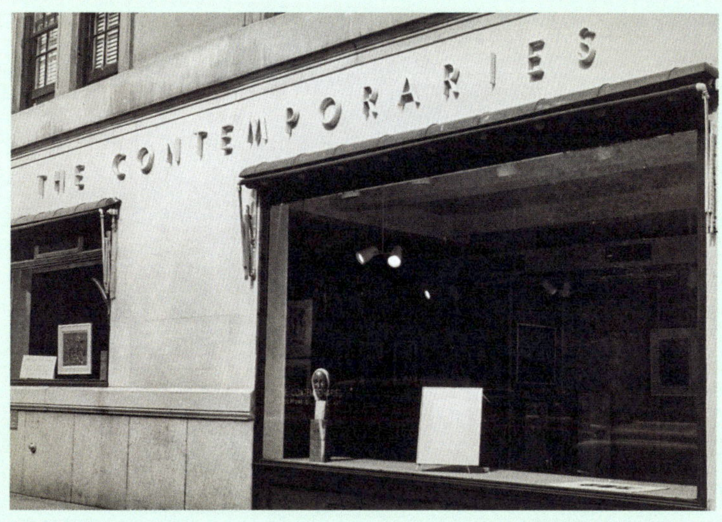

Exterior of The Contemporaries Gallery of Sculpture and Graphic Art, 992 Madison Avenue at Seventy-Seventh Street, New York, 1955. Photo by Robert Delson

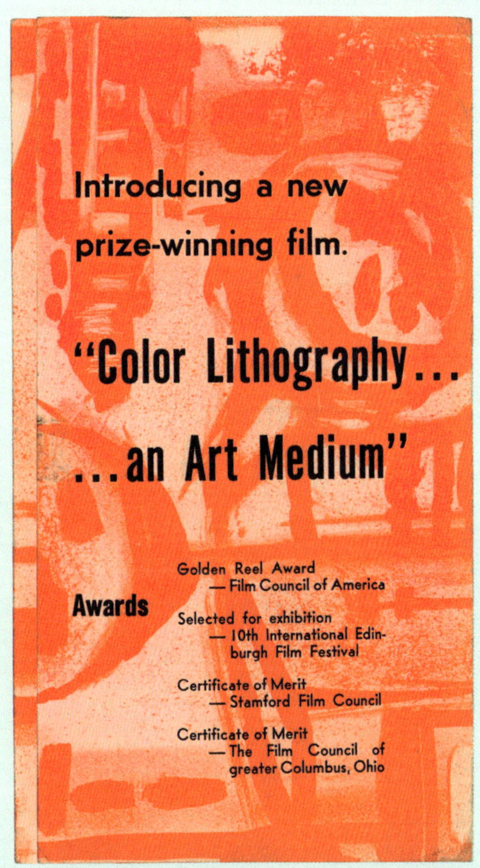

Brochure for Reginald Neal's film *Color Lithography: An Art Medium*, 1955

1956

January
Looking to increase revenue for the Graphic Art Centre, particularly during daytime hours, Lowengrund advertises courses for children and amateurs.

February
The Contemporaries Gallery launches the "Collector's Print," a print-of-the-month series marketed to "the discriminating collector" with the price capped at fifty dollars and edition size limited to forty.[6]

Seeking to grow the Graphic Art Centre and establish it on firmer financial footing, Lowengrund reaches out to possible nonprofit partners.[7] She forges a relationship with Fritz Eichenberg, chair of Pratt Institute's Graphic Arts Department, who had taught at the Centre.

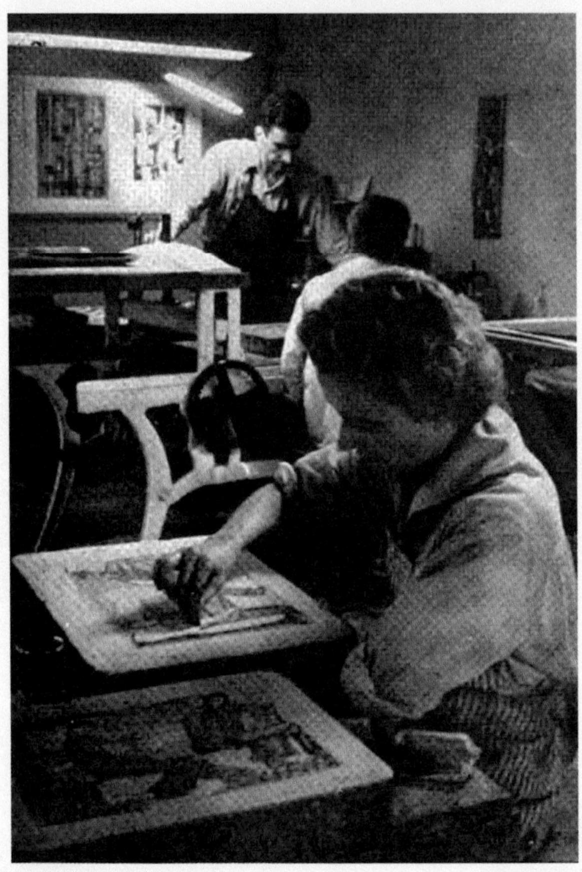

Joan Collins working on a lithographic stone with instructor Arnold Singer in background at the Contemporaries Graphic Art Centre, 1343 Third Avenue, 1956

March–July
Lengthy negotiations occur throughout the spring and summer regarding a possible merger between the Contemporaries Graphic Art Centre and Pratt Institute. There are issues surrounding the projected budget and Lowengrund's role in the newly merged entity, as well as resistance from Pratt's Board of Trustees about having an extension in Manhattan.[8]

August
Lowengrund and Pratt reach an agreement and formally submit a final proposal, which the Rockefeller Foundation accepts, providing $50,000 dispersed in tapering amounts over three years.[9]

October
The merger is actualized. Lowengrund and Eichenberg become codirectors of the Pratt-Contemporaries Graphic Art Centre.[10]

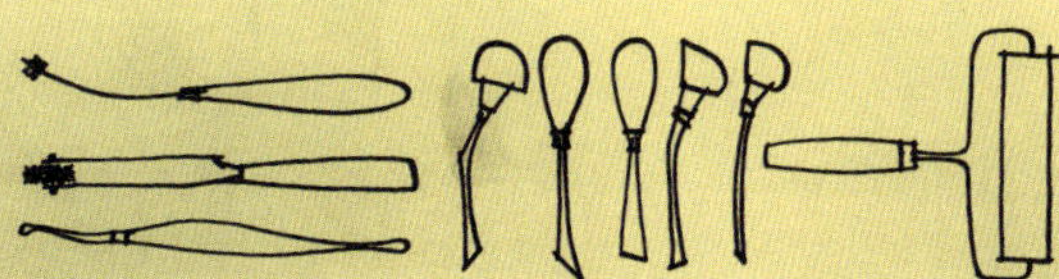

THE PRATT CONTEMPORARIES
GRAPHIC ART CENTRE
AN EXTENSION OF PRATT INSTITUTE
MARGARET LOWENGRUND • FRITZ EICHENBERG, DIRECTORS

WORKSHOP INSTRUCTION IN
ETCHING • ENGRAVING • WOODCUT
LITHOGRAPHY • COMBINED MEDIA

PROFESSIONAL PRINTING & RELATED SERVICES
EXHIBITIONS • FILMS • DEMONSTRATIONS AND LECTURES BY PROMINENT GRAPHIC ARTISTS

FACULTY Margaret Lowengrund, Seong Moy, Walter Rogalski, Michael Ponce de Leon
VISITING INSTRUCTORS: Federico Castellon, Antonio Frasconi, Irving Amen

THE CENTER IS OPEN MONDAY THROUGH FRIDAY FROM 2-5 AND 7-10 P.M. IT AIMS TO SERVE ARTISTS, ART TEACHERS, AND STUDENTS FROM ALL OVER THE WORLD WHO WISH TO FURTHER THEIR KNOWLEDGE IN THE GRAPHIC MEDIA UNDER EXPERT GUIDANCE AND WHO ALSO LIKE TO WORK IN A CONGENIAL AND STIMULATING WORKSHOP ATMOSPHERE.

ADVISORY BOARD UNA E. JOHNSON, Curator of Prints, The Brooklyn Museum
KARL KUP, Curator of Prints, The New York Public Library
WILLIAM S. LIEBERMAN, Curator of Prints, Museum of Modern Art
DONALD OENSLAGER, Professor of Stage Design, Yale University
GABOR PETERDI, Artist and Lecturer, Hunter College
THEODORE J. H. GUSTEN, International Graphic Arts Society
The Dean of the Art School, Pratt Institute, and the Two Directors of the Centre

THE PRATT-CONTEMPORARIES GRAPHIC ART CENTRE
1343 THIRD AVE. • (at 77th Street) NEW YORK 21, N. Y. Tel. LY 6-9180

CONTINUOUS OPEN REGISTRATION
MONTHLY RATES $25. — PLUS $5. — REGISTRATION FEE FOR NEW REGISTRANTS
TUITION FEES ARE PAYABLE IN ADVANCE

Paper, Etching Supplies and Other Materials Can Be Purchased at the Centre

Please fill out and return application with registration fee of $5.

Name..

Address..

Telephone..

Course..Registration fee $5.

Course announcement and enrollment flyer for The Pratt-Contemporaries Graphic Art Centre, 1955

1957

January

Lowengrund is hospitalized again, and she misses the second meeting of the Pratt-Contemporaries Graphic Art Centre's Advisory Board, composed of curators, artists, and Pratt faculty and administrators.

Pratt-Contemporaries Graphic Art Centre is open for instruction weekdays 2–5 p.m. and 7–10 p.m. Faculty includes Lowengrund, Seong Moy, Walter Rogalski, Ponce de León and visiting instructors Federico Castellón, Antonio Frasconi, and Irving Amen. Arnold Singer continues to serve as professional printer, along with Andrew Stasik.

February

Continuing its commitment to education, the Pratt-Contemporaries Graphic Art Centre hosts a Sunday afternoon film screening.[11] Building on their shared mission, Lowengrund and Eichenberg invite professional international artists to make editions at the Centre. Soon after, Rufino Tamayo makes a color lithograph with Singer (page 75).

October–November

Lowengrund, who has been quite ill since September, sells The Contemporaries Gallery to Ian Woodner, thus ending its relationship with Pratt-Contemporaries Graphic Art Centre. Lowengrund dies on November 19. Eichenberg initiates the Margaret Lowengrund Scholarship Fund, which he earmarks for young artists.[12]

THE PRATT-CONTEMPORARIES GRAPHIC ART CENTER
1343 THIRD AVE · AT 77th ST · NEW YORK 21 · Tel · LYceum 6-9180

A memorial exhibition of prints by Margaret Lowengrund will be held at the Graphic Art Centre from March 17. to April 25.

Miss Lowengrund, who was both a painter and a print-maker, studied in Philadelphia, London, England and with Andre L'Hote in Paris. She exhibited nationally and abroad from 1932 to 1951. Her works are in the British Museum and in several American collections, including a mural in the New York Labor Temple.

She was director of the Contemporaries Gallery and co-director of the Pratt-Contemporaries Graphic Art Centre in New York.

Exhibition announcement for *Memorial Exhibition of Prints by Margaret Lowengrund*, The Pratt-Contemporaries Graphic Art Centre, 1957

1958

March

Pratt-Contemporaries Graphic Art Centre mounts a memorial exhibition for Margaret Lowengrund.

April

Sekino Juni'ichirō is the first international artist to serve as a visiting instructor, offering a four-month course about woodcut. Throughout its earliest years, Pratt-Contemporaries Graphic Art Centre hosts many guest instructors and printers whose expertise advances its mission to engage both students and professional editioning services.

Ingram Merrill Foundation makes the first of many donations to a scholarship fund dedicated to bringing international students to the Centre. Among the first recipients were Maria Bonomi and Antonio Amaral (Brazil), Deli Sacilotto and Eric Bergman (Canada), Rudolfo Abularach (Guatemala), Jorge Damiani (Italy), and Gottfried Honegger and Warja Honegger-Lavater (Switzerland).[13]

October

Facing the severe taper of the Rockefeller Foundation grant, Eichenberg raises concerns with Pratt's administration about the long-term viability of Pratt-Contemporaries Graphic Art Centre. He considers staff cuts, moving the Centre to Brooklyn, or closing it entirely.[14]

1959

May

After months of negotiations, the Rockefeller Foundation awards Pratt-Contemporaries Graphic Art Centre another three-year grant. Contingent on this support, Pratt Institute pledges to cover any shortfalls in the Centre's projected annual operating.[15] Grant money is set aside to bring foreign artists as guest instructors.

August

Eichenberg changes the workshop's name to Pratt Graphic Art Center (PGAC).[16]

September

PGAC relocates to a two-thousand-square-foot studio at 795 Broadway at Eleventh Street, opposite Grace Church. With dedicated gallery walls, PGAC begins organizing a consistent program of exhibitions.

December

Jacob Landau offers a lecture about woodcut, continuing PGAC's long-standing commitment to public programming.

1960

January

In a fundraiser for the Margaret Lowengrund Scholarship Fund, PGAC holds a screening of *Ukiyo-e Print*, a film narrated by James Michener with additional commentary from Izumi Shigeru, then in residence at PGAC.

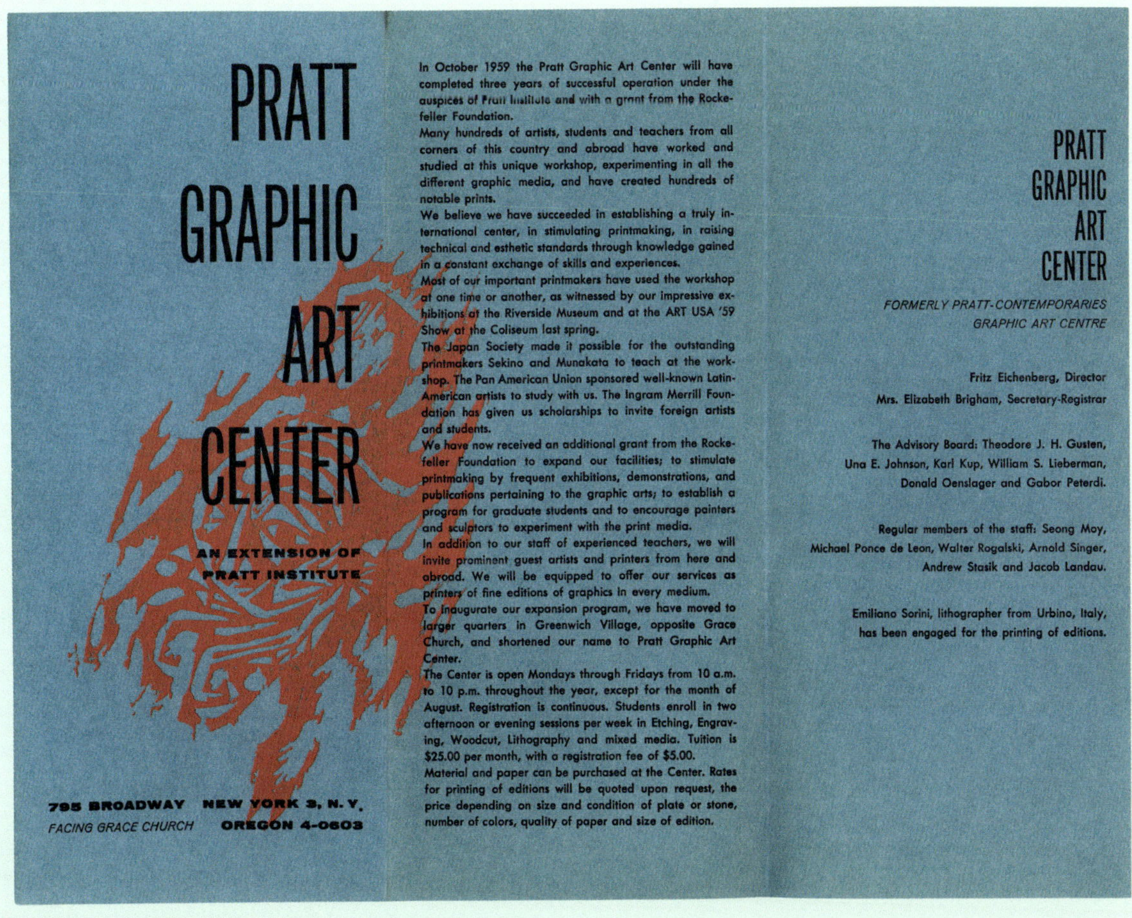

PRATT GRAPHIC ART CENTER

AN EXTENSION OF PRATT INSTITUTE

795 BROADWAY NEW YORK 3, N. Y.
FACING GRACE CHURCH OREGON 4-0603

In October 1959 the Pratt Graphic Art Center will have completed three years of successful operation under the auspices of Pratt Institute and with a grant from the Rockefeller Foundation.

Many hundreds of artists, students and teachers from all corners of this country and abroad have worked and studied at this unique workshop, experimenting in all the different graphic media, and have created hundreds of notable prints.

We believe we have succeeded in establishing a truly international center, in stimulating printmaking, in raising technical and esthetic standards through knowledge gained in a constant exchange of skills and experiences.

Most of our important printmakers have used the workshop at one time or another, as witnessed by our impressive exhibitions at the Riverside Museum and at the ART USA '59 Show at the Coliseum last spring.

The Japan Society made it possible for the outstanding printmakers Sekino and Munakata to teach at the workshop. The Pan American Union sponsored well-known Latin-American artists to study with us. The Ingram Merrill Foundation has given us scholarships to invite foreign artists and students.

We have now received an additional grant from the Rockefeller Foundation to expand our facilities; to stimulate printmaking by frequent exhibitions, demonstrations, and publications pertaining to the graphic arts; to establish a program for graduate students and to encourage painters and sculptors to experiment with the print media.

In addition to our staff of experienced teachers, we will invite prominent guest artists and printers from here and abroad. We will be equipped to offer our services as printers of fine editions of graphics in every medium.

To inaugurate our expansion program, we have moved to larger quarters in Greenwich Village, opposite Grace Church, and shortened our name to Pratt Graphic Art Center.

The Center is open Mondays through Fridays from 10 a.m. to 10 p.m. throughout the year, except for the month of August. Registration is continuous. Students enroll in two afternoon or evening sessions per week in Etching, Engraving, Woodcut, Lithography and mixed media. Tuition is $25.00 per month, with a registration fee of $5.00.

Material and paper can be purchased at the Center. Rates for printing of editions will be quoted upon request, the price depending on size and condition of plate or stone, number of colors, quality of paper and size of edition.

PRATT GRAPHIC ART CENTER

FORMERLY PRATT-CONTEMPORARIES GRAPHIC ART CENTRE

Fritz Eichenberg, Director
Mrs. Elizabeth Brigham, Secretary-Registrar

The Advisory Board: Theodore J. H. Gusten, Una E. Johnson, Karl Kup, William S. Lieberman, Donald Oenslager and Gabor Peterdi.

Regular members of the staff: Seong Moy, Michael Ponce de Leon, Walter Rogalski, Arnold Singer, Andrew Stasik and Jacob Landau.

Emiliano Sorini, lithographer from Urbino, Italy, has been engaged for the printing of editions.

Brochure and course list for Pratt Graphic Art Center, 1959

1960 (Continued)

February

In recognition of PGAC's contribution to advancing lithography, June Wayne ensures that a portion of her major Ford Foundation grant—to establish the Tamarind Lithography Workshop—is earmarked to bring several international lithographers to PGAC.[17]

March

Gabor Peterdi, longtime member of PGAC's Board of Advisors, gives a lecture in conjunction with an exhibition of his prints. PGAC repeats this model in the fall with Stanley William Hayter.

April

PGAC begins circulating *Graphic Techniques*, a didactic exhibition explaining the processes behind several graphic arts media, throughout arts venues in the United States and public schools in Westchester County and New York City. The show remains in circulation for three years.

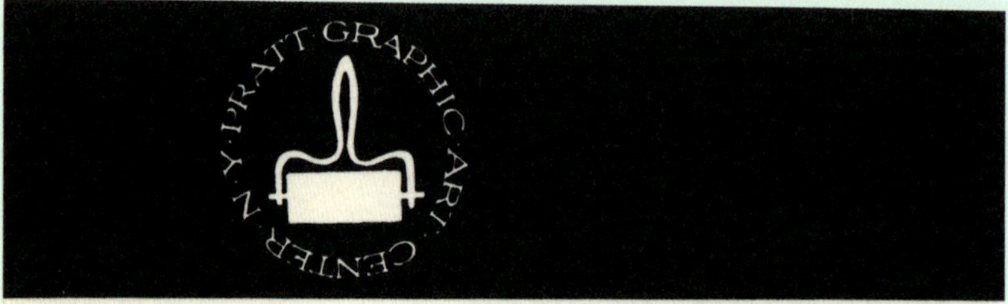

A LECTURE ON PRINTMAKING BY
GABOR PETERDI

To be held at lecture room 203 of the Cooper Union (north end off Astor Place) on TUESDAY MARCH 15 at 7:30 P.M. followed by a reception for the artist and a show of his prints at the PRATT GRAPHIC ART CENTER. The Peterdi prints will be on exhibition from March 2 to 16. *Only a limited number of places is available.*

R.S.V.P. Mrs. Brigham Pratt Graphic Art Center 795 Broadway Or 4-0603

Invitation for *A Lecture on Printmaking by Gabor Peterdi*, 1960

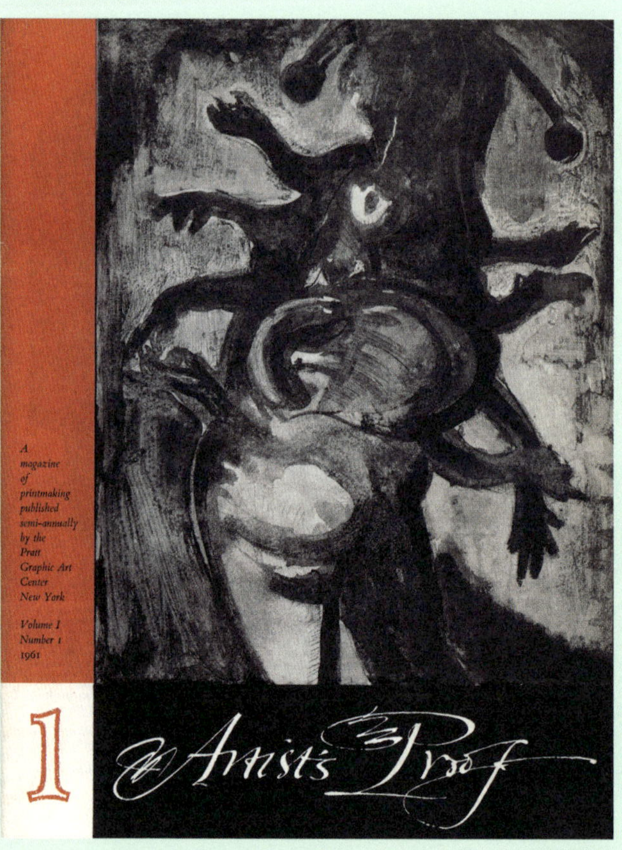

Artist's Proof, no. 1 (1961)

1961

February
The first issue of *Artist's Proof*, a semiannual journal from PGAC, is published. It presents a snapshot of PGAC's activities and captures international printmaking activity. In his foreword, Eichenberg acknowledges Lowengrund's "promising" vision for a contemporary printmaking center and describes the rationale behind *Artist's Proof*: "In this atmosphere filled with the smells of ink and turps and acids, the idea to start a publication devoted exclusively to printmaking seems a natural one; an informal publication which gives the printmaker a chance to be seen and heard, to exchange opinions, to discuss and show his work."[18]

Demonstrating its commitment to documenting, exhibiting, and engaging with international trends in printmaking, PGAC hosts a panel discussion about printmaking in Yugoslavia and Poland.

November
PGAC publishes *11 Prints by 11 Printmakers*, a portfolio featuring editions by PGAC faculty members. Associated American Artists serves as the sole distributor of the portfolio, with profits going to the Margaret Lowengrund Scholarship Fund.[19] In the coming years, PGAC produces additional portfolios benefiting the Center and spotlighting its professional members.

1962

September
PGAC moves two blocks north to 831 Broadway. In this much larger space, the in-house exhibitions program explodes. *Prizewinning American Prints*, the first exhibition at this location, subsequently tours to venues in North America. PGAC's subsequent exhibitions—ranging from student and faculty shows, surveys of international printmaking centers, and juried competitions—similarly travel widely.

The Pratt Graphic Art Center cordially invites you to an Open House at its new quarters
at 831 B'way, at 13th st., NYC, Monday, September 24th, 5-7 pm. Refreshments will be served.
The opening exhibition, PRIZEWINNING AMERICAN PRINTS, will be on view through October 15th.

OPEN HOUSE

Invitation to an open house celebrating PGAC's move to 831 Broadway and a preview of *Prizewinning American Prints*, 1962

October
With Pratt Institute's support, students, faculty, and professional members of PGAC participate in *Pratt Graphic Talent* at the Lever House on Park Avenue. These types of partnerships provide PGAC with greater visibility and funding sources through print sales.

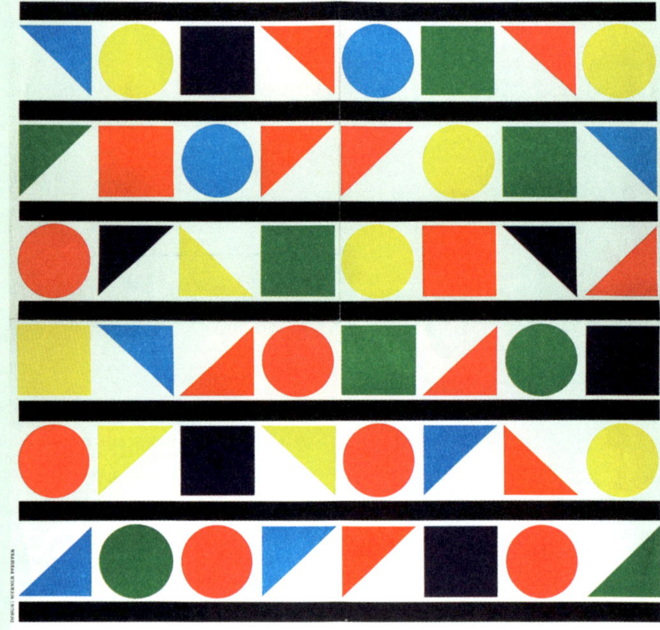

Announcement card for *Pratt Graphic Talent*, 1965

1963

February
PGAC launches a weekly lecture-demonstration series through the end of April. PGAC staff and invited artists review process and techniques, while curators and dealers discuss print history and current trends in the art market. A version of this series recurs in 1964 and 1965.

May
Eichenberg appeals to the Ford Foundation for the creation of the Pratt Intaglio Center, paralleling Tamarind's efforts for lithography, but he is turned down.

October
In keeping with PGAC's international scope, Yoshida Hodaka and Yoshida Masaji offer a workshop about woodblock printmaking and give a lecture about contemporary printmaking in Japan.

1964

February
Erich Mönch, head of the lithography workshop at the Staatliche Akademie der Bildenden Künste in Stuttgart, Germany, is in residence, continuing PGAC's ongoing commitment to hosting international experts in the graphic arts (pages 56–57). Concurrently, PGAC holds an exhibition of students from the Akademie.

April
Dovetailing with PGAC's traveling show *Contemporary Polish Prints*, Polish printmaker Tadeusz Lapinski lectures about artistic activity in Warsaw.

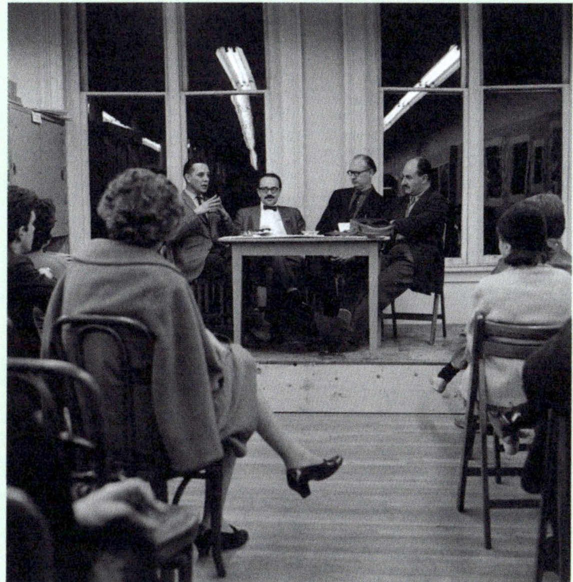

Printmaking and the Future: A Symposium, Pratt Graphic Art Center, April 24, 1963. Pictured at table: Michael Ponce de León, Jacob Landau, Will Barnet, and Gabor Peterdi

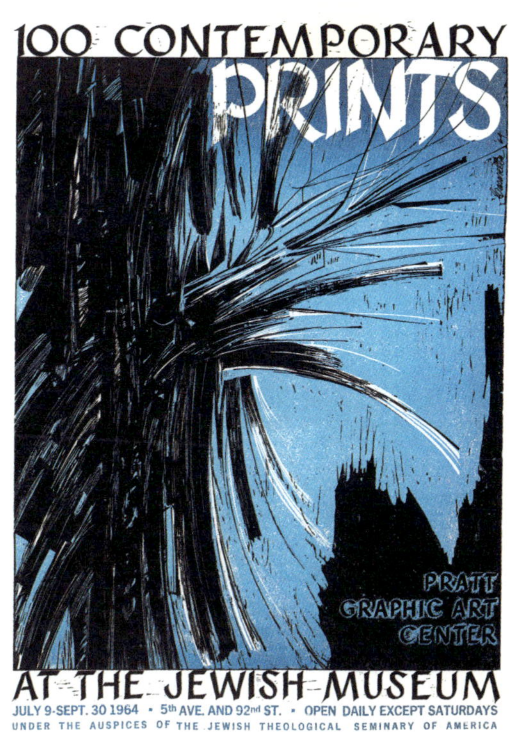

100 Contemporary Prints, Pratt Graphic Art Center, at the Jewish Museum, July 9–September 30, 1964. Designed by Edmond Casarella. Lithograph, sheet: 41 ⅞ × 30 15⁄16 in.

1965

March–April

Expanding its international outreach, PGAC hosts a roundtable discussion in conjunction with its exhibition about Romanian and Nigerian prints and Soviet posters, featuring Eichenberg, John Ross, and Jacob Lawrence discussing their visits to these countries.[20] Ponce de León visits Caracas, Venezuela, where he attends a loan exhibition of PGAC prints and lectures about the Center.[21]

May

Thirteen prints made at PGAC are exhibited in the *House of Good Taste* at the New York World's Fair. Exhibiting artists include Eichenberg, Stasik, Ponce de León, Moy, Ruth Kerkovius, Uchima Ansei, Edmond Casarella, and Arthur Deshaies.[22]

1966

September

The newly renamed Pratt Center for Contemporary Printmaking presents an exhibition about serigraphs, the first organized under its new banner. The show emphasizes the medium's increased relevance to contemporary printmaking.

Exhibitions at The Contemporaries 1951 to 1957

This chronology assembles the first comprehensive listing of exhibitions presented at The Contemporaries during Margaret Lowengrund's ownership between 1951 and 1957. Sources include the gallery's visitor book, calendar listings in newspapers and art magazines, and other archival sources. Exhibition dates often shifted, and the dates listed below represent the best approximation of when show changeovers occurred. The chronology retains some ambiguity, however, in cases where the gallery did not specify an opening or closing day—hence exhibitions listed by month.

Concurrent exhibitions are marked with an asterisk (*)
Shows without specific titles are given in square brackets [ ]

Unless otherwise noted, exhibitions took place at The Contemporaries at the following locations:

959 Madison Avenue (December 1951–August 1955)
992 Madison Avenue (October 10, 1955–November 30, 1957)

1951

Gallery Opening (December 10–January 1952)

1952

Painters and Their Prints (January 14–February 15)[1]

The Contemporaries, Well of the Sea Gallery, Hotel Sherman, Chicago, IL (February 1–29)

Large Prints (February 18–March 23)

Black and White (March 31–April 17)

Arthur Deshaies: New Processes in Modern Graphics (May 5–25)*

Richard Lippold (May 5–25)*

Homage to Lehmbruck (June 9–August 30)

The Graphic Workshop, Art Gallery, Woodstock Artists Association (opened July 19) and lobby, Woodstock Playhouse (opened July 25)[2]

Color Prints (August)

Evolution of a Contemporary Lithograph (September 15–30)[3]

52 Prints of the Year (October 15–November 8)

Graphic Britain: New Color Prints (November 10–30)

Christmas Collector (closed December 31)

1953

Emil Weddige: Color Lithography (January 5–25)

Warner Prins: Graphic Tiles and Drawings (February 1–21)

Graphic Proofs by Staff and Workshop (February 23–28)

Sculpture by Peter Lipman-Wulf (March 1–19)*

Lithographs by June Wayne (March 1–22)*

George Biddle: Lithographs and Ceramics Done in Rome, 1952 (March 23–April 4)

Three Media: Albers, Von Wicht, Jordan (April 6–25)

Original Prints from Sweden, Denmark, and the U. S. A. (April 27–May 9)

Danny Pierce: Graphics (May 11–25)

Lithographs by Richard Florsheim (May 25–June 6)

Degas to De Stijl (June 8 until August)

Methods in Modern Graphics (September 21–October 5)

Graphic Originals for Modern Walls (October 15–November 15)

André Racz: Fifteen Engravings (November 16–December 5)

Christmas Collector (December 5–January 5, 1954)

1954

Twenty Drawings (January 11–February 1)

Graphic Outlook '54 (February 8–March 15)

Hasegawa (March 21–April 10)

Predominantly French: Exhibition of International Graphic Art (April 19–May 15)

Prizewinners (closed June 1)

Third International Biennial of Contemporary Color Lithography, from Cincinnati Art Museum (June 1–30)

The Color Print Society (July 6–31)

The Graphic Workshop, lobby, Woodstock Playhouse, Woodstock, NY (July 27–August 15)

Michel Cadoret (August 2–30)

Abraham Hankins: Recent Woodcuts (September 7–23)

Midwest Printmakers (September 27–October 25)

Carol Summers: Woodcuts (October 31–November 27)*

Jane Wasey: Carved Weathervanes and Wall Sculpture (October 31–November 27)*

The Contemporaries Christmas Show: Original Prints from Immaculate Hearts College (November 29–December 24)

1955

Roloff Beny: Watercolors, Drawings, Prints (January 3–22)

Graphic Outlook '55 (January 31–February 19)

Graphics by Dean Meeker (February 27–March 19)*

Sculpture by Peter Lipman-Wulf (February 28–March 19)*

Beatrice Grover (March 28–April 16)

Irving Amen: Color Woodcuts (April 18–May 7)*

[Contemporary American, French, and British Graphics] (April 18–May 7)*

Fayga Ostrower: Etchings, Aquatints, Woodcuts (May 9–May 28)*

Sculptures by Irène Hamar (May 9–May 28)*

Prize-Winning Graphics (June 1–30)

[Summer Graphics] (July–August)

Today: An Exhibition of Sculpture and Graphic Art (October 10–November 9)

Michel Cadoret: Tapestries from Aubusson (November 15–December 10)*

South Sea & African Sculpture (November 15–December 10)*

[Graphic Art Exhibition], Kaufman Art Gallery, Ninety-Second Street Young Men's & Young Women's Hebrew Association, New York, NY (December 9–30)

Angelo Savelli: Serigraphs (December 12–January 1, 1956)*

Sculpted Jewelry, Prints, and Small Bronzes (December 12–January 1, 1956)*

1956

Fridl Loos: Collages (January 2–28)*

Modern Japanese Prints (January 2–28)*

Warrington Colescott: Watercolors, Drawings, Serigraphs (January 24–February 11)

George Biddle and Hélène Sardeau (February 15–March 10)

Americans in Two Fields: Painting and Graphic Arts (Barnet, Von Wicht, Lebrun, Erlanger, Casarella) (March 5–26)

Kiyoshi Saitō (opened March 27)

Photographs of Rooms by Members of the New York Chapter of the American Institute of Decorators (April 2–7)

Irène Hamar: Sculpture, Drawings, Marble Reliefs (April 9–28)

Dean Carter: Sculpture (May 7–31)*

Edward Giobbi and Thomas George: Woodblocks, Drawings, Prints (May 7–31)*

Brooklyn Museum Print Annual Prizewinners (June 1–July 31)*

[Raoul Dufy: "La Fée Electricité," Lithographic Mural; and French Post-Impressionist Prints] (June 1–July 31)*

Collector's Print Series (August 20–September 15)*

[European Paintings and Graphics] (August 20–September 15)*

Fourth International Biennial of Contemporary Color Lithography, from Cincinnati Art Museum (September 17–October 6)

Antoni Clavé: Paintings and Lithographs (October 8–27)

José de Creeft (October 27–November 17)*

Prints by Zoran Antonio Mušič and Giorgio Morandi (October 27–November 17)*

Christmas Selection (November 19–December 15)*

Prints by Sister Mary Corita (November 19–December 15)*

1957

Kazu Wakita (January)

Graphic Outlook '57 (January 14–February 6)

[The Contemporaries], Kaufman Art Gallery, Ninety-Second Street Young Men's & Young Women's Hebrew Association, New York, NY (February 15–28)

Marc Chagall (February 18–28)

Kazu Wakita: Oils, Watercolors, Lithographs (March 11–30)*

Lindsay Daen: Sculpture (March 11–30)*

Zoran Antonio Mušič: Oils, Lithographs, Etchings (March 11–30)*

Marino Marini: Paintings, Sculpture, and Graphic Work (April 1–20)

American Abstract Artists: 21st Annual Exhibition (April 22–May 11)

Daniel Serra-Badué: Paintings (May 14–31)

[Thirty-two prints by twenty-seven contemporary artists], Ringling Museum, Sarasota, FL (closed June 30)

[Modern Color Prints by British, Italian, French and American Artists] (June–September)

Pratt-Contemporaries Graphic Art Centre (September 16–October 5)

Religious Interpretation in Line and Color, Washington Cathedral, Washington, DC (September 23–October 29)

Ray Prohaska (October 7–25)

[Modern and Contemporary Graphics] (November)

Exhibitions at Pratt Graphic Art Center 1956 to 1966

This chronology provides a preliminary list of Pratt Graphic Art Center's exhibitions program. The name of this printmaking center changed three times during its first ten years, and the acronym "PGAC" used below stands variously for the Pratt-Contemporaries Graphic Art Centre, Pratt Graphic Art Center, and Pratt Center for Contemporary Printmaking. Locations for PGAC are as follows:

1343 Third Avenue (September 1956–August 1959)
795 Broadway (September 1959–August 1962)
831 Broadway (September 1962–December 1966)[1]

Exhibitions listed are only those directly involving PGAC—either shows hosted at PGAC's Manhattan locations or shows that PGAC organized for display elsewhere. PGAC widely circulated many of its exhibitions, and the chronology accounts for only a sliver of these venues.[2] PGAC-circulated exhibitions are noted with a diamond [♦].

As noted below, several PGAC exhibitions were also shown at Pratt Institute's Brooklyn campus in the Main Building's First Floor Gallery (alternately called the Institute Gallery) and Fourth Floor Gallery.[3] Although this chronology incorporates these Pratt Institute venues, it is distinct from an accounting of exhibitions featuring the undergraduates, graduate students, and faculty of the Pratt Institute's Department of Graphic Arts and Illustration.

Shows without specific titles are given in square brackets [ ].

1957

Pratt-Contemporaries Graphic Art Centre, The Contemporaries, 992 Madison Avenue (September 16–October 5)

[One-year anniversary show, featuring students and instructors], PGAC (opened November 7)

[Etchings and Woodcuts by Students of Irving Amen and Walter Rogalski], PGAC (December)

Caroline Durieux: Electron Prints, PGAC (December)

1958

Memorial Exhibition of Prints by Margaret Lowengrund, PGAC (March 17–April 25)

Fifth International Biennial of Contemporary Color Lithography, from Cincinnati Art Museum, PGAC (before June)

Pratt Institute Student Exhibition, Staatliche Akademie der Bildenden Künste Stuttgart (July 1–19)

1959

[PGAC faculty exhibition] ♦

- Los Angeles Art Center (January)
- De Beyerd Cultural Center, Breda, The Netherlands (opened September 16, 1960)
- Jacksonville Art Museum, Florida (until October 29, 1962)

Graphics, 1959, Riverside Museum, 310 Riverside Drive, New York (February 1–22)

Art:USA:59, Coliseum, Columbus Circle, New York (April 3–19)

Woodcuts by Shikō Munakata

- Fourth Floor Gallery, Pratt Institute (April)
- PGAC (until June 15)

Antonio Frasconi: Woodcuts, PGAC (June 15–July 3)

William Gropper: Lithographs, PGAC (November 18–December 1)

Max Kahn: Color Lithographs, PGAC (December 2–14)

Sister Mary Corita: Serigraphs, PGAC (December 15–31)

[Izumi Shigeru], PGAC (unknown)

Malcolm Myers: Etchings, PGAC (unknown)

1960

Woodblock Prints by Carol Summers, PGAC (February 17–29)

Prints by Gabor Peterdi, PGAC (March 1–16)

Contemporary Japanese Prints

- Fourth Floor Gallery, Pratt Institute (March 1–15)
- PGAC (March 15–30)

Prints by Professional Members of the Graphic Arts Workshop, PGAC (April) [4]

Graphic Techniques Exhibition ♦

- Miami Museum of Modern Art (April 1960)
- Little Gallery Frame Shop, Kansas City (May 15–June 25)
- Loeb Student Center, New York University (Summer)
- Oklahoma Art Center, Oklahoma City (November 6–31
- Free Library of Philadelphia (January 13–February 18, 1961)
- Patterson State College, Wayne, Texas (February 25–March 15, 1961)
- F. A. R. Gallery, New York (June 5–26, 1961)
- Stanford Art Gallery, Stanford, California (until October 2, 1961)
- Hudson River Museum, Yonkers, New York (January 4–31, 1962)
- Tour of high schools in Westchester County, New York (throughout 1962)
- Tour of high schools in New York City (October 1962 to early 1963)

Summer Instructors: Harold Paris and Ansei Uchima, PGAC (opened June 3)

Stanley William Hayter and Atelier 17, PGAC (reception October 28) [5]

Contemporary Dutch Prints, Fourth Floor Gallery, Pratt Institute (November 16–30)

Lasansky and the Iowa Group, PGAC (unknown)

Prints from the St. George's Gallery, London, PGAC (unknown)

[Kobashi Yasuhide], PGAC (unknown)

1961

Prints: 1961, Associated American Artists, New York (April 10–29)

[Uchima Ansei], PGAC (unknown)

[Ferdinand Springer], PGAC (unknown)

[Hans Fischer], PGAC (unknown)

1962

Romas Viesulas, PGAC (January)

Lithographs by Christian Kruck

- PGAC (opened February 2)
- Fourth Floor Gallery, Pratt Institute (September 17–24)

Contemporary Prints from Yugoslavia, PGAC (May)

Thirty-Five Prizewinning American Prints ♦ [6]

- PGAC (September 24–October 12)
- Art Guild Gallery, Paducah, Kentucky (until April 22, 1963)
- State College Iowa, Cedar Falls (June 23–July 5, 1963)
- SUNY New Paltz (August 1963)
- Ball State College, Muncie, Indiana (September 1963)
- Wustum Museum, Racine, Wisconsin (September 1963)
- University of Illinois Library, Bloomington (November 16–December 8, 1963)
- Duke Alumni Lounge Gallery, Durham, North Carolina (September 1964)
- New Mexico Highlands University Art Gallery (February 1965)
- Blauvelt Free Library, Hackensack, New Jersey (until November 10, 1965)
- Central Library, Regina, Saskatchewan (April 1966)

Pratt Graphic Talent—1962, Lever House, New York (October 1–14)

Contemporary Canadian Prints [7]

- PGAC (October 15–31)
- Fourth floor exhibit cases, Pratt Institute (November 26–December 17)

Contemporary British Lithographs from Curwen Press, PGAC (October 16–November 9)

Contemporary Polish Graphics ♦
Main/Institute Gallery, Pratt Institute (November 5–26)
PGAC (January 1–22, 1963; April 1–25, 1963)

Contemporary Japanese Prints ♦ [8]
PGAC (November 12–December 14)
Fourth floor exhibit cases, Pratt Institute (November 17–30)
Emily Lowe Gallery, Hofstra University (December 3–January 3, 1963)

Prints by Faculty & Students ♦
PGAC (December 14–30)
Oklahoma State University (until February 4, 1963)

1963

Faculty Print Show from PGAC, fourth-floor exhibit cases, Pratt Institute (January 7–21)

Prints by Allen Barber, PGAC (January 7–25)

[PGAC group show], Brooks Atkinson Theater, 256 West Forty-Seventh Street, New York (opened February 19)

Benefit Print Sale, PGAC (February 25–March 4)

Carl Pickhardt: Prints and Drawings on New Testament Subjects, PGAC (May 1–15)

Faculty-Student Exhibit, PGAC (May 15–June)

50 Years of American Prints: Homer to Hopper, PGAC (September 23–October 29) [9]

Hodaka Yoshida and Masaji Yoshida: Woodblock Prints, PGAC (October 29–November 7)

1964

Benefit Print Sale, Associated American Artists, 605 Fifth Avenue (January 6–11)

Exhibition of Lithographs by Students of the Staatliche Akademie der Bildenden Künste, Stuttgart, Germany
Fourth floor exhibit cases, Pratt Institute (January 7–20)
PGAC (February 26–March 20)

Lithography from the Herron School of Art, PGAC (February 19–March 2)

First International Miniature Print Show, PGAC (April 6–30) ♦

Students of Sid Hammer, Arnold Singer, and Michael Ponce de León, PGAC (May 11–29)

Summer Session Faculty: Ed Casarella, Andrew Stasik, Benton Spruance, Clare Romano, Sergio Gonzalez-Tornero, PGAC (June 1–30)

100 Contemporary Prints, Jewish Museum, New York, NY (July 9–September 20)

Printmaking–A Family Affair, PGAC (September 21–October 16) ♦

Faculty Show: Prints by Al Blaustein and Andrew Stasik, PGAC (October 24–November 20)

Contemporary Prints from Yugoslavia, Bulgaria, and Poland, PGAC (November 23–December 31) ♦ [10]

PGAC Prints and Ten Prints by M. C. Escher, Fourth Floor Gallery, Pratt Institute (until November 13)

1965

Salute to 1965, American Greeting Gallery, Pan Am Building (January 5–February 5)

Faculty Prints #2: Michael Ponce de León and Arnold Singer, PGAC (February 1–28)

Contemporary Prints: Graphics by 100 Artists, Gallery 288, St. Louis, Missouri (until February 20)

Contemporary Prints from Nigeria and Romania and Russian Posters, PGAC (March 1–26)

Pratt Graphic Talent—1965, Lever House, New York (April 4–18)

Eugene Feldman: Off-Set Lithograph Prints, PGAC (opened April 26)

Woodcuts from Hong Kong and Taiwan, PGAC (April 2–23) [11]

[PGAC faculty and students], Gallery on the Green, Huntington, New York (April 4–30)

[Lithographs by PGAC students of Erich Mönch], Amerika-Haus, Stuttgart (unknown)

1966

Benefit Print Sale, Associated American Artists Gallery, 605 Fifth Avenue (January 3–8)

Second International Miniature Print Show, PGAC (April 8–30) ♦

Contemporary Serigraphs 1966, PGAC (opened September 30) ♦

Joryū Hanga Kyōkai, PGAC (opened November 11) [12]

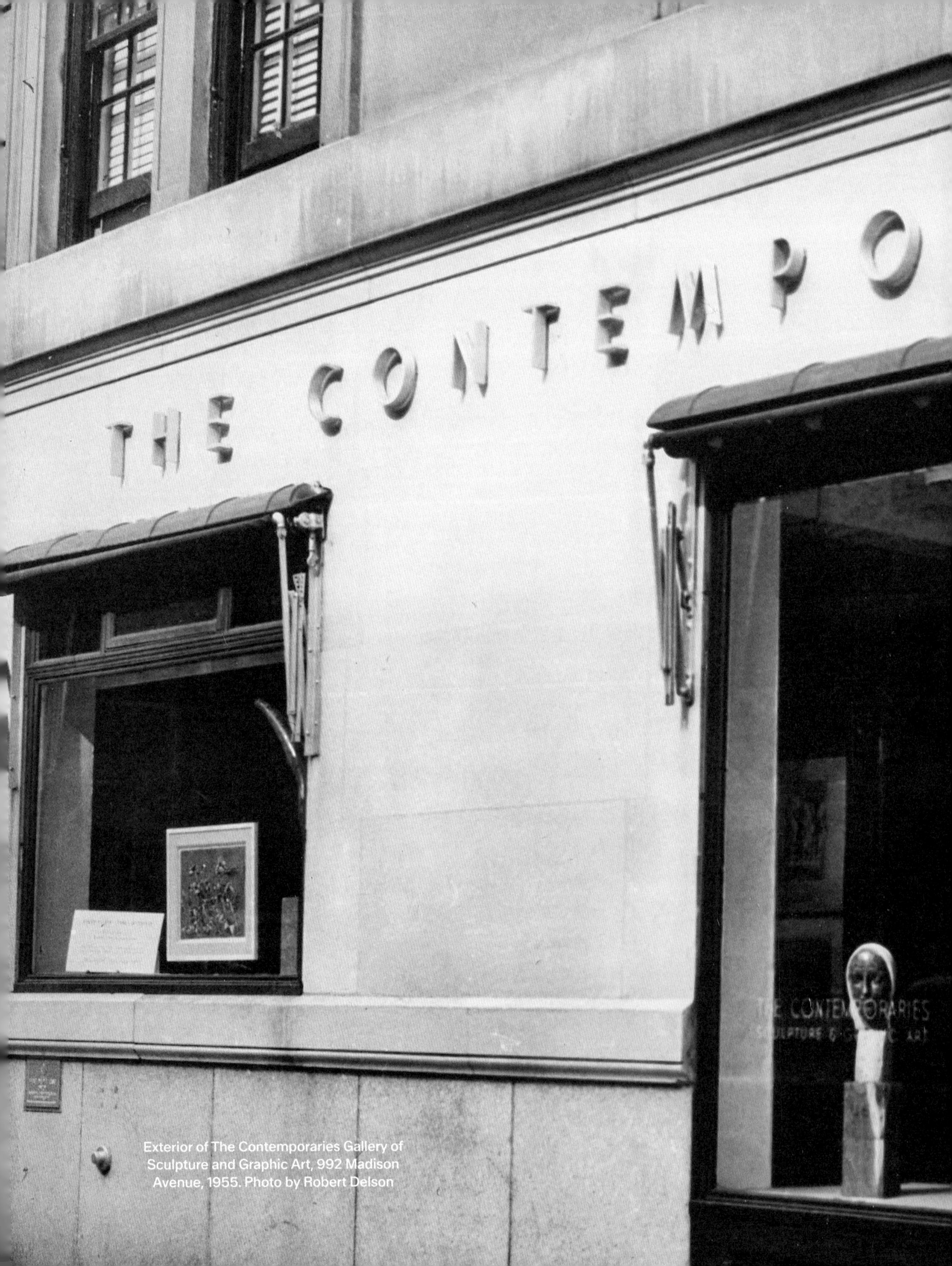

Exterior of The Contemporaries Gallery of Sculpture and Graphic Art, 992 Madison Avenue, 1955. Photo by Robert Delson

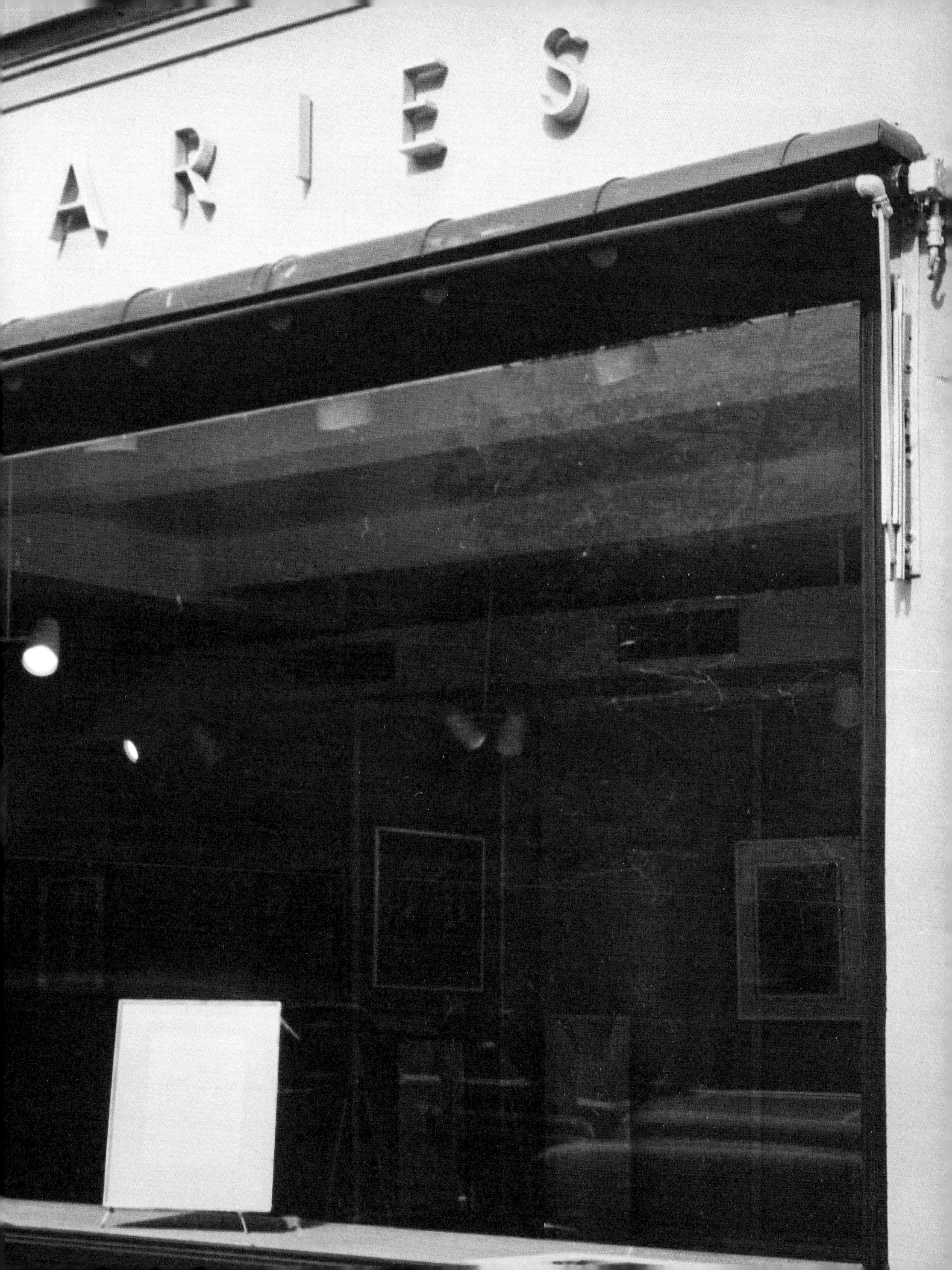
A R I E S

The following abbreviations for archival collections appear in the Notes.

AAA/SI
Archives of American Art, Smithsonian Institution, Washington, DC
CAP Clinton Adams Papers, 1934–2002
PCA Print Council of America records, 1951–2020

FEP
Fritz Eichenberg Papers, Robert B. Haas Family Arts Library, Yale University Library, New Haven, CT

MLP
Margaret Lowengrund Papers, courtesy The Lowengrund Family

MoMA
The Museum of Modern Art Archives, New York, NY
ALS Art Lending Service and Art Advisory Service Records

MOORE
Connelly Library, Moore College of Art & Design, Philadelphia, PA

NYPL MAD
Contemporaries Gallery records, 1951–57, Manuscripts and Archives Division, New York Public Library, New York

NYPL APP
The Miriam and Ira D. Wallach Division of Art, Prints and Photographs, New York Public Library, New York, NY

PAFA
Pennsylvania Academy of the Fine Art Archives, Philadelphia, PA

PIA
Pratt Institute Archives, Brooklyn, NY

RAC PGAC
Pratt Institute – Graphic Arts Center, Rockefeller Foundation records, Rockefeller Archive Center, Sleepy Hollow, NY

SUA
Special Collections Research Center, Syracuse University Libraries, Syracuse, NY
EMP Edward Millman Papers
RFP Richard Florsheim Papers

INTRODUCTION

1 For a compact list of this historicizing literature, see Regina Freyberger, "Into the New: Menschsein in der US-amerikanischen Kunst von Pollock bis Bourgeois," in *Into the New. Menschsein: Von Pollock bis Bourgeois* (Frankfurt am Main: Städel Museum, 2022), 22n3.
2 The earlier origins of the Print Boom are explored further in Lauren Rosenblum's forthcoming dissertation, "The Art, Craft and Labor of Lithography during the American Print Renaissance, 1952–68," Graduate Center of the City University of New York.
3 John Muench, as quoted in Judith Sobel and Martin Dibner, *John Muench: Paintings and Prints 1950–1990* (Freeport, ME: Maquoit Press, 1991), 9.
4 The new owners of The Contemporaries, which existed under the same name at 992 Madison Avenue until 1968, likely discarded materials left on site after Lowengrund's death.
5 Clinton Adams, *American Lithographers, 1900–1960: The Artists and Their Printers* (Albuquerque: University of New Mexico Press, 1983), 182–89; Clinton Adams, "Margaret Lowengrund and The Contemporaries," *The Tamarind Papers* 7 (Spring 1984): 17–23; Richard S. Field and Ruth Fine, *A Graphic Muse: Prints by Contemporary American Women* (New York: Hudson Hills Press in association with the Mount Holyoke College Art Museum, 1987), 5; Elizabeth G. Seaton, ed., *Paths to the Press: Printmaking and American Women Artists, 1910–1960* (Manhattan, KS: Marianna Kistler Beach Museum of Art, Kansas State University, 2006), 186–87.
6 Lowengrund attended the organization's earliest meetings in 1954, before its formal incorporation in 1956, and sat on subcommittees centered on university printmaking programs, workshops, and print clubs. "Meeting of the National Print Council," Alverthorpe Gallery, November 19, 1954, folder 4, box 1, PCA; Meeting minutes of the Print Council of America. September 22 and April 26, 1957, folder 25, box 1, PCA, AAA/SI.
7 Deborah Wye, *Artists & Prints: Masterworks from the Museum of Modern Art* (New York: Distributed Art Publishers, 2004), 23; Jennifer Field, "The New York School and the Evolution of Avant-Garde Printmaking in America" (PhD diss., Institute of Fine Arts, 2016), 11–14.
8 The definition of an "original print" was much debated in these midcentury decades (and still today). In the 1950s, the term meant artists personally marking an original design onto a matrix and, if possible, printing the matrix themselves. For a recent review of the effort to define the concept, see Debora Wood, "What is an Original Print? The Evolution of a Definition," *Print Quarterly* 39, no. 3 (September 2022): 274–286.
9 Esther Sparks, *Universal Limited Art Editions: A History and Catalogue: The First Twenty-Five Years* (New York: Abrams, 1989), 17.
10 Sparks, *Universal Limited Art Editions*, 53. Mary Callery visited The Contemporaries in January 1955, signing the gallery's visitors' register, NYPL MAD. Since the only extant visitor book for The Contemporaries ends in March 1955, there is no way to say for sure whether the Grosmans attended the opening for *Today (September 1955)*.
11 Riva Castleman, *Tatyana Grosman: A Scrapbook* (Bay Shore, NY: Universal Limited Art Editions, 2008), 60.
12 June Wayne, letter to Linda Sweeney, March 3, 1958, MLP; June Wayne, letter to Theo Gusten, November 1, [1957], folder 1, box 11, PCA, AAA/SI.
13 June Wayne, letter to Linda Sweeney.

ROSENBLUM

1 "A Model Workshop," *Art Digest* 29, no. 4 (November 15, 1954): 12.
2 "A Model Workshop," 12.
3 For a discussion on the importance of training in illustration for early twentieth-century print artists and the sidelining of this foundational art education in dominant histories of modern art, see Richard S. Field, *American Prints: 1900–1950* (New Haven, CT: Yale University Art Gallery, 1983).
4 Oscar Loeb, "The Observation Car," *Philadelphia Jewish Exponent*, January 9, 1931. For an overview of historic immigration patterns in relation to socioeconomic and religious differentiation between German and Russian Jewry in Philadelphia, see Murray Friedman, "Introduction: The Making of a National Jewish Community," in *Jewish Life in Philadelphia, 1830–1940* (Philadelphia: Institute for the Study of Human Issues, 1983), 1–25.
5 Lowengrund was a winner of the annual children's drawing competition sponsored by Wanamaker's Department Store. "Personal and Social," *Philadelphia Jewish Exponent*, January 5, 1917. As an older child she took classes at the Graphic Sketch Club, a free art center founded in 1898 by philanthropist Samuel S. Fleisher and located in the then predominantly Eastern European Jewish community in South Philadelphia. "Philadelphia Artist Triumphs Abroad," *Philadelphia Evening Public Ledger*, November 29, 1927. For more on the life and career of Margaret Lowengrund, see Ellen J. Benjamin, "Remembering the Imprint of an Artist, Trailblazer, and Mid-Twentieth-Century Promoter of American Printmaking" (unpublished typeset manuscript, September 14, 2022).
6 Philadelphia School of Design for Women, School List, 1916–1923, MOORE; Christine Jones Huber, *The Pennsylvania Academy and Its Women, 1850 to 1920* (Philadelphia: Pennsylvania Academy of the Fine Arts, 1973), 26–27.
7 School Circular, 1923–1924, RG.03.04.01, Records of PAFA the School, PAFA.
8 While the Philadelphia School of Design for Women's "School List" does not organize students by teacher, George Harding was the only faculty teaching illustration. Well-credentialed, he had studied at PAFA and with Howard Pyle, published in the *Saturday Evening Post* (starting in 1906), and served as an international correspondent for *Harper's Monthly Magazine* (between 1912 and 1914). Walter Kelly Hood, "Words, Wars, and Walls: The Art Life of George Matthews Harding," (PhD diss., Northwestern University, 1966); and Henry C. Pitz, "George Harding," *American Artist* 21, no. 10, issue 210 (December 1957): 29–34.
9 School Circular, 1923–1924.
10 For more on Lowengrund's published illustrations, see Ellen J. Benjamin's essay in this catalogue.
11 For a discussion of PAFA's descent into institutional conservatism by the 1930s, see Frank H. Goodyear, "History of the Pennsylvania Academy of the Fine Arts, 1805–1976," in *In This Academy: The Pennsylvania Academy of the Fine Arts, 1805–1976: A Special Bicentennial Exhibition*, ed. Frank H. Goodyear (Philadelphia: Pennsylvania Academy of the Fine Arts, 1976), 44–45. The ASL was founded in 1875 by defecting National Academy of Design students who sought a modern education in which emerging artists learned directly from established figures. Art Students League, *No Day Without a Line* (New York: Art Students League of New York, 1999).
12 Elizabeth Robins Pennell, *The Life and Letters of Joseph Pennell*, vol. II (Boston: Little, Brown, and Co., 1929), 271, 273.
13 While the European revival in etching arrived in the United States before the turn of the twentieth century, the 1910s saw a reemergence of etching that, by the 1920s, transformed into a vast commercial enterprise producing an overabundance of derivative and inexpensive graphics. Gladys Engel Lang and Kurt Lang described the "etching craze" in *Etched in Memory: The Building and Survival of Artistic Reputation* (Chapel Hill: University of North Carolina Press, 1990), 72–73.
14 Having attended the Ohio Mechanics Institute to study commercial printing before attending the ASL, Charles Locke was at first a graphics student alongside Lowengrund before taking over lithography instruction. Pam Koob, "Printmaking Instruction at The Art Students League of New York," in *A Century on Paper: Prints by Art Students League Artists, 1901–2001* (New York: Art Students League of New York, 2002), 3–4.
15 Helen T. Reinthaler, "Teaching the Graphic Arts in America," *American Printer and Lithographer* 79 (August 5, 1924): 66. Reinthaler describes a visit to Heywood Strasser & Voigt Litho. Co., NY, which in 1918 had printed Pennell's poster supporting the Allied forces' war effort.
16 While it was uncommon for artists working in lithography during this period to participate in edition printing, Pennell, who had begun seriously working in the medium around 1895, initiated a collaboration with the Ketterlinus Lithographic Manufacturing Company, Philadelphia for *The Panama Canal Series* (1912). James Watrous, *A Century of American Printmaking, 1880–1980* (Madison: University of Wisconsin Press, 1984), 46.
17 Invented in 1796 by Alois Senefelder, lithography experienced varied reception in England, France, and the United States, the countries around which Pennell circulated at the turn of the nineteenth century. Georgia Barnhill, ed., *With a French Accent: American Lithography to 1860* (Worcester, MA: American Antiquarian Society, 2012); Peter C. Marzio, *The Democratic Art:*

Chromolithography, 1840–1900 (Boston: David R. Godine, 1980); Kate Nichols, Rebecca Wade, and Gabriel Williams, eds. *Art versus Industry?: New Perspectives on Visual and Industrial Cultures in Nineteenth-Century Britain* (Manchester: Manchester University Press, 2018).

18 Pennell, *"Life and Letters,"* II: 277.

19 In a review of the Anderson Galleries exhibition, one art critic observed that "Mr. Pennell has the gift of infusing his pupils with his own enthusiasm for work and insistence upon craftsmanship." Continuing that "the women students make an unusually brave showing," the critic then cites Lowengrund by name. "Pennell's Class in Graphic Arts Makes Good Showing," *Brooklyn Daily Eagle*, April 5, 1925.

20 Notably, Whistler had recruited his friend Pennell to travel to Paris in 1893 to print a series of etchings of shopfronts. Joseph Pennell and Elizabeth Robins Pennell, *The Life of James McNeill Whistler*, vol. 1 (Philadelphia: J. B. Lippincott Company, 1908), 141–2. Examples of Lowengrund's early work, including *Fish Market, Bronx* (1922) and *Poultry Market* (1922), can be found in collection of The Lowengrund Family.

21 The Curtis Publishing Company of Philadelphia owned both the *Philadelphia Evening Ledger* and the *New York Evening Post*. Lowengrund produced work for the same editor at both papers over a four-year span. Margaret Lowengrund, "Fine Art and Commercial Art," in *The Art of the Artist: Theories and Techniques of Art by the Artists Themselves*, ed. Arthur Zaidenberg (New York: Crown Publishers, 1951), 151.

22 Lowengrund, "Fine Art and Commercial Art," 1951, 151.

23 Hartrick taught illustration at the London County Council's Central School of Arts and Crafts from 1914 to 1929. During the 1890s, the Scotland-born artist worked for weekly newspapers in London, including the *Graphic*, *Daily Graphic*, and *Pall Mall Budget* and was a committed lithographer throughout his lifetime. Archibald Standish Hartrick, *A Painter's Pilgrimage through Fifty Years* (Cambridge, England: The University Press, 1939); Michael MacLeod, *Archibald Standish Hartrick, Thomas Barclay Hennell, Vincent Henry Lines* (London: Goldsmiths College, 1979), 8–11.

24 Kemille S. Moore, "The Revival of Artistic Lithography in England, 1890–1913" (PhD diss., University of Washington, 2002), 205–236; and Joseph Pennell, "The Senefelder Club," in *The Senefelder Club* (London: XXI Gallery, Adelphi, 1922), 21.

25 For more on this topic, see Ellen J. Benjamin's essay in this volume.

26 "American Girl Artist Back with Honor Record Abroad," *New York Evening Post*, November 26, 1927. This Salon gained a reputation for the launch of cubism during the first two decades of the century and then, after World War I, for showcasing international artists—primarily displaced Europeans—who were working across style and who were mostly based in the Montparnasse neighborhood. During the 1920s it would become known as the School of Paris. Kate Kangaslahti, "Foreign Artists and the École de Paris: Critical and Institutional Ambivalence between the Wars," in *Academics, Pompiers, Official Artists and the Arrière-garde: Defining Modern and Traditional in France, 1900–1960*, ed. Natalie Adamson and Toby Norris (Newcastle upon Tyne: Cambridge Scholars, 2009), 165–91.

27 Dodgson selected the print out of an exhibition held by members of the Senefelder Club. "American Girl Artist Back."

28 "American Girl Artist Back."

29 "American Girl Artist Back."

30 The studio in which this series of approximately a dozen prints were executed remains unidentified.

31 Lilly received a Pulitzer Prize in 1932 while working for the *New York World-Telegram*. Public service defined his later career, including stints on New York City's Tax Commission and at the United Nations. He eventually founded a public relations firm. "Joseph Lilly, 64, Ex-City Official," *New York Times*, February 24, 1965.

32 For more on this topic, see the essay by Ellen J. Benjamin in this volume.

33 Max Fraser, "Hands Off the Machine: Workers' Hands and Revolutionary Symbolism in the Visual Culture of 1930s America," *American Art* 27, no. 2 (Summer 2013): 95–117.

34 Operating between 1935 and 1943, the state-administered FAP had sections dedicated to various visual arts. The Graphic Arts Division (1935–42) offered opportunity in all printmaking processes with particular emphasis on lithography and screenprint. Elizabeth Olds, "Prints for Mass Production," in *Art for the Millions: Essays from the 1930s by Artists and Administrators of the WPA Federal Art Project*, ed. Francis V. O'Connor (Greenwich, CT: New York Graphic Society, 1973), 142–144.

35 Lowengrund likely worked in the printshop while it was located at 6 East Thirty-Ninth Street, its first address.

36 Helen Langa, "Introduction: Social Viewpoint Prints, Cultural Democracy, and Leftist Politics," in *Radical Art: Printmaking and the Left in 1930s New York* (Berkeley: University of California Press, 2004), 1–9.

37 Russell T. Limbach, "Lithography: Stepchild of the Arts," in O'Connor, *Art for the Millions*, 145–47. Elizabeth Gaede Seaton also identifies period rhetoric around the democracy of federally sponsored printmaking standing in distinction from the "elitist tendencies" of the Etching Revival and discusses printmaking as a function of New Deal programs' advocacy of "cultural democracy." See Seaton's "Federal Prints and Democratic Culture: The Graphic Arts Division of the Works Progress Administration Federal Art Project, 1935–1943" (PhD diss., Northwestern University, 2000), 9–10. See also Langa, *Radical Art*, 1–2.

38 Clinton Adams, *American Lithographers, 1900–1960: The Artists and Their Printers* (Albuquerque: University of New Mexico Press, 1983), 123–26.

39 Founded in 1919, the school began hosting studio art courses in 1932 and added printmaking in 1936. Andrew Hemingway, *Artists on the Left: American Artists and the Communist Movement, 1926–1956* (New Haven: Yale University Press, 2002), 31. During the 1939–40 academic year, Lowengrund taught in the art department alongside printmakers Will Barnet, Harry Sternberg, and Fritz Eichenberg, her future colleague at Pratt Institute. *Curriculum The New School for Social Research, 1939–1940*, NS050101.01, New School course catalog collection, The New School Archives, The New School for Social Research, New York.

40 The school hosted the breakout sessions associated with the three-day convening of the AAC in February 1936. Peter M. Rutkoff and William B. Scott, *New School: A History of the New School for Social Research* (New York: Free Press, 1986). For a succinct history of the AAC, see Hemingway, *Artists on the Left*, 123–25.

41 While Lowengrund clearly engaged with the key cultural organizations, the vehemence of her party-line politics remains unstated and therefore unknown. She could be characterized as a less radical "fellow-travelling liberal" or a "small-c communist." Helen Langa, "'At Least Half the Pages Will Consist of Pictures': New Masses and Politicized Visual Art," *American Periodicals* 21, no. 1 (2011), 26; Michael Denning, *The Cultural Front: The Laboring of American Culture in the Twentieth Century* (New York: Verso, 1996), xvii, 5. Regardless of Lowengrund's CPUSA status, she was later mentioned in the 1944 Senate hearings on un-American propaganda activities due to these affiliations. Special Committee on Un-American Activities, *Investigation of Un-American Propaganda Activities in the United States: Hearings Before a Special Committee on Un-American Activities*, 78th Congress, 2nd session (1944), Committee Print, Appendix pt. 9: Communist Front Organizations, 1071, 1073, 1093.

42 Matthew Baigell and Julia Williams, eds., *Artists Against War and Fascism: Papers of the First American Artists Congress* (New Brunswick, NJ: Rutgers University Press, 1986), 13.

43 Exhibitions included: *America Today*, Guild Gallery, NY, December 1936; *Framed and Hung*, ACA Gallery, NY, February–March 1937; *Second Annual Exhibition*, John Wanamaker Department Store, NY, May 1938; and *Art in a Skyscraper*, 444 Madison Avenue, NY, February 1939, among others. For a discussion of An American Group exhibitions, see Hemingway, *Artists on the Left*, 125–30.

44 Exhibitions included: *Waterfront Art Show*, New School for Social Research, NY, February 1937; *Roofs for 40,000,000*, La Maison Française, Rockefeller Center, NY, April 1938; *Contemporary American Art*, American British Art Center, NY, March 1944; and their annual exhibitions between 1937 and 1940. For a review of An American Group, see Hemingway, *Artists on the Left*, 133–36.

45 Langa, *Radical Art*, 217. For a discussion of the Artists' Union, see Hemingway, *Artists on the Left*, 85–87.

46 *The Woman Today* 2, no. 2 (May 1937): 22; John T. Bernard, "Give Us a Program," *New Masses* 24, no. 10 (August 31, 1937): 3–5. Helen Langa observed that the image program for *New Masses*, as it deradicalized its Marxist politics to align with the Popular Front in the mid- to late 1930s, drew from the FAP Graphic Arts Division. Langa, "'At Least Half,'" 37.

47 Mary Ellen Green, "Artist Dropped in at the Labor Temple Just to Dance, and She Has Been at the Bar for Weeks—Doing a Mural," *New York Post*, November 20, 1939. Anton Refregier's program for a mural in the building's dining room remains unknown. "New York Labor Temple, 1939–1940," folder 28, box 16, Anton Refregier Papers, ca. 1900–ca. 1990, AAA/SI. The American Socialist Party oversaw this uptown organization for unionists in the heart of the German-American Yorkville neighborhood, and it is not to be confused with the radical, Presbyterian-affiliated Labor Temple located downtown (1910–57). Charles Clos, "Memories," *New York Times*, April 14, 1985.

48 Lowengrund hosted a "regular morning program" on WKNY, according to a clipping in MLP from the *Kingston Evening Leader* describing her broadcast at the 1947 Ulster County Fair and Farmers' Field Day. For more on Lowengrund's work as a columnist in the Woodstock area, see Ellen J. Benjamin's essay in this catalogue.

49 The scope of Lowengrund's involvement with WAA's leadership is not yet fully known, but she at least served on the executive board between 1951 and 1953, variously as recording secretary and head of publicity. Richard S. Thibault, Jr., "Five New Members Voted by Artists," *The Kingston Daily Freeman*, August 15, 1952; Letter from Ralph L. Wickiser to David Smith, August 26, 1952, folder 1952 May–September No. 3, box 2, Estate of David Smith, New York; "Woodstock Artists Elect," *Art Digest* 25, no. 20 (September 15, 1951): 3.

50 By 1940, the town's population grew to approximately two thousand year-round residents. Alf Evers, *Woodstock: History of an American Town* (Woodstock: Overlook Press, 1987), 611. See also Tom Wolf and Bruce Weber, *Woodstock Artists Association: One Hundred Years of Community and Art* (Woodstock: Woodstock Artists Association, 2019).

51 Tom Wolf, *Woodstock's Art Heritage: The Permanent Collection of the Woodstock*

Artists Association (Woodstock: Overlook Press, 1987), 27. For a discussion of Woodstock during the war years see Richard Heppner, "Homeland Security–Woodstock during the First Months of World War II," in *Remembering Woodstock: From the Archives and Publications of the Historical Society of Woodstock* (Charleston, SC: History Press, 2008), 83–89.

52 "Margaret Lowengrund, in the ACA Gallery," *Sun* (New York), April 7, 1945; "The Good Life," *Art Digest* 19, no. 2 (April 1945): 22. The Rudolph Galleries opened in 1939 under the direction of Rudolph Frederick Fiolic. It was the first commercial gallery in Woodstock and exhibited prominent members of its artist community. "Rudolph, of Famed Rudolph Galleries, Celebrates His 65th Birthday This Month," *Woodstock Townsman*, July 13, 1955. Barry Shank, "Subject, Commodity, Marketplace: The American Artists Group and the Mass Production of Distinction." *Radical History Review* 76 (2000): 25–52.

53 Edward Alden Jewell, "Prints Displayed of America in War," *New York Times*, October 5, 1943; Ellen Landau, *Artists for Victory* (Washington, DC: Library of Congress, 1983), 3, 65–66.

54 The press, set up in WAA's basement in the late 1920s, was the first that was widely accessible to area artists. Its first master printer, Grant Arnold, arrived in 1930 under the auspices of the FAP. He left Woodstock in 1939. Clinton Adams, *The Woodstock Ambience, 1917–1939* (Albuquerque: Tamarind Institute and the University of New Mexico, 1981), 7–8.

55 B. K., "Painter-Printers at Seligmann," *Art Digest* 25, no. 5 (December 1950): 16–17.

56 From the late 1940s through the 1950s, a number of modern printmaking groups promoted the medium through exhibitions. These included: the Graphic Circle (founded 1947), the Printmakers (exhibitions began in 1950 and involved Lowengrund), and 14 Painter-Printmakers. Christina Weyl, "Networks of Abstraction: Postwar Printmaking and Women Artists of Atelier 17," *Archives of American Art*, January 8, 2014, https://www.aaa.si.edu/essay/christina-weyl.html.

WEYL

1 Margaret Lowengrund, "The Director," from proposal for "The Contemporaries Graphic Arts Gallery and Workshop," December 19, 1955, folder 3494, box 405, RAC PGAC.

2 Lowengrund, "The Director."

3 Lowengrund, "The Director."

4 "New Studio and Gallery for Graphics," *Art Digest* 26, no. 4 (November 15, 1951): 16; Advertisement for "Lithography Studio-Workshop," *Art Digest* 26, no. 4 (November 15, 1951): 30. Lowengrund's original press release, referenced in *Art Digest*, is no longer extant.

5 "New Studio and Gallery."

6 "New Studio and Gallery."

7 Dore Ashton, "S. A. G. A. Annual Lacks Character," *Art Digest* 28, no. 2 (February 15, 1954): 17.

8 The Contemporaries' Visitors' Register, NYPL MAD. John Muench, briefly professional printer at The Contemporaries, also noted the exceptional crowd, as quoted in Judith Sobel and Martin Dibner, *John Muench: Paintings and Prints 1950–1990* (Freeport, ME: Maquoit Press, 1991), 9.

9 On the size of the workshop, see Charles B. Fahs, memo dated February 1, 1955, folder 3494, box 405, RAC PGAC. On the budget, see John Muench, letter to Clinton Adams, December 6, 1981, Lithography File–General "M," CAP, AAA/SI.

10 For Lowengrund's career as a critic, see Ellen J. Benjamin's essay in this catalogue.

11 Margaret Lowengrund, "Art Today," *Ulster County Sunday News*, [November 2], 1947, MLP.

12 Lowengrund herself worked with Miller. See her print, *Along the Road* (ca. 1930s), Ben and Beatrice Goldstein Foundation Collection (no. 301), Prints & Photographs Division, Library of Congress, Washington, DC.

13 Margaret Lowengrund, "Metropolitan Surveys the Art of Lithography," *Art Digest* 23, no. 6 (December 15, 1948): 19. Italics in the original.

14 June Wayne, "To Restore the Art of the Lithograph in the United States," folder 0008, box 186, June Wayne Papers (Collection 562), UCLA Library Special Collections, Charles E. Young Research Library, University of California, Los Angeles.

15 Although eyewitness accounts describe Lowengrund as a confident printer, Clinton Adams, who laid the foundation of scholarship on Lowengrund during the 1980s, was skeptical of her abilities. See Richard E. Thibaut, "Lithographic Presses Available to Artists," *Kingston Daily Freeman*, July 17, 1952. John Muench, letter to Clinton Adams, January 3, 1983, Lithography File-General "M"; Arnold Singer, letter to Clinton Adams, September 21, 1979, Lithography File-General "S"; and Michael Ponce de León, letter to Clinton Adams, February 23, 1983, Lithography File-General "N-R," CAP, AAA/SI.

16 Margaret Lowengrund, letter to Edward Millman, February 28, 1952, "Lowengrund, Margaret," box 2, EMP, SUA.

17 *Laughing Bug* is likely not the stone with the "subtle wash" that Lowengrund and Millman corresponded about in winter 1952 (see note 16), since he decided not to edition it.

18 Lowengrund resurrected WAA's basement studio, which Grant Arnold first used to print lithographs during the 1930s. By 1952, it had two double-geared lithographic presses, and she further equipped it with donations from the community. WAA hosted a festive opening party on July 17, 1952 for "The Graphic Workshop," as The Contemporaries' seasonal outpost was called. Richard E. Thibaut, "Association Unique," *Kingston Daily Freeman*, June 17, 1952; Thibaut, "Lithographic Presses"; Janice La Motta, Tom Wolf, and Bruce Weber, *Woodstock Artists Association: One Hundred Years of Community and Art* (Woodstock: Woodstock Artists Association, 2019), 53–55, 273–74.

19 Michael Ponce de León, letter to Clinton Adams, March 12, 1983, Lithography File-General "N-R," CAP, AAA/SI.

20 Richard E. Thibaut, "Woodstock News: Lowengrund Exhibit Extended in New York," *Kingston Daily Freeman*, March 13, 1952. Prominent Woodstock residents—Milton Avery and Sally Michel, Andrée Ruellan and John Taylor, Adolf Dehn, Alexander Archipenko, and Marion Greenwood—fill the pages of the gallery's visitors' register.

21 Advertisement for "The Contemporaries," *Art Digest* 27, no. 2 (October 15, 1952): 28; advertisement for Day's class, *Art Digest* 27, no. 4 (November 15, 1952): 28.

22 Lowengrund presented her first extended vision for The Contemporaries in "New Course in Lithography, New York & Woodstock," ca. spring 1952, "The Contemporaries" folder, box 11, RFP, SUA.

23 Lowengrund, "New Course in Lithography"; Thibaut, "Lithographic Presses."

24 Lowengrund's assistant Susanne Spaeth outlined fees in a letter to Alexander Archipenko, February 21, 1956, Box 2, Alexander Archipenko Papers, 1904–1986, bulk 1930–1964, AAA/SI. Thank you to Alexandra Keiser, Research Coordinator at The Archipenko Foundation, for sharing a copy of this letter.

25 A screening of Neal's thirty-minute film, *Color Lithography: An Art Medium* (1955), took place at The Contemporaries' new Graphic Art Centre at 1343 Third Avenue on November 6, 1955. The Contemporaries, postcard to Karl Kup, October 29, 1955, Margaret Lowengrund folder, NYPL AAP. For an advertisement describing the film, see "Introducing a New Prize-Winning Film: 'Color Lithography ... an Art Medium,'" 1955, box 17, FEP.

26 "A Model Workshop," *Art Digest* 11, no. 2 (November 15, 1954): 12.

27 The gallery did not consistently produced checklists, and this roster is based on reviews and archival research. Lowengrund sold the gallery to Ian Woodner sometime in fall 1957, and the gallery continued as "The Contemporaries" until 1968, but with different priorities and no ties to the Pratt-Contemporaries Graphic Art Centre. Theo Gusten, letter to June Wayne, December 3, 1958, folder 1 (Tamarind), box 11, PCA, AAA/SI; Robert Kipniss, *A Working Artist's Life* (Hanover, NH: University Press of New England, 2011), 156.

28 Lowengrund had many gallery assistants, including Kay Vaczek, Lovell Wood, Suzanne Berry, Marcia London, and Karl Lunde. Lunde ran the gallery until 1966.

29 Margaret Lowengrund Lilly, "Artist at Large," *Woodstock Weekly Window*, [April 15], 1948. For more on the ICA manifesto, see Richard Meyer, "Midcentury Contemporary (1948)," chap. 4 in *What Was Contemporary Art?* (Cambridge, MA: MIT Press, 2013).

30 Margaret Lowengrund, "Modern Museum Shows Master Prints," *Art Digest* 23, no. 1 (June 1949): 12. In the "modern school," she featured masters from Europe (Van Gogh, Bonnard, Toulouse-Lautrec) and the United States (Hopper, Marin, Sloan, Bellows). Among the "latest work," she cited Sue Fuller, Stanley William Hayter, Harold Paris, Boris Margo, Minna Citron, Harry Bertoia.

31 Margaret Lowengrund, letter to Richard Florsheim, April 22, 1953, "The Contemporaries" folder, box 11, RFP, SUA.

32 Dore Ashton directly contrasted the vivacity of *Graphic Outlook '54* to the "malaise" of the Society of American Graphic Artists' 1954 annual: "Prints: S. A. G. A. Annual Lacks Character," *Art Digest* 28, no. 2 (February 15, 1954): 17. For discussion of the many postwar print annuals, see Christina Weyl, "Circulating Modernist Prints," chap. 5 in *The Women of Atelier 17: Modernist Printmaking in Midcentury New York* (New Haven: Yale University Press, 2019).

33 Press release for *Graphic Outlook 1957*, ca. January 1957, NYPL MAD.

34 Rosalie Berkowitz, "Graphic Arts Workshop," *The Wasp* 1, no. 5 (July 26, 1952): 2; Dore Ashton, "Painters as Printers," *Art Digest* 26, no. 1 (February 1, 1952): 9.

35 Margaret Lowengrund, "The Purpose," from proposal for "The Contemporaries Graphic Arts Gallery and Workshop," December 19, 1955, folder 3494, box 405, RAC PGAC.

36 For more, see Sarah Archer's essay in this catalogue.

37 With small edition sizes, The Contemporaries differentiated itself from the International Graphic Arts Society, which issued editions of 210. Margaret Lowengrund, "The Activities," from proposal for "The Contemporaries Graphic Arts Gallery and Workshop," December 19, 1955, folder 3494, box 405, RAC PGAC.

38 The Art Lending Service, begun in 1951, was an initiative of the museum's Junior Council. Artists who consigned prints through The Contemporaries included Thomas George, E. Powis Jones, Zoran Antonio Mušič, Hasegawa Saburō, Gabor Peterdi; see "The Contemporaries," folder V.102, ALS, MoMA.

39 Lee Chesney, for one, believed The Contemporaries and Weyhe Gallery were the only two galleries dedicated to contemporary graphic artists. Lee Chesney, "Printmaking Today," *College Art Journal* 19, no. 2 (Winter 1959): 158–65.

40 Pairings included Arthur Deshaies and Richard Lippold (1952); Peter Lipman-Wulf and June Wayne (1953); Jane Wasey and Carol Summers (1954); Dean Meeker and Peter Lipman-Wulf (1955); Irène Hamar and Fayga Ostrower (1955); George Biddle and Hélène Sardeau (1956); Edward Giobbi, Thomas George, and Dean Carter (1956); José de Creeft, Zoran Antonio Mušič, and Giorgio Morandi (1956); Lindsay Daen, Zoran Antonio Mušič, and Wakita Kazu (1957).

41 Names of exhibitors are pulled from this widely reviewed show: "New York Notes," *Arts* 30 (October 1955): 8; Dore Ashton, "The Contemporaries Gallery Reopens,"

New York Times, October 10, 1955; Emily Genauer, "Print-and-Sculpture Gala," *New York Herald Tribune*, October 16, 1955; L. G., "Contemporaries Group," *Arts* 30 (November 1955): 50; Charles Z. Offin, "From the Editor's Notebook," *Pictures on Exhibit* 19 (November 1955): 14.

42 Margaret Lowengrund, letter to David Smith, August 12, 1954, Estate of David Smith. Hirshhorn purchased two pieces by José de Creeft during Lowengrund's lifetime, and he continued to buy from The Contemporaries after 1957.

43 Fahs memo, February 1, 1955.

44 In fall 1954 Lowengrund circulated an appeal to curators, collectors, gallerists, and philanthropists looking for support for an enlarged Graphic Art Center. See Margaret Lowengrund, letter to James Johnson Sweeney, October 15, 1954, folder 41, box 261, James Johnson Sweeney records (A0001), Solomon R. Guggenheim Museum Archives, New York.

45 Edward F. D'Arms, memos dated October 24, December 5, and December 9, 1955, and February 9, 1956; Edward F. D'Arms, letter to Margaret Lowengrund, January 16, 1956, folder 3494, box 405, RAC PGAC.

46 Lowengrund, "The Director."

47 See Jillian Russo's essay in this catalogue.

48 For inventories, see Margaret Lowengrund, "Notes on The Contemporaries Graphic Art Centre," February 27, 1956; Fritz Eichenberg, letter to Charles B. Fahs, September 14, 1956, folder 3494, box 405, RAC PGAC.

49 D'Arms memo, December 9, 1955.

50 Charles B. Fahs, notes from meeting with Margaret Lowengrund, February 9, 1956, folder 3494, box 405, RAC PGAC.

51 Fritz Eichenberg, confidential memo to Albert Christ-Janer, October 17, 1960, box 18, FEP. Eichenberg had known Lowengrund since 1938 when both taught at The New School for Social Research.

52 Fritz Eichenberg, memo to Francis Horn (president of Pratt Institute), ca. February 1956, folder 3494, box 405, RAC PGAC.

53 Francis Horn, letter to Charles B. Fahs, August 29, 1956, folder 3494, box 405, RAC PGAC.

54 Tentative budget, Pratt-Contemporaries Graphic Art Centre, October 1, 1956, folder 3494, box 405, RAC PGAC.

55 Francis Horn, letter to Charles B. Fahs.

56 Edward F. D'Arms, memo regarding first meeting of Advisory Committee, Pratt-Contemporaries Graphic Art Centre, January 17, 1957, folder 3495, box 405, RAC PGAC. Lowengrund had been diagnosed and operated on as early as spring 1955. Margaret Lowengrund, letter to Carroll Edward Hogan (Albright Art Gallery), June 4, 1955, Contemporaries Gallery Records, NYPL MAD.

57 Margaret Lowengrund, "Report: The Pratt-Contemporaries Graphic Art Centre," June 20, 1957, Annual Reports, 1956–57, Records of the President's Office, PIA.

58 Fritz Eichenberg, letter to Charles B. Fahs, December 5, 1957; Meeting minutes, Advisory Board of Pratt-Contemporaries Graphic Art Centre, December 9, 1957, folder 3495, box 405, RAC PGAC.

59 Charles B. Fahs, notes from phone conversation with Fritz Eichenberg, October 23, 1958, folder 3495, box 405, RAC PGAC.

60 See Seong Moy's comments in Edward F. D'Arms, memo, January 17, 1957.

61 Meeting minutes, Advisory Board of Pratt-Contemporaries Graphic Art Centre, January 17, 1957, folder 3495, box 405, RAC PGAC. After her passing, Lowengrund became a scapegoat for the presence at PGAC of "dilettantes" and "dear old ladies." Just after the new Graphic Arts Centre opened, Lowengrund ran advertisements explicitly marketing classes to amateurs and children, recognizing tuition was essential to the Centre's bottom line. Lowengrund cited increased enrollment in a profit and loss statement she shared with the Rockefeller Foundation. See income and expenses listed in her "Notes on The Contemporaries Graphic Art Centre," February 27, 1956; advertisement for The Contemporaries Graphic Art Centre, *Arts* 30 (January 1956): 65; Aaron Berkman, "Graphic Arts for the Amateur," *Art News* 54, no. 10 (February 1956): 8. For posthumous discussion of Lowengrund, see Fritz Eichenberg, Report to the Advisory Board of PGAC, March 8, 1962, box 17, FEP; Arnold Singer, interview with Clinton Adams, September 21, 1979, Lithography File-General "S," CAP, AAA/SI. June Wayne, Lowengrund's posthumous champion, vehemently rejected the "dilettante" label when reviewing a draft of Clinton Adams's *American Lithographers, 1900–1960*. June Wayne, letter to Clinton Adams, August 2, 1982, Wayne File, folder 1: Correspondence, 1975–84, CAP, AAA/SI.

62 Fritz Eichenberg, letter to Boyd Compton, August 26, 1959, folder 3495, box 405, RAC PGAC.

63 Reporting about enrollment was not consistent across time. Figures generally count unique students and not the number of courses in which these students enrolled. Cited figures are pulled from: Fritz Eichenberg, "Annual Report to Members of the Advisory Board, Pratt-Contemporaries Graphic Art Centre," June 1958, Reports, 1955–63, Records of the School of Art and Design, Reports, 1955–63, PIA; Fritz Eichenberg, "Final Report to the Rockefeller Foundation," 6, December 1962, folder 3496, box 405, RAC PGAC.

64 Fritz Eichenberg and Andrew Stasik, "Progress Report," 1, ca. 1964, folder 3496, box 405, RAC PGAC.

65 Eichenberg, "Final Report," 5; Eichenberg and Stasik, "Progress Report," 1.

66 "Pratt Graphic Art Center: Extension and Adventure," *Pratt Alumnus* 67, no. 2 (April 1965): 6. For more about the international dimensions of PGAC, see Noriko Kuwahara's and Rachel Vogel's essays in this catalogue.

67 No resource yet exists to catalogue the hundreds of editions printed at PGAC. Some prints have an identifying blind stamp, but many do not.

68 Eichenberg, "Annual Report," June 1958, 1.

69 Eichenberg and Stasik, "Progress Report," ca. 1964, 1.

70 Eichenberg, "Final Report," 8.

71 Clinton Adams, *American Lithographers, 1900–1960: The Artists and Their Printers* (Albuquerque: University of New Mexico Press, 1983), 200.

72 Although Ford Foundation funding was intended for only three printers, a larger number likely shared this money due to visa and travel issues. Like much of PGAC's history, documentation is sparse and spotty. Albert Christ-Janer, "Financial Accounting" sent to Ford Foundation, January 25, 1963, 06000134, box R0941, Series Grants, Ford, RAC.

73 "Print Sale at Pratt Graphic Art Center," February 8, 1963, Press Releases: 1961–67, Records of the Pratt Graphics Center, PIA.

74 "Prints to Be Sold for Pratt Center," *New York Times*, December 26, 1963; John Canaday, "A Wee Plug for a Worthy Cause," *New York Times*, January 5, 1964.

75 Nonprofit and university-based workshops founded in the years after PGAC also relied heavily on sales. Sarah Kirk Hanley, "INK Blog: University-Based Workshops Respond to the Crisis in Higher Education," *Art in Print* 5, no. 1 (May 2015), https://artinprint.org/article/ink-blog-university-based-workshops-respond-to-the-crisis-in-higher-education.

76 "Minutes of Discussion Following the Report of the Director to the Members of the Advisory Board of the PGAC," April 18, 1963, box 18, FEP.

77 June Wayne recognized this skills gap, realizing that Tamarind-trained printers did not necessarily have business backgrounds nor the ability to market and sell the editions they printed. In the mid-1960s, she developed several practical guides to close that gap. See *A Study of the Marketing of the Original Print* (Los Angeles: Tamarind Lithography Workshop, 1964) and *Gallery Facility Planning for Marketing Original Prints* (Los Angeles: Tamarind Lithography Workshop, 1967).

78 Dore Ashton, "Art: A Long Tradition in Printmaking," *New York Times*, February 5, 1959.

79 The group included Gabor Peterdi, Stanley William Hayter, Yoshida Hodaka and Yoshida Masaji, Mario Avati, Douglass Howell, and Sheldon Keck, among others.

80 "Ingram Merrill Foundation Grant Awarded to Pratt Center for Contemporary Printmaking," January 31, 1967, Communications June 1966–June 1967, box 2, Records of the Department of Communications and Marketing, PIA.

81 Fritz Eichenberg, "Report to the Advisory Board of the Pratt Graphic Art Center, April 18, 1963, box 18, FEP. *Artist's Proof* offers one of the best records of PGAC's history since Pratt Institute did not systematically preserve the Center's archives.

82 Fritz Eichenberg, untitled report, April 29, 1964, box 1.

BENJAMIN

1 Lowengrund's artistic skills gained local attention during her teens. According to her niece, she began circulating sketches while in high school. Joan Dowling, conversation with the author, 2018–19. Lowengrund quipped in her high school yearbook, "To be funny and to paint, / Makes Life seem like what it ain't!" Philadelphia High School for Girls, Yearbook, 1921, Philadelphia, 24, private collection of Shannon Sweeney (Lowengrund's granddaughter). Soon after, Lowengrund created illustrations for the Philharmonic Society of Philadelphia while Josef Pasternack served as musical director. The Philharmonic Society of Philadelphia, *Sixth Season 1923–24* (Philadelphia: Philharmonic Society of Philadelphia, 1923), Lowengrund, Margaret Accounts, private collection of Tom Wolf.

2 The columns comprise part of the Margaret Lowengrund Papers (henceforth MLP), which also contain original newspaper clippings, exhibition materials, and sundry ephemera about Lowengrund. They were a gift to the author from Linda Sweeney, Lowengrund's daughter, on May 26, 2007.

3 Margaret Lowengrund, "The Old Scissors Man at Fifteenth and Cherry," *Philadelphia Evening Public Ledger*, February 28, 1923.

4 Margaret Lowengrund, "A Willing's Alley Serenade," *Philadelphia Evening Public Ledger*, n.d., MLP.

5 Lowengrund, "A Willing's Alley Serenade."

6 These are a selection of Lowengrund's columns from *New York Evening Post*, which ran between March 18, 1924 and November 6, 1925, MLP.

7 "American Girl Artist Back with Honors Record Abroad," *New York Evening Post*, November 26, 1927. "Phila. Artist Triumphs Abroad: Phila. Girl Sketcher Wins Fame in Paris and London Art World," *Philadelphia Evening Public Ledger*, November 29, 1927.

8 Lowengrund's lithograph *Café du Lapin Agile* was reproduced in a French periodical. MLP contains a clipping on which there is the handwritten note, "Paris s'amuse." Efforts to identify this publication have not yet been successful. She also referenced "Paris s'amuse" in a 1936 interview: Douglas Gilbert, "Observant Artist Rambles Around Town Putting Reactions on Canvas: Says Cubists Influenced All Art, but Traditional Is Favored Again," *New York World-Telegram*, February 3, 1936.

9 Joseph Lilly, "A Dutch Treat," *American Traveler* 2, no. 2 (February 1934): 8–9, 23; Margaret Lowengrund, "Ten Days to Callao," *American Traveler* 2, no. 3 (March 1934): 8–9, 22; and "Frontispiece," *American Traveler* 2, no. 4 (April 1934): 4.

10 "Painting Under Fire: Margaret Lowengrund Interrupted by Shots at Peru President," *Brooklyn Times Union*, February 2, 1936, 9.

11 Lowengrund completed several weekly insertions in the *New York World-Telegram* to accompany articles by Earl Sparling. See Earl

Sparling, "Mirrors of Manhattan," *New York World-Telegram*, September 9–12, 1931; Sparling, "Crossroad of Manhattan," *New York World-Telegram*, October 12–17, 1931; and A. J. Liebling, "Ellis Island, This Way Out," *New York World-Telegram*, March 20–24, 1933.

12 "U. S. Tightens Net in Nazi Spy Trial," *Paramount News*, October 1938, Neg. 7428, Issue 23. The Sherman Grinberg Film Library lists this newsreel in their catalogue but the footage is missing from their vault; the story does appear in Paramount release sheets. Lance Watsky, e-mail messages to the author, July 24–31, 2020.

13 Samuel Merwin, *Rise and Fight Againe* (New York: A. & C. Boni, Inc., 1935); Sinclair Lewis, *Main Street* (Cleveland: The World Publishing Company, 1946); and Fay Ingalls, *The Valley Road* (Cleveland: The World Publishing Company, 1949).

14 Margaret Lowengrund, "Art Today," *Ulster County Sunday News*, n.d., 1947; Margaret Lowengrund, "Art Today," *Ulster County Sunday News*, n.d., 1947, MLP.

15 Margaret Lowengrund, "Art," in *World Scope Encyclopedia: Book of the Year, 1949* (New York: Universal Educational Guild, Inc., 1950), n.p. For her typeset manuscript, see Margaret Lowengrund, "This Year in Art," 1949, NYPL MAD.

16 Rep. George Anthony Dondero, speaking on "Communism in the Heart of American Art—What to Do about It," on May 17, 1949, 81st Congress, 1st session, *Congressional Record* 95, pt. 5: 6374–75.

17 Dondero, "Communism in the Heart of American Art," 6375. A few years earlier Congress flagged Lowengrund's affiliation with American Artists' Congress and An American Group. Special Committee on Un-American Activities, *Investigation of Un-American Propaganda Activities in the United States: Hearings Before a Special Committee on Un-American Activities*, 78th Congress, 2nd session, 1944, Committee Print, Appendix pt. 9 (Communist Front Organizations): 1071, 1073, 1093.

18 Peyton Boswell, "A Plea for Tolerance," *Art Digest* 23, no. 17 (June 1949), 7.

19 John T. Bernard, "Give Us a Program!," *New Masses* 23, no. 10 (August 1937): 3–5.

RUSSO

1 There is growing interest in the contributions of female gallerists. Recent exhibitions and catalogues include Rebecca Shaykin, *Edith Halpert: The Downtown Gallery and the Rise of American Art* (New York: The Jewish Museum/Yale University Press, 2019); Jillian Russo, *Wild and Brilliant: The Martha Jackson Gallery and Postwar Art* (New York: Hollis Taggart Gallery, 2021). The Women Art Dealers Digital Archives (WADDA), cofounded by Véronique Chagnon-Burke and Caterina Toschi, is working on a forthcoming anthology, *Women Art Dealers, Makers of the Modern Art Market, 1940–1990*.

2 In this essay, "modern" art refers to art produced before 1940, and "contemporary" art to work created in the decades straddling the opening of The Contemporaries (1940–60)—definitions in line with Lowengrund's use of these terms.

3 Grace Borgenicht, as quoted in Judy K. Collischan Van Wagner, *Women Shaping Art: Profiles of Power* (New York: Praeger, 1984), 85.

4 Van Wagner, *Women Shaping Art*, 86.

5 Virginia Zabriskie, as quoted in Van Wagner, *Women Shaping Art*, 91.

6 Marian Willard, as quoted in Van Wagner, *Women Shaping Art*, 33–34.

7 Martha Jackson, oral history interview by Paul Cummings, May 23, 1969, 19, AAA/SI.

8 Lawrence Campbell, "The Ray Johnson History of the Betty Parsons Gallery," *Art News* 72 (January 1973): 56–57.

9 Margaret Lowengrund, "Art," in *World Scope Encyclopedia: Book of the Year, 1949* (New York: Universal Educational Guild, Inc., 1950), n.p.

10 Cristopher Gray, "Streetscapes: The Weyhe Bookstore and Gallery; From Books to Baked Goods," *New York Times*, September 29, 1991.

11 Erika Doss, "Catering to Consumerism: Associated American Artists and the Marketing of Modern Art, 1934–1958," *Winterthur Portfolio* 26, no 2/3 (Summer-Autumn 1991): 163.

12 Robert Kipniss, *A Working Artist's Life* (Hanover, NH: University Press of New England, 2011), 128.

13 Sidney Delson, "Robert Delson: An Anecdotal Biography" (unpublished manuscript, December 1995), 6–11, courtesy Irma Delson Canan.

14 Charles Z. Offin, "From the Editor's Notebook," *Pictures on Exhibit* 19 (November 1955): 14.

15 Katherine Goodman, interview by Mary Berlow, June 30, 2008, Martha Jackson Oral History Project, Anderson Gallery, University at Buffalo, Buffalo, NY.

ARCHER

1 "Model Suite in Briar Oaks, Fisher Brothers' Apartment Project in Riverdale," *New York Herald Tribune*, July 26, 1953, 1C.

2 "Beryl S. Austrian, 83, A Decorator of Lobbies," *New York Times*, October 6, 1982.

3 "Model Suite in Briar Oaks."

4 Lynn Spigel, *Make Room for TV: The Television and the Family Ideal in Postwar America* (Chicago: University of Chicago Press, 1992), 2.

5 The Contemporaries' Visitors' Register, January 1955, NYPL MAD.

6 "Beryl S. Austrian: Contract Designer," *Wallpaper & Wallcoverings*, March 1966, 39.

7 "Model Suite in Briar Oaks."

8 Russell Lynes, "High-Brow, Low-Brow, Middle-Brow," *Life*, April 11, 1949, 99–102.

9 Lynes, "High-Brow, Low-Brow, Middle-Brow," 101.

10 Erika Doss, "Catering to Consumerism: Associated American Artists and the Marketing of Modern Art, 1934–1958," *Winterthur Portfolio* 26, no. 2/3 (Summer–Autumn 1991): 143.

11 Gail Windisch, "Delivering Art to American Homes: Associated American Artists and the Two Men Who Shaped It, 1934–1984," in *Art for Every Home: Associated American Artists, 1934–2000*, ed. Elizabeth G. Seaton, Jane Myers and Gail Windisch (New Haven: Yale University Press, 2015): 24.

12 *Full Color Masterpieces* (New York: Associated American Artists, 1950), 2, as quoted in Kristina Wilson, "'Apology Areas': Interior Decorating and the Marketplace in the 1950s," in *Shaping the American Interior: Structures, Contexts and Practices*, ed. Paula Lupkin and Penny Sparke (London: Routledge, 2018): 157–68.

13 Margaret Lowengrund, "The Circle Expands," *Art Digest* 23, no. 11 (March 1, 1949): 24.

14 Letter from Margaret Lowengrund to Edward Millman, February 28, 1952, box 2, EMP, SUA.

15 Dore Ashton, *Art Digest* 28, no. 3 (November 1953): 27. Lowengrund, herself, was keenly aware of the trend towards oversized or mural-like prints.

16 Margaret Lowengrund, proposal for "The Contemporaries Graphic Arts Gallery and Workshop," December 19, 1955, folder 3494, box 405, RAC PGAC. After suffering from prolonged financial threat, Lowengrund sought support for The Contemporaries from the Rockefeller Foundation.

17 Barbara Kessler, "Speaking of Art," *Vassar Chronicle*, December 5, 1953.

18 "Speaking of Art," *Vassar Chronicle*, November 14, 1953.

19 *Full Color Masterpieces*, 2, as quoted in Kristina Wilson, "'Apology Areas': Interior Decorating," 157–68.

KUWAHARA

1 For more, see my essay, "Onchi's *Portrait of Hagiwara Sakutarō*: Emblem of the Creative Print Movement for American Collectors," *Impressions* 29 (2007–08): 121–39.

2 For more on Hasegawa, see Dakin Hart and Mark Dean Johnson, *Changing and Unchanging Things: Noguchi and Hasegawa in Postwar Japan* (Oakland: University of California Press, 2019).

3 A. B. S., "On Abstract Art: A Symposium," *New York Times*, March 21, 1954.

4 Hasegawa Saburō, letter to Shibata Yōzō, April 13, 1954, Letters (to Shibata Yōzō) 1947–1955, Hasegawa Saburo Memorial Gallery Archive, Konan Boys' High School, Hyogo Prefecture. Hasegawa signed The Contemporaries' visitors' register, February 8, 1954, NYPL MAD.

5 William Liberman, transcript of phone call with John Marshall, June 15, 1954, folder 3494, box 405, RAC PGAC.

6 Margaret Lowengrund, transcript of phone call with Edward D'Arms, December 5, 1955, folder 3494, box 405, RAC PGAC.

7 Yoshida Chizuko, Hodaka's wife, and Saitō Kiyoshi also exhibited. Barbara Guest, "Gallery Groups," *Art Digest* 30, no. 5 (February 1956): 59.

8 Noriko Kuwahara, "The Art of Saitō Kiyoshi: Internationalism and Regionalism," in *Saitō Kiyoshi: Graphic Awakening*, ed. Rhiannon Paget (New York: Scala Art Publishers, 2021): 1–15.

9 Saitō Kiyoshi, "Diary," April 2 and 3, 1956, private collection, Fukushima, Japan.

10 Postwar Japanese lithography had two points of confluence: first, Izumi Shigeru and others of the Democrat Artists Association (formed in 1951); second, the Cercle de la Gravure du Japon, a lithography studio for painters to professionally print their work in 1954. Wakita Kazu, who had practiced lithography in Germany prior to World War II, belonged to the latter group.

11 Wakita's January exhibition was reviewed by Herbert D. Hale, "Kazu Wakita," *Art News* 55 (January 1957): 57. The Contemporaries also advertised a March duo show with Zoran Antonio Mušič. Wakita himself refers to the March show as his solo exhibition in "Wakita Kazu Chronology," in *Wakita Kazu hanga sakuhin shū* (Tokyo: Bijutsu Shuppansha, 1976), 15.

12 Douglas Overton, letter to Charles B. Fahs, August 23, 1956, folder 3226, box 356, Graphic Arts, Japan Society, RAC PGAC.

13 Gordon facilitated bilateral cultural exchange at the Japan Society. Austrian by birth, she lived in Japan before the war and returned afterward as a staff member of the Occupation force.

14 Kobashi Yasuhide, *Iisutoribaa no unagitsuri: waga Nyuyooku seikatsu no 20 nen* (Tokyo: Miraisha, 1981), 11–13.

15 George sent a few letters to Lowengrund while in Kyoto (see the archived collection at NYPL MAD). Bridgestone Museum, Tokyo, held a solo show for George in October 1957.

16 Uchima became an instructor in woodcut at Sarah Lawrence College (September 1962) and at Columbia University (September 1968).

17 The two Yoshidas (no relation) were in New York to attend the general meeting of the International Association of Plastic Arts. For the women's show, see *PI Newsletter* 17, no. 8 (November 7, 1966), PIA.

18 Fritz Eichenberg, "Forward," *Naoko Matsubara, Kyoto Woodcuts* (Tokyo: Kodansha International, 1978), n.p.

VOGEL

1 Luis Camnitzer, *Luis Camnitzer in Conversation with Alexander Alberro* (New York: Fundación Cisneros/Colleccíon Patricia Phelps de Cisneros, 2014), 48.

2 John Canaday, "A Wee Plug for a Worthy Cause," *New York Times*, January 5, 1964.

3 Andrea Giunta, "A Conversation with Liliana Porter and Luis Camnitzer," in *The New York Graphic Workshop, 1964–1970*, eds. Gabriel Pérez-Barreiro, Ursula Davila-Villa, and Gina McDaniel Tarver (Austin: Blanton Museum of Art, 2009), 44; *Luis Camnitzer in Conversation*, 49.

4 Liliana Porter, *Liliana Porter in Conversation with Inés Katzenstein* (New York: Fundación Cisneros/Colleccíon Patricia Phelps de Cisneros, 2013), 32.

5 Liliana Porter, conversation with the author, April 6, 2022.
6 Liliana Porter, conversation with the author, April 6, 2022. Porter and Camnitzer began spending more and more time together, both inside and outside the workshop. They quickly grew close, marrying the following year; they divorced in 1979.
7 *Liliana Porter in Conversation*, 34; Luis Camnitzer and Jane Farver, *Luis Camnitzer: Retrospective Exhibition 1966–1990* (Bronx, NY: Lehman College Art Gallery, 1991), 52.
8 Judith Richards, oral history interview with Liliana Porter, June 27–28, 2012, AAA/SI.
9 *Luis Camnitzer in Conversation*, 55; Giunta, "A Conversation," 46.
10 *Liliana Porter in Conversation*, 34.
11 Luis Camnitzer, "Printmaking: A Colony of the Arts (1999)," in *On Art, Artists, Latin America, and Other Utopias*, Luis Camnitzer, ed. Rachel Weiss (Austin: University of Texas Press, 2021), 107. Camnitzer is likely referring to PGAC faculty members Michael Ponce de León, who produced deep intaglio prints using a hydraulic press and handmade paper, and Arthur Deshaies, who used sheets of Plexiglas as the printing matrix.
12 *Luis Camnitzer in Conversation*, 55.
13 Luis Camnitzer, "Manifesto of the New York Graphic Workshop," in Pérez-Barreiro et al., *The New York Graphic Workshop*, 87.
14 New York Graphic Workshop, "Manifesto," in Pérez-Barreiro et al., *The New York Graphic Workshop*, 88.
15 New York Graphic Workshop, "Manifesto," 88.
16 Camnitzer, "Manifesto of the New York Graphic Workshop," 87.
17 Exhibition brochure for *New York Graphic Workshop: Luis Camnitzer, José Guillermo Castillo, Liliana Porter* (Caracas: Museo de Bellas Artes, 1969), in Pérez-Barreiro, Davila-Villa, and Tarver, *New York Graphic Workshop*, 93.
18 New York Graphic Workshop, "Manifesto," 88.
19 Porter's color intaglio, *The Yellow Chair* (1964), was included in PGAC's sponsoring membership portfolio issued in 1966. Camnitzer's *Fragment of a Cloud* (1967), a stencil on cotton batting, was included in PCCP's 1969 portfolio "Ten Prints by Ten Printmakers."
20 Luis Camnitzer, "A Redefinition of the Print," *Artist's Proof: A Journal of Printmaking* 6, no. 9–10 (1966): 103.
21 Walter Benjamin, "The Work of Art in the Age of Its Technological Reproducibility, Second Version," in *Walter Benjamin: Selected Writings, Volume 3: 1935–1938*, ed. Howard Eiland and Michael W. Jennings (Cambridge, MA: Harvard University Press, 2002), 103–105.
22 Fritz Eichenberg, "Editorial," *Artist's Proof: A Journal of Printmaking* 6, no. 9–10 (1966): 4.
23 Eichenberg, 4.
24 Eichenberg, 4.
25 NYGW exhibition brochure for *Towards FANDSO* (New York: The Pratt Center for Contemporary Printmaking, 1967), n.p.
26 NYGW exhibition brochure for *Towards FANDSO*, n.p.
27 Luis Camnitzer, *Art in Editions: New Approaches* (New York: The Pratt Center for Contemporary Printmaking, 1968), n.p.
28 Camnitzer, *Art in Editions*, n.p.
29 Camnitzer, *Art in Editions*, n.p.

CHRONOLOGY

1 Richard E. Thibaut, "Woodstock News," *Kingston Daily Freeman*, October 16, 1951.
2 Helen Carson, *Pictures on Exhibit* 14, no. 1952 (February 1952): 25.
3 Una Johnson, letter to Elizabeth Mongan, August 15, 1954, Alverthorpe Galleries, Records of the Department of Prints, Drawings, and Photographs, Brooklyn Museum.
4 "Partial List of Sponsors for The Graphic Art Center," James Johnson Sweeney Records (A0001), folder 141, box 261, Solomon R. Guggenheim Museum Archives, New York, NY.
5 Margaret Lowengrund, letter to Carroll Edward Hogan (Albright Art Gallery), June 4, 1955, NYPL MAD.
6 Press release for The Collector's Print, ca. 1956, Contemporaries Graphic Art Centre (MDAAZ), NYPL APP.
7 See in folder 3494, box 405, RAC PGAC: Suzanne M. Spaeth, "Memo to Margaret Lowengrund regarding the Long Island University Project," November 16, 1955; Edward F. D'Arms, telephone conversation with Lowengrund, December 5, 1955; Charles B. Fahs, memo from visit with Margaret Lowengrund, February 9, 1956.
8 See in folder 3494, box 405, RAC PGAC: Charles B. Fahs, letter to Margaret Lowengrund, February 29, 1956; Charles B. Fahs, notes from telephone conversation with Margaret Lowengrund, July 23, 1956. Richardson (Jerry) Pratt, who served as chairman of the Board of Trustees, had doubts about the Manhattan location.
9 Francis Horn, letter to Charles Fahs, August 29, 1956, folder 3494, box 405, RAC PGAC.
10 For specifics about the arrangements, see Lowengrund's contract with Pratt Institute, dated October 25, 1956, MLP.
11 *PI Newsletter* 7, no. 19 (February 25, 1957): 1.
12 Fritz Eichenberg, letters to Joyce Espen, November 26, 1957 and Linda Sweeney, December 11, 1957, MLP. By June 1958, Eichenberg had raised $1,062.58, which he awarded to seventeen recipients in equal amounts. Fritz Eichenberg, "Annual Report to Members of the Advisory Board, Pratt-Contemporaries Graphic Art Centre," June 1958, Reports, 1955–63, Records of the School of Art and Design, PIA.
13 For more on the Ingram Merrill Foundation's gifts, see FEP.
14 For the third year of its grant, the Rockefeller Foundation's contribution to Pratt-Contemporaries shrank to $12,000 (down from $22,000 for the first year). Stretched thin on a bare-bones budget, the Centre had no extra funds for advertising. Fritz Eichenberg, memo to Albert Christ-Janer, October 14, 1958, FEP.
15 Flora M. Rhind, letter to Robert Oxnam, May 26, 1959, folder 3495, box 405, RAC PGAC. The Rockefeller Foundation's second grant also provided for $60,000, again tapered over three years. Eichenberg estimated the Centre's annual budget at $30,000. Fritz Eichenberg, draft memo to Rockefeller Foundation, April 15, 1959, folder 3495, box 405, RAC PGAC.
16 Fritz Eichenberg, letter to Boyd Compton, August 26, 1959, folder 3495, box 405, RAC PGAC.
17 Request for Grant Action, February 4, 1960, 06000134, reel 0941, Series Grants, Ford, RAC. The Ford Foundation awarded Wayne $186,000 for the creation of Tamarind Lithography Workshop; from this amount, $21,000 went to PGAC.
18 Fritz Eichenberg, "Foreword," *Artist's Proof* 1, no. 1 (1961): 1.
19 Planning for the portfolio began in October 1961 according to memos located in the Associated American Artists records, circa 1934–1983, folder 9 (Pratt Graphic Art Center), box 26, AAA/SI. For details about the sale and distribution, see "Details of all arrangements made regarding the Portfolio Project," March 10, 1962, FEP. Portfolio sales added $593 to the Margaret Lowengrund Scholarship Fund, bringing the total amount raised over four years to $1,655.58. Fritz Eichenberg, "Final Report to the Rockefeller Foundation," 5, December 1962, folder 3496, box 405, RAC PGAC.
20 John Ross collected the Romanian prints while traveling. Similarly, Jacob Lawrence had acquired the Nigerian prints. The Soviet posters were part of PGAC's collection. Press release, March 8, 1965, Loose Press Releases, 1964–65, Records of Department of Communications and Marketing, PIA.
21 Press release, March 1, 1965, Loose Press Releases, 1964–65, Records of Department of Communications and Marketing, PIA.
22 *PI Newsletter* 15, no. 32 (May 3, 1965), 2.

EXHIBITIONS AT THE CONTEMPORARIES

1 Una Johnson included this exhibition in her "Chronology of Important Exhibitions of Painters Who Are Also Printmakers," *14 Painter-Printmakers* (Brooklyn, NY: Brooklyn Museum, 1955). Johnson used a generic title, *Color Prints by 10 Well-Known Painters*, and a slightly different roster of exhibitors.
2 This exhibition, organized by Jerry Jerominek, may have been the first "Graphic Outlook." The announcement card for the Graphic Outlook in 1955 counts it as the "Fourth Annual" but only two previous versions are known (1952 and 1954). Richard E. Thibaut, "Woodstock News, Lithograph Display Now at Playhouse," *Kingston Daily Freeman*, July 25, 1952, 21.
3 It is possible this exhibition toured. The collection of Contemporaries Gallery material at NYPL MAD contains a photograph depicting the installation of an exhibition called "Evolution of a Contemporary Print."

EXHIBITIONS AT THE PRATT GRAPHIC ART CENTER

1 PGAC remained in operation until March 1986 at various Manhattan locations.
2 By early 1967, PGAC had fifteen shows in circulation. Press release, January 31, 1967, Loose Press Releases, 1966–67, Records of Department of Communications and Marketing, PIA.
3 During the period covered in this chronology, Pratt Institute's Department of Graphic Arts and Illustration exhibited in the Main Building in a fourth-floor space known as the "G. A. I. Gallery." It is unclear if this space was the same as the "Fourth Floor Gallery" in the Main Building or an entirely separate gallery. Thank you to Cristina Fontánez Rodríguez, PIA archivist, for helping to disambiguate these spaces.
4 *Graphic Technique* was first developed for PGAC's participation in *Art:USA:59* at the Coliseum, New York City.
5 Associated American Artists loaned work for this show. Andrew Stasik to Sylvan Cole, November 10, 1960, folder 9 (Pratt Graphic Art Center), box 26, Associated American Artists records, circa 1934–1983, AAA/SI.
6 Andrew Stasik organized *Prize-winning American Prints*, which was on tour throughout Western Canada before its display at PGAC. "Of Graphic Interest," *Artist's Proof* 2, no. 2 (Fall-Winter 1962): 47.
7 The magazine, *Canadian Art*, facilitated this exhibition featuring young Canadian printmakers. James Boyd, "A Survey of Printmaking in Canada," *Artist's Proof* 2, no. 2 (Fall Winter 1962): 4.
8 Izumi Shigeru organized this show, per press release, November 1, 1962, Loose Press Releases, 1962–63, Records of Department of Communications and Marketing, PIA.
9 This show originated with the Smithsonian Institution's Traveling Exhibition Service and featured prints from the Library of Congress purchased through the Pennell Fund.
10 Zoran Krzisnik, director of the Modern Gallery in Ljubljana, made selections. "Of Graphic Interest," *Artist's Proof* 4, no. 1 (1964): 56.
11 Sheila Isham, wife of an American diplomat stationed in Hong Kong, arranged the exhibition with the assistance of the Chatham Gallery, Hong Kong. Press release, March 30, 1965, Loose Press Releases, 1964–65, Records of Department of Communications and Marketing, PIA.
12 *PI Newsletter*, November 8, 1966: This exhibition was acquired by the prominent printmaker and former faculty member, Uchima Ansei, on his recent trip to Japan. At the reception, there was a screening of the color film *Japanese Printmaking*, produced by Yoshida Tōshi.

Sarah Archer is the author of several books, including *The Midcentury Kitchen* and *Midcentury Christmas*. Her writing has appeared in *The Atlantic*, *The Cut*, *Architectural Digest*, *The New Yorker*, *Hyperallergic*, and the peer-reviewed *Journal of Modern Craft*, among other outlets. Archer has contributed essays to exhibition catalogues by institutions such as the Renwick Gallery of the Smithsonian Institution, the Peabody Essex Museum, and the Museum of Arts and Design. Previously, she was senior curator at the Philadelphia Art Alliance at the University of the Arts.

Ellen J. Benjamin is Emerita Associate Professor in DePaul University's School for New Learning, where she taught for 18 years on the university's Chicago, Hong Kong, and Bangkok campuses. She has also held Fulbright Professorships in Turkey, Romania, and Mongolia. Benjamin has worked with nonprofits such as the American Friends Service Committee, Planned Parenthood, the American Civil Liberties Union, and Amnesty International USA. She holds an MA in Social Work from The University of Michigan and a PhD in Social Service Administration from The University of Chicago. Margaret Lowengrund was Benjamin's great-aunt, sister to her mother's mother.

Noriko Kuwahara is Professor of Japanese Art History, Faculty of Literature, at Seitoku University in Chiba, Japan. She has published extensively on Onchi Kōshirō and modern Japanese prints, and received the Ringa Prize for her 2012 publication *Onchi Kōshirō Kenkyū: hanga no modanizumu [A Study of Onchi Kōshirō: Modernity in Japanese Prints]*. She has contributed English-language texts to several publications, including *Saitō Kiyoshi: Graphic Awakening* (The John and Mable Ringling Museum of Art, 2021). Kuwahara holds an BA and MA from Ochanomizu Women's University and a PhD from the University of Tsukuba.

Lauren Rosenblum is a doctoral candidate in art history at The Graduate Center, CUNY. Her research situates twentieth-century printmaking in the United States within social contexts that account for such factors as the rise of second-wave feminism, the assertion of countercultures, and progressive labor relations. She has taught art history at several institutions, including most recently at Purchase College, and has worked in prints and drawings departments at The Museum of Fine Arts, Houston, and the Philadelphia Museum of Art.

Jillian Russo is an independent curator and art historian. Previously, she was curator at the Art Students League of New York (2013–2018) and then Director of Exhibitions at Hollis Taggart Gallery (2019–2021), where she curated the exhibition *Wild and Brilliant: The Martha Jackson Gallery and Post-War Art*. She is a regular contributor to *The Brooklyn Rail* and has written for *American Quarterly*, *Panorama*, and *CAA Reviews*. She received her PhD from The Graduate Center, CUNY with a focus on modern and postwar art in the United States.

Rachel Vogel is the Assistant Curator at the Addison Gallery of American Art, where she specializes in modern and contemporary art. She has contributed to numerous exhibitions and publications at the Johnson-Kulukundis Gallery at the Harvard Radcliffe Institute, and has curated exhibitions at Art League Houston and Rice University's Media Center Gallery, among other institutions. Her writing has been published in the *Oxford Art Journal*, *Art Journal*, *CAA Reviews*, and is forthcoming in *American Art*. She received her PhD in the History of Art and Architecture from Harvard University.

Christina Weyl is an independent curator and scholar, and the author of *The Women of Atelier 17: Modernist Printmaking in Midcentury New York* (Yale University Press, 2019). Her writing has appeared in *Art in Print*, *Print Quarterly*, the *Archives of American Art Journal*, and several anthologies and exhibition catalogues. From 2014 to 2018, Weyl served as Co-President of the Association of Print Scholars, a nonprofit professional organization she cofounded in 2014. She holds a BA from Georgetown University and a PhD in Art History from Rutgers University.

In reproducing the images in this publication, Print Center New York has made every reasonable and good-faith effort to locate, and obtain permission from, rights holders. If errors or omissions are identified, please contact Print Center New York so that corrections can be made in any future editions.

All works by Margaret Lowengrund © 2023 Heirs of Margaret Lowengrund / Artists Rights Society (ARS), New York.

Photo by Argenis Apolinario: 92 (top, bottom)

Image courtesy Archives of American Art, Federal Art Project, Photographic Division, Washington, DC: 15, 27

Image courtesy Art Students League, New York: 23

Image courtesy Avery Architectural & Fine Arts Library, Columbia University, New York: 67

© Maurice Berezov Photographer / A.E. Artworks, LLC. Image courtesy Woodstock Artists Association and Museum Archives, Woodstock, NY: Cover, 64

© Mary Callery and Universal Limited Art Editions. Image courtesy Universal Limited Art Editions, Bay Shore, NY: 16

© 2023 Luis Camnitzer / Artists Rights Society (ARS), New York. Image courtesy Tate Gallery UK. Photo: Tate: 89

© Estate of Edmond Casarella and Susan Teller Gallery, New York. Image courtesy The Jewish Museum/New York, NY/U.S.A.: 105

Image courtesy Chicago Design Archive: 95

© 2023 Revocable Trust of Judith Childs / Estate of Bernard Childs / Licensed by VAGA at Artists Rights Society (ARS), New York. Image courtesy National Gallery of Art, Washington, DC: 77 (bottom)

© 2023 Corita Art Center / Immaculate Heart Community / Licensed by Artists Rights Society (ARS), New York. Image courtesy National Gallery of Art, Washington, DC: 78

© 2023 Estate of Stuart Davis / Licensed by VAGA at Artists Rights Society (ARS), New York. Image courtesy Philadelphia Museum of Art, Gift of Mrs. Edith Gregor Halpert, 1958, 1958-53-7: 76

© Estate of Robert Delson, courtesy Irma Delson Canan. Image courtesy The Wolfsonian–Florida International University, Miami Beach, Gift of Sidney Delson, XC1998.300.41.52. Photo by Lynton Gardiner: 17; image courtesy The Wolfsonian–Florida International University, Miami Beach, Gift of Sidney Delson, XC1998.300.41.43. Photo by Lynton Gardiner: 66 (left); image courtesy The Wolfsonian–Florida International University, Miami Beach, Gift of Sidney Delson, XC1998.300.41.51. Photo by Lynton Gardiner: 66 (right); image courtesy The Wolfsonian–Florida International University, Miami Beach, Gift of Sidney Delson, XC1998.300.41.52. Photo by Lynton Gardiner: 97 (top); image courtesy Manuscripts and Archives Division, The New York Public Library: 45, 63; image courtesy Instituto Fayga Ostrower: 96

© Arthur Deshaies. Image courtesy The Museum of Modern Art, New York. Purchase. Digital Image © The Museum of Modern Art/Licensed by SCALA / Art Resource, NY: 70

© 2023 Estate of Fritz Eichenberg / Licensed by VAGA at Artists Rights Society (ARS), New York. Photo by Argenis Apolinario: 93

© Estate of Louis Faurer: 65

© Beatrice Grover. Image courtesy Guild Hall, East Hampton, NY. Photo by Gary Mamay Photography: 73

Image courtesy Robert B. Haas Family Arts Library, Yale University, New Haven: 97 (bottom), 99, 100, 101, 102

© Estate of Hasegawa Saburō. Image courtesy The Museum of Modern Art, New York, Gift of Mr. and Mrs. E. Powis Jones. Digital Image © The Museum of Modern Art/Licensed by SCALA / Art Resource, NY: 80

Photo by Evan Jenkins: 24, 25, 29, 32, 33, 34 (top, bottom), 35, 38 (bottom), 39, 58, 59, 60, 61 (left)

Image courtesy Noriko Kuwahara: 81

© 2023 The Jacob Landau Institute / Licensed by VAGA at Artists Rights Society (ARS), New York. Photo by Argenis Apolinario: 91 (right)

© Estate of Basil Langton. Image courtesy Liliana Porter: 86

Image courtesy Prints and Photographs Division, Library of Congress, Washington, DC: 30

© Estate of Peter Lipman-Wulf. Image courtesy the Estate of Peter Lipman-Wulf. Collection of Michael Henkel, East Hampton, NY: 73 (bottom)

Image courtesy Marianna Kistler Beach Museum of Art, Kansas State University, Manhattan, KS: 28

Image courtesy Marxists Internet Archive: 61 (right)

© Seong Moy. Image courtesy Davison Art Center, Wesleyan University, Middletown, CT. Purchase funds, 1962.25.1. Photo by J. Giammatteo: 79 (left)

Image courtesy Municipal Archives, City of New York: 49 (bottom)

Image courtesy National Gallery of Art, Washington, DC: 36

Image courtesy National Park Service, Weir Farm National Historical Park, Wilton, CT: 21

© New York Graphic Workshop, Liliana Porter / Luis Camnitzer. Image courtesy Blanton Museum of Art, The University of Texas at Austin: 87 (left); image courtesy Liliana Porter: 87 (right)

Image courtesy Art & Architecture Collection, The New York Public Library: 13

© Estate of Fayga Ostrower. Image courtesy Instituto Fayga Ostrower: 74 (top)

Image courtesy Philadelphia Museum of Art, Print Club of Philadelphia Permanent Collection, 1956, 1956-55-36: 77 (top)

© Liliana Porter. Image courtesy Liliana Porter: 88

© Pratt Institute. Image courtesy Pratt Institute Archives Negatives Collection, Brooklyn: 54, 56, 57, 82, 83, 84, 102 (bottom), 103, 104, 105 (top)

Image courtesy Princeton University Art Museum, Princeton, NJ: 26

Image courtesy private collection: 69

Image courtesy Rockefeller Archive Center, Sleepy Hollow, NY: 50, 51

Image courtesy Konan Gakuen, Saburo Hasegawa Memorial Gallery, Hyogo, Japan: 40

Image courtesy San Francisco Museum of Modern Art. The United States General Services Administration, Formerly Federal Works Agency, Works Projects Administration (WPA), allocation to the San Francisco Museum of Modern Art. Photo by Don Ross: 37 (top)

© Estate of Lee Sievan. Image courtesy Woodstock Artists Association and Museum Archives, Gift of Estate of Lee Sievan, Woodstock, NY: 95 (top)

© 2023 The Estate of David Smith / Licensed by VAGA at Artists Rights Society (ARS), New York. Image courtesy Smithsonian American Art Museum, Museum purchase, Washington, DC: 79 (right)

© Estate of Andrew Stasik. Photo by Argenis Apolinario: 90

© 2023 Tamayo Heirs / Mexico / Artists Rights Society (ARS), New York. Image courtesy Denis Bloch Fine Art, Beverly Hills: 75

© Uchima Anju. Photo by Argenis Apolinario. 91 (left)

© 2023 The June Wayne Collection / Licensed by VAGA at Artists Rights Society (ARS), New York: 74 (bottom). Image courtesy Fine Arts Museums of San Francisco, Gift of Dr. George J. Wayne. Photo by Jorge Bachmann.

Image courtesy Whitney Museum of American Art, Gift of Robinson A. Grover. Inv.: 2003.27. Digital image © Whitney Museum of American Art / Licensed by Scala / Art Resource, NY: 72

Image courtesy The Wolfsonian–Florida International University, Miami Beach, Gift of Sidney Delson, XC1998.300.41.21. Photo by Lynton Gardiner: 47

Image courtesy Woodstock Artists Association & Museum, Woodstock, NY, Gift of Linda Sweeney, 1990-10-01: 37 (bottom)

Image courtesy Woodstock Artists Association & Museum, Woodstock, NY, Gift of Peter and Chagit Heller, 2006-08-02: 38 (top)

Image courtesy Woodstock Artists Association & Museum, Woodstock, NY. WAA Annual Print Award, 1975-11-02: 43 (top)

Image courtesy Woodstock Artists Association and Museum Archives, Woodstock, NY: 43 (bottom)

Image courtesy Library Special Collections, Charles E. Young Research Library, University of California, Los Angeles: 71

COLOPHON

Published on the occasion of the exhibition *A Model Workshop: Margaret Lowengrund and The Contemporaries*, presented at Print Center New York September 21–December 23, 2023. Curated by Lauren Rosenblum and Christina Weyl

Published by
Hirmer Publishers
Bayerstraße 57–59
80335 Munich
Germany
www.hirmerpublishers.com

Edited by Lauren Rosenblum and Christina Weyl

Project Manager, Print Center New York: Jenn Bratovich
Project Manager, Hirmer Publishers: Rainer Arnold
Senior Editor, Hirmer Publishers: Elisabeth Rochau-Shalem
Design: CHIPS
Copyediting: Flatpage
Proofreading: Michael Pilewski
Lithography: Reproline Mediateam
Printing and binding: Printer Trento s.r.l.
Printed in Italy

Bibliographic Information published by
the Deutsche Nationalbibliothek
The Deutsche Nationalbibliothek lists this publication in the Deutsche Nationalbibliografie; detailed bibliographic data is available on the internet at www.dnb.de

ISBN 978-3-7774-4152-8

Print Center New York gratefully acknowledges our Board of Trustees and Jordan Schnitzer for their leadership support.

This exhibition is made possible with support from Getty through The Paper Project initiative. Additional support is provided by Wyeth Foundation for American Art, The Kaleta A. Doolin Foundation, and the Helen Frankenthaler Foundation.

Print Center New York is funded, in part, by the New York State Council on the Arts with the support of Governor Kathy Hochul and the New York State Legislature, and the New York City Department of Cultural Affairs in partnership with the City Council.

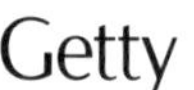

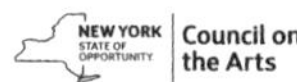

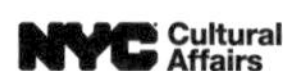

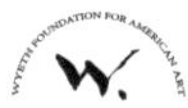

Cover image: Margaret Lowengrund inside The Contemporaries at 959 Madison Avenue, ca. 1952–55. Gelatin silver print. Photo by Maurice Berezov